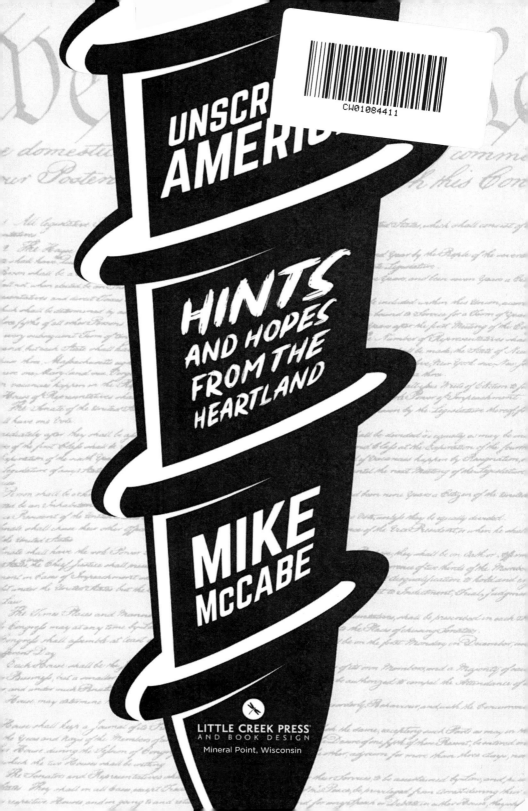

UNSCR
AMERI

HINTS
AND HOPES
FROM THE
HEARTLAND

MIKE
McCABE

LITTLE CREEK PRESS®
AND BOOK DESIGN
Mineral Point, Wisconsin

Little Creek Press*
A Division of Kristin Mitchell Design, Inc.
5341 Sunny Ridge Road
Mineral Point, Wisconsin 53565

Book Design and Project Coordination:
Little Creek Press

First Edition
February 2020

Printed in Wisconsin, United States of America

For more information or to order books,
please visit: www.littlecreekpress.com

Library of Congress Control Number: 2020900411

ISBN-13: 978-1-942586-70-8

US Constitution background art on front cover;
ID 126552207 © Todd Taulman | Dreamstime.com

Red barn art on back cover:
ID 124428146 © Paulacobleigh | Dreamstime.com

TABLE OF CONTENTS

Dedicated to those who know and practice true patriotism

Neither the extensive travels that inspired this book nor the writing of it would have been possible without the love, patience and support of my wife, Marilyn Feil, and my son, Casey McCabe. They put up with a lot and sacrificed much.

Thank you to Kristin Mitchell for believing in this book and making me glad I trusted her with its production.

An immense debt of gratitude also is owed to all who accompanied me on the journey and helped shape the experience as well as my thinking. Among them: Christine Welcher, Beth Hartung, Katie and Dan Schierl, Andre Walton, Dmitri Martin, Kyle Puckhaber, Jeff Perzan, Elizabeth Feil, Jackie Clark, Doug Holmes, Alice Schneiderman, Rökker Smith, Rick Adamski, Dan Weidert, Mike Weidert, Geoff and Christine Davidian, Ralph Knudson, Nancy Heerens-Knudson, Karen Lund, Patti Trotter, Connie Myers, Ed Jeannette, James Zumstein, Nik Novak, Glen Orsburn, Dave and Diane Pauly, Craig Lamberton, David Ermisch, Gail Bos, Sarah Lloyd, Hiroshi and Arlene Kanno, Mark Neumann, Allen and Marisa Pruitt, Ron Berger, Al Sulzer, Lorene Vedder, Mike Brandt, Mary Schneider, Martin Campbell, Alejandro Alonso Galva, Avi and Dannette Lank, John Calabrese, Mat Derrico, Pat Skogen, Mark Scheffler, Joe and Linda Mastalski, Jeanne and Dan Patenaude, Mary Dougherty, Amanda Zehren, Kathy and Chuck Ivey, Zachary Baeseman, Scott Kunkel, David Barnhill, Myron Buchholz, Steve Carlson, Julie and Bob Crego, Jim Crist, Pat Jursik, Lynn Jaskowiak, Alyssa Maus, Cheryl Mader, Christine Lilek, Art and Dawn Shegonee, Dennis Uhlig, John Fease, Leanne Wied, Rick Ziolkowski, Mary B. Hayes, Jane and Dan Bucks, Rick Melcher, Mark Taylor, Scott Wittkopf, Joe Pourroy, Sean Downing and hundreds of others who were my eyes and ears in places where I wasn't and lent their support and shared their insights with me. ✏

INTRODUCTION

The president was joking. Sort of.

After all, it was the White House Correspondents' Dinner. The annual gala was started way back in 1921 and by tradition has featured an after-dinner show with big-name performers. Presidents started attending in 1924. Since 1983, the featured speaker has typically been a comedian who roasts the president and his administration.

On an evening in late April 2016, Barack Obama took the stage, casting himself in the role of roaster in chief.

"I see Mike Bloomberg," Obama said early in his routine. "Mike, a combative, controversial New York billionaire is leading the GOP primary, and it is not you. (Laughter.) That has to sting a little bit. (More laughter.) Although it's not an entirely fair comparison between you and The Donald. After all, Mike was a big-city mayor. He knows policy in depth. And he's actually worth the amount of money that he says he is." (Laughter and applause.)

The president picked on other targets, pointing out Vermont Senator Bernie Sanders in the audience.

"Bernie, you look like a million bucks. (Laughter.) Or to put it in terms you'll understand, you look like 37,000 donations of twenty-seven dollars each."

Obama kept rolling. "Just look at the confusion over the invitations to tonight's dinner. Guests were asked to check whether they wanted steak or fish, but instead, a whole bunch of you wrote in Paul Ryan. (Laughter.) That's not an option, people. Steak or fish. (Laughter.)

"And then there's Ted Cruz. Ted had a tough week. He went to Indiana—Hoosier country—stood on a basketball court, and called the hoop a 'basketball ring.' (Laughter and applause.) What else is in his lexicon? Baseball sticks? Football hats? (Laughter.) But sure, I'm the foreign one. (Laughter and applause.)"

Then the president circled back.

"You know I've got to talk about Trump. Come on! (Laughter and applause.) We weren't just going to stop there. Come on. (Laughter and applause.)

"Although I am a little hurt that he's not here tonight. We had so much fun the last time. (Laughter.) And it is surprising. You've got a room full of reporters, celebrities, cameras, and he says no? (Laughter.) Is this dinner too tacky for The Donald? (Laughter.) What could he possibly be doing instead? Is he at home, eating a Trump Steak—(laughter)— tweeting out insults to Angela Merkel? (Laughter.) What's he doing? (Laughter.)

"The Republican establishment is incredulous that he is their most likely nominee—incredulous, shocking. They say Donald lacks the foreign policy experience to be president. But, in fairness, he has spent years meeting with leaders from around the world: Miss Sweden, Miss Argentina, Miss Azerbaijan. (Laughter and applause.) And there's one area where Donald's experience could be invaluable, and that's closing Guantanamo. Because Trump knows a thing or two about running waterfront properties into the ground. (Laughter and applause.)

"All right, that's probably enough. I mean, I've got more material— (applause)—no, no, I don't want to spend too much time on The Donald. Following your lead, I want to show some restraint. (Laughter.) Because I think we can all agree that from the start, he's gotten the appropriate amount of coverage, befitting the seriousness of his candidacy. (Laughter and applause.) I hope you all are proud of yourselves. (Laughter.) The guy wanted to give his hotel business a boost, and now we're praying that Cleveland makes it through July. (Laughter.)"

As the president hinted at with his remark about having "so much fun the last time," this wasn't the first time Obama took to the stage at the White House Correspondents' Dinner to poke fun at Trump. Five years earlier, he roasted him for a full five minutes—with Trump seated in the audience—delighting in slinging zingers at the man who questioned his presidency's legitimacy.

"No one is happier, no one is prouder to put this birth certificate matter to rest than The Donald," Obama said that evening. "That's because he can finally get back to focusing on the issues that matter, like: Did we fake the moon landing? What really happened in Roswell? And where are Biggie and Tupac? All kidding aside, obviously, we all know about your credentials and breadth of experience. For example, no, seriously, just recently in an episode of *Celebrity Apprentice*, at the steakhouse, the men's cooking team did not impress the judges from Omaha Steaks. And there was a lot of blame to go around. But you, Mr. Trump, recognized that the real problem was a lack of leadership. And so, ultimately, you didn't blame Little John or Meatloaf—you fired Gary Busey. And these are the kinds of decisions that would keep me up at night. Well-handled, sir. Well-handled."

Trump sat frozen in the audience, lips tightly pursed, eyes squinting, staring straight ahead with a scowl on his face. Multiple media accounts suggested this was the moment that fueled Trump's presidential ambitions. *The New York Times* later wrote: "That evening of public abasement, rather than sending Mr. Trump away, accelerated his ferocious efforts to gain stature within the political world. And it captured the degree to which Mr. Trump's campaign is driven by a deep yearning sometimes obscured by his bluster and bragging: a desire to be taken seriously."

The *National Review* published an article titled "How the White House Correspondents' Dinner Gave Us the Trump Campaign." Adam Gopnik of *The New Yorker* wrote about how he had been at the dinner in 2011, seated only a few tables away from Trump. "On that night, Trump's own sense of public humiliation became so overwhelming that he decided, perhaps at first unconsciously, that he would, somehow, get his own back—perhaps even pursue the Presidency after all, no matter how nihilistically or absurdly, and redeem himself."

Trump himself denied that the 2011 dinner had anything to do with his eventual bid for the White House. "There are many reasons I'm running. But that's not one of them."[1]

Whatever his reasons, American politics went to a weird place as the 2016 election approached. The *National Review*, the journal founded by the godfather of American conservatism William F. Buckley, wrote that "Donald Trump is a menace to American conservatism who would take the work of generations and trample it underfoot on behalf of a populism as heedless and crude as The Donald himself." The magazine also published a series of essays by twenty-two prominent conservatives denouncing Trump's candidacy. Flamboyant conservative radio and TV personality Glenn Beck said voting against Donald Trump was the "moral, ethical choice" even if it meant Hillary Clinton was elected president.[2] Beck wasn't alone among conservative pundits lying awake at night anguishing over what the Republican Party was turning into. Milwaukee's conservative radio host Charlie Sykes owned up to his role in creating an environment where the likes of Trump could thrive, acknowledging that he and other right-wing media personalities had "created this monster."[3] And then Sykes announced he was ending his radio show.[4]

That would have been all well and good, if not for the fact that the rest of us were going to have to suffer the side effects of their sleep disorders.

Most of Sykes' conservative media peers went to great lengths to deflect responsibility. Acting as if he and right-wing commentators like him had no hand in making the Frankenstein that was laying waste to the GOP, Jonah Goldberg self-righteously proclaimed that Trump's supporters were "oblivious to the fact that he needs more than his base to win. And once again, conservatives who've made a career thumping their chests or their Bibles about the importance of character and morality found themselves making excuses for a man who personifies everything they claimed to oppose."[5] Other conservative heavyweights like George Will and David Brooks expressed horror at the ugly turn American conservatism had taken, with Brooks writing that "Trump breaks his own world record for being appalling on a weekly basis" and his "performances look like primate dominance displays—filled with chest beating and looming growls. But at least primates have bands to connect with, whereas Trump is so alone, if a tree fell in his emotional forest, it would not make a sound." Brooks concluded:

"It's all so pathetic."[6] Will called Trump an "arrested-development adolescent" with "feral appetites and deranged sense of entitlement." He went on to say he is a "marvelously efficient acid bath, stripping away his supporters' surfaces, exposing their skeletal essences" without displaying a hint of awareness of his own culpability as an intellectual architect of modern conservatism that has now morphed into Trumpism. Will grasped for straws, wishfully speculating that maybe "Trump is the GOP's chemotherapy, a nauseating but, if carried through to completion, perhaps a curative experience."[7]

The right-wing pundits were hardly alone in expressing horror at the events that were unfolding. More than one hundred Republican national security leaders, many of them former Republican administration officials, signed a letter stating they are "unable to support a party ticket with Mr. Trump at its head." Christine Todd Whitman, the former Republican governor of New Jersey and one-time Environmental Protection Agency administrator under George W. Bush, publicly vented that "Trump … is employing the kind of hateful rhetoric and exploiting the insecurities of this nation, in much the same way that allowed Hitler and Mussolini to rise to power in the lead-up to World War II." Mitt Romney, the 2012 Republican presidential nominee, former governor of Massachusetts and now Utah senator, said Trump "has neither the temperament nor the judgment to be president." Rosario Marin, the nation's treasurer under George W. Bush, was personally offended by Trump. "He's insulted me, the people I love, the community I represent." Bush's treasury secretary Henry Paulson said, "The GOP, in putting Trump at the top of the ticket, is endorsing a brand of populism rooted in ignorance, prejudice, fear, and isolationism." Bush's commerce secretary Carlos Gutierrez piled on, saying, "I haven't heard an economic concept come out of Trump's mouth except for protectionism and lower taxes. If you put those two together, that is a recipe for disaster." The former Republican senator from New Hampshire, Gordon Humphrey, said, "I am ever more confirmed in my belief that Trump is a sociopath, without a conscience or feelings of guilt, shame, or remorse."[8]

When a video surfaced showing Trump bragging about how he could force himself on women, more party leaders reached their breaking point. Among them was Ohio's John Kasich, himself a presidential candidate, who said, "I will not vote for a nominee who has behaved in a manner that reflects so poorly on our country. Our country deserves better." Arizona Senator John McCain: "Donald Trump's behavior this week, concluding with the disclosure of his demeaning comments about women and his boasts about sexual assaults, make it impossible to continue to offer even conditional support for his candidacy." Nevada Governor Brian Sandoval: "This video exposed not just words, but now an established pattern which I find to be repulsive and unacceptable for a candidate for president of the United States. I cannot support him as my party's nominee."[9]

So there we stood, with a looming presidential election featuring the two most unpopular major party nominees ever.[10] Someone was going to be elected. But it was hard to see how anyone would win.

Wall Street and Main Street Republicans alike had to be hoping and praying for Trump to lose. It would be hard enough to stitch together the mangled body of the rampaging monster that was tearing their party limb from limb if he lost. If he won, the party would be his. Their worst fears were realized. In the end, an uneasy alliance of wealthy capitalists, the religious right, and working-class whites—a fragile coalition of strangers cobbled together by Republican operatives and right-wing media personalities—put Donald Trump in the nation's highest office, leaving establishment Republicans struggling to come to terms with the unsettling reality of having Donald Trump as the party's national standard-bearer. And leaving even the leaders of the Never Trump movement within the party little choice but to stand united behind a deeply polarizing figure they clearly could not stand.

Whether they can see it or not, Trump is a perfect reflection of what the Republican Party has made itself. In other more important ways, Trump exposes the party leaders' biggest blind spots. Trump understands something the party brass can't bring themselves to accept. Most voters—including many who consider themselves either Republicans or Democrats but also the self-described independents who make up the biggest single voting bloc—hate both major parties and believe that your average politicians are nothing but self-dealers, interested first and foremost in advancing their own careers and feathering their own nests. Paradoxically, a narcissist like Trump appeals to quite a few of those who are thinking this way because they figure he's already rich and famous and doesn't need to hold any office to make a name for himself or line his pockets, even though he has done just that.[11] [12]

The other blind spot Trump is exploiting is that Republican insiders figure most Americans hate the government. For decades they have demonized anything having to do with government. Their message has been self-centered, putting the individual on a pedestal, and their policies have torn at the fabric of society. It is clear Trump saw a miscalculation there. He found sizeable numbers of disenchanted voters—especially working-class white men—who yearned for some common aim or uniting cause. He seems to instinctively sense that it's not the government they hate, it's a government that they believe stopped working on their behalf quite some time ago that has them exasperated. He's offered them common enemies to unite around, tapping into powerful feelings of nativism and nationalism. Trump's pitch appeals to the darkest impulses, the fear of outsiders, the fondness for walls. But it also zeroes in on how everyday Americans have been betrayed by ruling elites and how the government is serving a few at everyone else's expense. All of this leaves the Republican Party at greater risk of splintering and disintegrating than at any time in living memory.

You'd think this would put the Democrats in the proverbial catbird seat. But Democratic establishment types have conspicuous blind spots too. Those blind spots explain why they couldn't see the Bernie Sanders insurgency coming in 2016 and why they still can't seem to fathom his appeal and that of younger protégés, especially to young millennials.[13] Like Trump, but for very different reasons, Sanders is immune from the "typical politician" characterization. With Sanders, the immunity was built up over a lifetime of standing for principles when they weren't fashionable. And like Trump, but in a vastly different way, Sanders calls

Americans to a common purpose, while Democratic insiders continue to cater to their most loyal constituencies and ignore other vast swaths of the population. To party regulars, both Trump and Sanders are seen as unwelcome intruders. But the fact that the inner circles on both sides see both Trump and Sanders as such says a lot about the similar mindsets in the two major parties and the glaring vulnerabilities both parties have. All this leaves American politics more up in the air than it has been in living memory, and leaves America divided and without a clear sense of national purpose.

At some point we will come to our senses. Sooner or later, we will ring in the year one A.T.

After Trump, that is.

Anyone wishing to get a head start on preparing for that moment would do well to pay close attention to places like where I am from. Clues to the puzzle can be found there. ✛

CHAPTER ONE
CANARY IN THE COAL MINE

America is screwed.

You know it, I know it. Not because media pundits on cable news or power brokers on Capitol Hill say so. Not because college professors have clued us in on how empires fall. You can tell on your own. You've got eyes. I can tell because the place I've called home my whole life—the flyover state of Wisconsin—is America's weather vane. As Wisconsin goes, so goes the U.S. of A.

Wisconsin was instrumental in putting Donald Trump in the White House.[1] Before that, my home state played a crucial role in making Barack Obama the nation's first black president and then re-electing him.[2]

Like litmus, the mixture of dyes extracted from lichens that is red under acid conditions and blue under alkaline conditions, Wisconsin readily changes colors. Politically speaking, it is a swing state, not bright Republican red or solid Democratic blue but rather deep purple. People here voted mostly Republican through 1928, then (like most states) turned Democratic during the Great Depression and World War II. From the mid-1940s through 1984, Wisconsin again voted Republican more often than not. Democrats won the seven presidential elections from 1988 through 2012, though usually not by much. The 2000 and 2004 elections, in particular, could have gone either way in Wisconsin. The Democrats' winning streak was broken in 2016 when Trump won the state by 0.7 percent over Hillary Clinton. After losing Wisconsin's April 5 Democratic primary to Vermont's Bernie Sanders, Clinton didn't come back to the state to campaign before the November general election. Not once.

Clinton evidently did not consider that whenever major change has come to America, Wisconsin has been on the cutting edge. Wisconsin established the first kindergartens and was first to set up a vocational, technical, and adult education system. First to pass a law providing workplace injury compensation[3] and first to create an unemployment compensation program.[4] First to create primary elections to take the business of nominating candidates away from party bosses in smoke-filled rooms and put it in the hands of the people. First to base taxation on the ability to pay.[5]

Social Security was invented here.[6] When Americans were spooked by communism after defeating the Nazis, it was Wisconsin's Joseph McCarthy who most aggressively fanned the flames of the Red Scare and popularized Cold War thinking. As environmental degradation began to take a noticeable toll, Wisconsin's Gaylord Nelson founded Earth Day, celebrated on April 22, to raise consciousness. Time and again, Wisconsin has blazed trails. The state even has shown the way to mark the route, creating the first highway numbering system in 1917 that was later adopted nationwide. In 1919, Wisconsin became the first state to ratify the amendment to the U.S. Constitution, giving women the right to vote. In 1982, Wisconsin led the way again by passing the country's first statewide gay rights law.

Once a state of firsts, Wisconsin now is bringing up the rear by many measures. The state lags the rest of the country in job and wage growth[7] and was slower to recover from the last recession.[8] Once an industrial powerhouse, Wisconsin has lost manufacturing jobs at a disturbing clip[9] and has been slow to adapt to the changing nature of the economy, ranking dead last in the country in new business start-ups and entrepreneurial activity.[10] So far in the twenty-first century, no state in America has seen its middle class shrink more than Wisconsin.[11] The roads are going to hell.[12] As of 2018, the state ranked forty-ninth in internet speed[13] and was lagging badly in renewable energy development.[14] We used to pride ourselves on having some of the best schools in the nation but have watched them slip toward mediocrity in recent years.[15] Many parts of the state now have a public health crisis on their hands when it comes to drinking water.[16] Long known as America's Dairyland, Wisconsin's family farmers are in crisis. The state is losing more than a family farm a day, and western Wisconsin led the nation in farm bankruptcies in 2017.[17] There also was a record number of suicides in Wisconsin that year,[18] driven by a surge in the numbers of farmers taking their own lives. One sector that is booming is the prison industry. In a country with the most prisoners of any nation in the world, Wisconsin's biggest city has the dubious distinction of being home to the most incarcerated zip code in America.[19]

Wisconsin has lost its way and is becoming a shadow of its former self. Same goes for the country as a whole. The gap between rich and poor is wider in America than in any other major developed country.[20] And the gap continues to widen. Barely half of Americans now qualify as middle class. That compares to 61 percent in 1971.[21] More challenging was the uneven recovery from the Great Recession geographically, with the coasts rebounding faster and more completely than the heartland.[22] All of this gravely threatens the country's cohesiveness. It's hard to remain the *United* States of America with such stark divisions.

Small towns across America are dying,[23] and it's not too much of an overstatement to say that rural life faces extinction. This breeds political resentment[24] and is a threat to all of America,[25] and conditions cry out for a Marshall Plan for small towns across America. Problems in inner cities are just as alarming, and urban renewal is needed every bit as much as rural revitalization. Wisconsin's largest cities are the state's biggest economic engines, and the same goes for other states. America cannot thrive if our biggest cities struggle and crumble. Decaying cities need a Marshall Plan too. We can't just seek refuge in the suburbs.

Hate and fear of outsiders are on the rise and lead nowhere good. Walling ourselves off is the wrong impulse, especially when there's an increasingly acute labor shortage that threatens to throttle the U.S.

economy.[26] For all those who have lost good-paying, family-supporting factory jobs, few seem to recognize that the primary culprits are automation and economic globalization, not immigration. Now more than ever, it is important to remember that ours is a nation of immigrants. Openness to foreigners has been a defining characteristic of America and is essential to who we are as a nation. Immigration has always made our country stronger, never has it made us weaker.

We have to face facts about climate change. Our survival as a species depends on it. It should be America's goal to be the first nation in the world fully powered by renewable energy. Building the green economy to that scale is not only the right thing to do environmentally, but is also a way to resuscitate American manufacturing and replace all those lost factory jobs. American ingenuity once made us a world leader in making things. Now much of that ingenuity is devoted to cooking up hedge funds, derivatives, subprime mortgages, credit default swaps, mortgage-backed securities, collateralized debt obligations, and other such financial flimflam. Putting our minds to building a new clean energy infrastructure can get us focused on making useful goods again while also saving the planet.

If Wisconsin's history of being a bellwether foreshadowed what's to unfold in the future, my state should be leading the way on all these fronts. It is not. Not for now anyway.

After working for close to two decades as a government watchdog exposing corruption in Wisconsin's state capitol, I was arm-twisted into making a run for governor in 2018. Our campaign traveled over 100,000 miles in eleven months—the equivalent of more than four trips around the world without once leaving the state of Wisconsin. The journey was as eye-opening as it was exhausting.

The stories I heard and the conditions I saw varied widely from place to place, but plenty of common threads ran through all of them. Go west to Trempealeau County, not far from the Minnesota border, and you see hills and bluffs disappearing due to sand excavation and hear fears expressed over the effects of breathing the fine dust that hangs in the air or drinking water that has been turned an amber color. In the

Central Sands region you see lakes and streams drying up because a few are being allowed to drill high-capacity wells and hog all the water. Head east to Kewaunee County near Green Bay and you are told about massive industrial feedlots and how a third of private wells have been poisoned, and you see someone turn on a water tap and what comes out of the faucet is brown and smells like cow manure. A few counties away parents are frightened about what old lead pipes in their community's water system might be doing to their children.

Somewhere else you run into young millennials buried under a mountain of student debt. One owes $30,000. Another $80,000. A third carries over $100,000 in debt. All of them wonder how they are going to dig out of the hole they are in. All of them wonder when—or if— they will ever be able to buy a car or make a down payment on a house. Debt is spiraling in Wisconsin because students and their families are increasingly being left to their own devices to pay for college, as state support has dwindled. Wisconsin had the fourth-steepest decline in per-student higher education spending in the country, from $7,002 in 2013 to $6,435 in 2018, when the national average was about $7,800 per student.[27]

At another stop you meet a farmer who now is expected to file payroll taxes online but has no internet access out on the farm. At the next stop in the inner city, everyone is talking about the criminal justice system and racial profiling and mass incarceration. And how impossible it is to make ends meet earning the minimum wage. Then you meet some former factory workers who used to make twenty-five dollars an hour working on an assembly line but could only find work paying eleven or twelve dollars an hour after the plant closed. Their standard of living has been cut in half. They find little comfort in the news that the state's unemployment rate is coming down some. They can find a job. Many have two or three. What's next to impossible to find is work that keeps them in the middle class.

Down the road a piece, town officials are agonizing over a decision to tear up paved roads and go back to gravel because they can't afford to maintain the pavement and keep filling all the potholes. Next you arrive in a community where the townspeople are resigned to their local school closing. They know how that school is a hub of local activity, and they know losing it will be a death sentence for their town.

Along the way, I met more Trump voters than I can count. I knew some were Trump voters because they told me so, some because of a baseball cap they wore or a bumper sticker displayed on their vehicles. Some were satisfied with his presidency so far, some clearly admired him greatly, some had their doubts, and some even showed signs of buyer's remorse. Others had specific misgivings but remained generally supportive. No two were exactly alike. Each story was unique.

In two different places on two separate days, two men approached me at campaign events. I have no idea what prompted them to attend, but both offered a handshake, and each introduced himself not by name but rather by saying, "I'm a deplorable."

Heck of a way to start a conversation. Maybe they were trying to pick a fight. Maybe they were testing me or trying to throw me off balance. Maybe it was just their way of identifying themselves as Trump supporters. They did a good job of concealing their motives. What they couldn't hide so well is that they were hurting.

It was no mystery what and who they were referring to when they identified themselves the way they did.[28] I didn't take the bait. I didn't bring up the president. I asked them where they were from and what kind of work they did. In their answers were threads found in my own family's tapestry. We got to talking. I think we all were surprised by how many similarities there were in our life experiences.

Both men stayed to hear me speak to the small groups attending the events. One listened quietly. The other was visibly agitated and couldn't help interrupting me several times to challenge things I said. Afterward, both men approached me again. The one who stood in the back listening made it clear he didn't agree with many of the things I said but told me he still was impressed with what he heard and was glad he came. The other man said he thought he would be put down or berated at such an event and was surprised he wasn't.

I highly doubt either of these two men ended up voting for me, but that's beside the point. I found nothing deplorable about them. What I did find is that they both have reasons to be frustrated and afraid and angry. Both are hurting. Both are frantically searching for a way to make the pain go away.

Trump's America First rhetoric was music to their ears. His promise to renegotiate trade deals and slap steep tariffs on foreign products gave them hope that maybe the kinds of factory jobs they once had could be brought back. They both acknowledged it might not work, but they hadn't heard a better idea. One took Trump's commitment to building a border wall literally, while the other considered it more of a metaphor for tightened border security. As with trade, both found some hope in Trump's stance on immigration. They figured a wall—either literal or figurative—might improve their chances to find work that would restore their ability to make ends meet.

One of the men told me he found Bernie Sanders' message and platform appealing and even claimed to have voted for Sanders in Wisconsin's presidential primary election on April 5, 2016 before going on to join more than 1.4 million others in Wisconsin who enabled Trump to narrowly win this key battleground state in November. Neither man expressed even a hint of regret about helping land him in the White House.

Others are wondering if Wisconsin isn't cutting off its nose to spite its face. For example, dairy farmers who rely heavily on immigrants—some documented, some not—to tend and milk their herds are beginning to voice misgivings about President Trump's trade wars and anti-immigration policies. Clark County, where I did most of my growing up on my family's dairy farm, has nearly twice as many cows[29] as people.[30] As of the 2010 census, a majority of the 216 people living in my hometown of Curtiss identified as Hispanic or Latino.

When Trump said in early 2019 that there was no room in the U.S. for more immigrants, the middle-of-the-road *Wisconsin State Journal* editorialized that "Wisconsin has lots of space and a dire need for more skilled and entrepreneurial workers to fill jobs and keep our economy strong."[31] The newspaper reached this conclusion after examining a study showing that Wisconsin doesn't have enough young people to replace retiring baby boomers over the next fifteen years and that from 2010 to 2015 "the state lost population among key workforce groups, with the most troubling being the net outmigration of young families, a group that Wisconsin typically attracted." In 1990, Wisconsin had 1.75 residents under age sixteen for every resident fifty to sixty-four years of age, producing a growing workforce. By 2000, the ratio was down to 1.42. As of 2017, it was 0.87, indicating a shrinking labor pool.[32]

The number of people in their prime working years living in Wisconsin fell in all seventy-two counties but two from 2007 to 2017. The same is true for 80 percent of counties across America, which now have fewer residents ages twenty-five to fifty-four than a decade ago.[33] That prompted the *State Journal* to counter Trump's claim with this: "Our state needs more people to work and contribute here, including immigrants."

In my old stomping grounds of Clark County, with all its cows and immigrant farmworkers, Trump defeated Hillary Clinton by more than a two-to-one margin. This drives Democrats up a wall. Many jump to the conclusion that people in such places are foolishly voting against their own interests. That has become a mantra among highly educated urban professionals who make up a large portion of the Democratic Party's base. That belief is as wrong as it is condescending. Rural voters are not voting against their own interests. They know their interests well but feel invisible and forsaken. They wonder if politicians in Washington, D.C. or state capitals even know they are out there. They vote in anger. They vote out of desperation. They vote hoping against hope that they might get the attention of policymakers who haven't given them a second thought in ages. They vote in hopes of shaking up a system they are convinced is rigged against them. That's why dozens of rural counties in Wisconsin and many hundreds across America voted for Barack Obama and then turned around and voted for Donald Trump. The line between hope and change on the one hand and fear and hate on the other is far thinner than you might think.

Large segments of our nation's population are feeling left behind, struggling to make ends meet and watching their standard of living erode. Places like Wisconsin have more than their share of people in this predicament. Wisconsin is to the nation what canaries are to coal miners. What's been happening to Wisconsin—politically, socially, and economically—is an unmistakable warning that there's something toxic about current conditions in our country.

The challenges vary from place to place. But they all grow from the same taproot, a poisoned culture that glorifies greed, dooming us to a government that works for a wealthy and well-connected few at everyone else's expense and an economy that richly rewards those at the top and leaves so many out in the cold. There is grotesque inequality, both political and economic, that breeds resentment, anger, and hate. There is privilege, both political and economic, that erodes trust in others and destroys faith in the idea that we are all in this together and need to look out for each other. There is looming ecological catastrophe that causes many to bury their heads in the sand.

America is screwed. It's up to us to unscrew it.

If you don't see it as your job, my job, *our* job, then ask yourself these questions: Do you have a high level of confidence that Congress will unscrew the country? Will the White House? Will governors or state legislators?

Nope. This is up to we the people.

Unscrewing America starts with remembering the countless forgotten people living in forgotten places in our country.

Unscrewing America depends on democracy being rescued. Democracy as Lincoln defined it—government of the people, by the people, and for the people—is an endangered species. The will of the people has to be the law of the land, and that won't be the case as long as voting districts are drawn in a way that produces elections where one party wins the most votes, but the other ends up holding the most offices. It won't be the case as long as voting is suppressed. And it won't be the case as long as we have the best government money can buy, with the wealthiest in our society allowed to put elected officials in a stranglehold and dictate how our country should be run.

Unscrewing America depends on aligning our politics and economics. That means bringing democracy to our economy. Just as we need the government Lincoln envisioned, we also need to imagine—and construct—an economy that is truly of the people, by the people, and for the people.

Unscrewing America depends on rediscovering our sense of national purpose. It depends on a moral reckoning. It depends on rethinking our relationship with the earth.

It's not too late. America can be unscrewed once we overhaul the thinking, the practices, and the systems that screwed us over in the first place. ✪

CHAPTER TWO
A LOG AMONG CROCODILES

A *Wisconsin State Journal* profile of my candidacy started with this: "For Mike McCabe, running for governor was never part of the plan."[1]

Got that right.

I was fifty-seven years old, going on fifty-eight. I had never held public office. In fact, I had spent close to two decades doing work that pretty much guaranteed I never would hold office. As an independent watchdog, I had been making enemies in both major parties for years.

The group I led, the Wisconsin Democracy Campaign, specialized in following the money. We had produced a vast storehouse of studies connecting the dots between campaign money and public policy favors. One of our reports showed how state commerce programs meant to help low- and middle-income people get good jobs were redirected to corporate welfare, with the biggest handouts going to contributors to state election campaigns. Another study detailed the auctioning of the state budget to wealthy special interest contributors. A series of reports put a price tag on the value of perks special interest contributors receive. One found that on average big campaign contributors were getting a 33,000 percent return on their "investments" in the political process.

Democracy Campaign research revealed numerous other problems that are at the root of political corruption in the state. One report titled "Legal Laundering" documented how campaign money is routed through a tangled web of campaign committees to conceal the special interest origins of donations. Another we called "Tax Code Two-Step" described how wealthy donors danced around a federal ban on tax-exempt groups surreptitiously funneling what came to be known as "dark money" into election campaigns. We reported how lawmakers' campaigns are largely paid for by people who cannot vote for them. We illustrated how campaign donations come from an elite sliver of society and pack the discriminatory wallop of poll taxes and literacy tests. We described how big donors hedge their bets, giving to both sides to ensure access to and influence over elected officials regardless of party. We analyzed how local television stations systematically overcharge candidates for campaign ads. We showed how local government decisions were being systematically overruled by state lawmakers doing the bidding of wealthy special interest campaign contributors.[2]

We didn't just shine light in dark places. We acted on what we uncovered.[3]

In response to formal complaints filed by the Democracy Campaign, the notoriously weak state elections board fined nineteen wealthy donors and an ex-governor a total of nearly $7,800 in 2003 for making or accepting illegal campaign donations.[4] The board also fined another target of a WDC complaint, a self-described "political hitman," $5,500 for filing false reports of his campaign activities. In 2008, after the Democracy Campaign and allied groups had successfully advocated for the creation of a new government accountability board to oversee ethics, elections, lobbying, and campaign finance, the GAB imposed more sizable penalties on wealthy donors we flagged for breaking campaign donation limitations.[5] In March 2010, the GAB collected more than $23,000 in fines from seven people we accused of exceeding contribution limits. In 2011, more than $40,500 in fines were assessed to twelve donors against whom the Democracy Campaign filed complaints.

In 2007, we filed an ethics complaint against state Supreme Court Justice Annette Ziegler with the Wisconsin Judicial Commission that triggered an investigation and resulted in Ziegler becoming the first sitting member of the high court to be found guilty of judicial misconduct and disciplined for ethics violations.[6]

We played a key role in prompting a criminal investigation that mushroomed into the biggest political scandal in Wisconsin's history.[7] We issued a report showing how taxpayer-funded legislative caucus offices staffed by state employees were being used to run election campaigns. We were the first and only group to challenge the legitimacy of these leadership-controlled offices before an investigative series in the *Wisconsin State Journal* started in 2001. The study served as a road map for the reporter who broke the story. We met with *State Journal* reporters for over six months before the first stories appeared in print.

After the newspaper series, we filed legal complaints triggering criminal investigations into apparent violations of state ethics, campaign finance, and open records laws.[8] The probes produced nearly four dozen state and federal felony charges against five current or former state legislators from both major parties and one capitol staffer as well as misdemeanor charges against another legislator and several other staffers. All of the lawmakers and staffers were convicted. Two of the former legislators received jail sentences, and two others were sentenced to prison, although one of them was granted a new trial on a technicality and eventually reached a plea agreement dismissing felony charges and imposing a $5,000 fine after more than eight years of legal maneuvering.

Veteran reporter Dee Hall, the one who spearheaded the newspaper's investigations, was named Journalist of the Year in Wisconsin for her exposés of the abuse of taxpayer funds by state employees doing illegal campaigning. She dropped me a note saying, "Thanks again for all of your help…. Your group was integral in laying the groundwork…. I just had to convince people to fess up and confirm it."

After blowing the whistle on illegal activities in the caucus offices, the Democracy Campaign worked with other reformers to pass legislation abolishing the partisan state offices. The bill was approved by the senate on a 30–3 vote and the state assembly on an 86–8 vote. The legislation was signed into law by the governor. Effective January 1, 2002, the scandal-plagued legislative caucuses ceased to exist. Along with the formal abolition of the taxpayer-funded political caucuses, new workplace rules governing all legislative employees took effect in November 2001 to prevent future abuses of state offices and resources for campaign purposes.

As all this was unfolding, I got my hands on a copy of a memo from a prominent lobbyist describing Senate Democratic Leader Chuck Chvala's demands for campaign contributions from the lobbyist's clients.[9] In the memo, the lobbyist informed his clients that Chvala told him he "will not look favorably upon groups" that give more collectively to the fifty-six Assembly Republicans than they give the eighteen Senate Democrats.

A friend of the Chvala family gave me the copy of the document, saying only, "He's crossed the line," and, "You know what to do with this." I discreetly passed the memo on to news reporters, and the story was on the front page the next day.[10] We followed up months later with an analysis of subsequent campaign finance reports showing that special interest donors abruptly changed their giving patterns to meet the demands that the lobbyist said Chvala made. The donors had followed orders with amazing precision.[11] Chvala was criminally charged with nineteen felony counts, including extortion. He ended up pleading guilty to two felonies for misconduct in office and served a nine-month jail sentence.

This kind of work made me no friends in the state capitol. It did get the Democracy Campaign recognized as "Citizen Openness Advocate of the Year" in 2012 by the Wisconsin Freedom of Information Council. In bestowing the award, the council said, "No one has done more than this nonpartisan watchdog group to hold public officials accountable by demanding transparency, not only in campaign financing but in the operations of government, and no one has taken more heat for it, especially this year."

No good deed goes unpunished.

By 2017, Wisconsin was restless. You could find people in every part of the state who were tiring of Governor Scott Walker's divide-and-conquer politics and feed-the-rich policies. They wanted something different. Some of those people wanted to break the mold altogether and started looking in my direction, urging me to consider running for governor. My answer was no for quite some time. More like hell no.

If only they'd taken no for an answer. Instead, they started petition drives to draft me. A handful of community leaders from around the state wrote a letter and got close to 200 people to sign it.[12] They were business owners, farmers, doctors, clerical workers, cooks, librarians, teachers, students, nurses, pharmacists, police officers, social workers, prison guards, chaplains, veterinarians, landscapers, janitors, bartenders, insurance agents, and realtors. Some were from fair-sized cities like Appleton, Green Bay, Janesville, La Crosse, Oshkosh, Stevens Point, and Wausau. Others were from tiny specks on the map like Amery, Eleva, Eureka, Seymour, Stoddard, and Redgranite.

In their pitch, they said, "The levers of political power have been seized and are being manipulated by those interested primarily in self-enrichment and personal power. The actions of those who currently control the capitol are extremely short-sighted as well as morally and ethically corrupt, and sap our state of its underlying strength and vitality."

The letter writers went on to describe themselves as "hungry for a different kind of leadership. You are the right answer. You are an upright man, not interested in self-enrichment or power for power's sake, with a feeling for the needs of others and your country. We are aware that you would rather not run for office."

They had that last part right but were undaunted: "With the landscape littered with professional politicians and career officeholders, your understandable and admirable reluctance to run only makes you more appealing to us...."

Lamenting that the "rural-urban divide is growing disturbingly wide," they told me, "You have what so few of today's politicians have, namely an understanding of rural life and the challenges small-town residents face and an ability to speak their language." They rested their case with this: "We need you to run because the major parties are broken, and you belong to no political party. You are a true independent and have been speaking truth to power for decades.... For decades you have shined light on the misdeeds of Republicans and Democrats alike and have blown the whistle on them without fear or favor. That makes you a public servant in the truest sense. That's what Wisconsin needs now more than ever. We need you to run because Wisconsin politics has grown corrupt, and there is no one in our state who has worked harder for a longer time and done more to fight political corruption than you. Truth is becoming an increasingly scarce commodity in our society, and no one in our state has demonstrated a greater devotion to truth telling than you and been more willing than you to speak the truth even when few want to hear it, and some actively seek to silence it."

Others followed up that letter with an online petition that 500 more signed.[13] I was honored and flattered, of course, but the idea of running for any office, much less the state's highest one, still struck me as lunacy. As they correctly noted, I belong to no political party. I had not spent my life building relationships in party circles and lining up supporters. I had spent so much of my life pissing off the establishment.

As more people reached out to push me to take the plunge, a Bambara proverb I learned while living and working long ago in the West African country of Mali as a Peace Corps volunteer came to mind: "No matter how long a log floats on the river, it will never be a crocodile." That was their way of saying be who you are. I had a hard time seeing myself in the role of candidate. It was easy to see myself as a log among crocodiles.

Hell, in June 2016 I wrote an article for the Blue Jean Nation blog under the headline "You and I can't run for governor." The commentary started with this observation: "Representation is the foundation our political system is supposed to be built on. For authentic representation to be possible, it has to be realistic for people who are truly reflective of the general public to run for office. By this measure, you can see that American democracy is on very thin ice when you consider what's involved in seeking and holding an office like governor."

You see, those doing the campaigning in Wisconsin's previous election for governor collectively spent well over $80 million.[14] The popular assumption is that candidates need to have as much money as their opponents—or close to it—to be taken seriously. That thinking is mistaken but widely accepted. That fact alone leaves nearly everyone on the outside looking in. Only a select few can put millions of dollars of their own money into a political campaign. Among the multitudes who can't, most are unwilling to sell out their beliefs and principles to win over special interests capable of supplying them with the financing to compete.

Not having a personal fortune or a willingness to take out a second mortgage on your soul is not the only characteristic separating those who can run from others who think they can't. Elections for governor are partisan contests, and America has a strong two-party system. The major parties expect candidates to join their ranks. Most Americans are not fond of either major party at the moment and have little interest in joining one of them. Candidates not only are supposed to be dues-paying party members, but are also expected to take the position that their party can do no wrong and the other party can do no right. Most Americans don't believe that and aren't comfortable pretending to.

There's another thing about getting to be governor that rubs me the wrong way. To my way of thinking, serving in public office puts you below the people you are elected to represent, not above them. Governors are supposed to be servants, not masters. In Wisconsin, getting elected governor entitles you to a salary of close to $150,000 a year, more than three times what the average worker makes.[15] Governors take up residence in a 20,000-square-foot lakefront mansion. Servant quarters it is not.

Never in my life have I made $150,000 in a year, and I have trouble with the idea of taking such a lofty salary at taxpayer expense just for winning an election. I've never lived in a mansion and wouldn't feel right moving into one in the name of public service. To my mind, governors should pay for their own housing, just like everyone else.

Putting governors up on a pedestal is only one way the ideal of representation is debased. Ever notice how the House of Representatives is hardly representative of the American electorate? To this day, the House's membership is far older, richer, whiter, and more likely to be male than the average American. That's because it's next to impossible for most Americans to run for the office. Our country is poorer for it.

Scott Walker, consummate career politician, friend of the wealthy and well-connected, had spent virtually his entire adult life seeking and holding office: first the state assembly, next a stint as Milwaukee County executive, then governor in 2010. He survived a recall election in 2012 before winning another full four-year term in 2014. Three times Democrats had cleared a path for a well-financed, stand-for-little centrist to oppose him in races for Wisconsin's highest office. Three times those establishment favorites had come up short against Walker. Wisconsin was restless. People were hungry for something different. With all this going through my mind, still thinking it was madness, and against my better judgment, I decided to answer the call.

I was in. ✛

CHAPTER THREE
BUCKING THE ODDS

It didn't take me long to start wondering if I'd made a horrible mistake. It felt weird telling people I was running for governor. I often got one of those who-do-you-think-you-are looks when I did say it. I couldn't be offended. Those same thoughts were occurring to me. Memories from my past flooded my mind, swamping my self-confidence. One day during my senior year of high school, a bunch of us were standing around in the gym during lunch, and the conversation turned to future plans. When I told that circle of classmates I was planning to head off to Madison to attend the University of Wisconsin, one of the girls who was tops in our class shot me that same kind of skeptical look and said in front of the others, "You'll be back."

I don't think she intended to be mean. Very few from my high school were going to college, and the farm kid didn't fit the profile of the few who might dare to do it. Even in a small-town environment, the kids from out on the farm were looked down upon by some. I was accustomed to being seen as the hick, the hayseed. It was out of character to go to college. It sure as hell was out of character for someone like me to think of being governor. Those who-do-I-think-I-am thoughts visited regularly. I pushed ahead anyway. Who cares what others think, I reminded myself.

Running for office, especially statewide, is a daunting, humbling, and all-consuming undertaking. I had plenty of company. More than a dozen and a half people announced their intention to run for governor in 2018. Some were established officeholders and seasoned campaigners. Others were more like me. I had a small but passionate following but was unknown to most of Wisconsin's nearly six million residents except at the state capitol, where I was known—and hated.

The first thing that happens when you throw your hat in the ring is everyone starts categorizing you and slapping labels on you. Given my life's work, I'm not all that easy to pigeonhole. I choose *commoner* as my label for two reasons. First, I am the son of dairy farmers. I don't know what else a farm boy could be but a commoner. It's who I am. The second reason has to do with what I want. I want more common sense in government. I want more searching for common ground and less dividing and conquering people who could and should be united. And I want concern for the common good to become far less uncommon.

Still, many can't shake their dependence on the old labels. They asked again and again if I am liberal or conservative, left or right. Never mind that those terms no longer mean what they once meant. They don't even mean what today's dictionaries say they mean. The word *liberal* comes from the same root as *liberty*. It means freedom. People who call themselves conservative think they are the pro-liberty ones and consider modern-day liberals to be anti-freedom. The word *conservative* shares the same root as *conserve* and *conservation*. People who consider themselves liberals think they are pro-conservation and can't see how today's conservatives are for conserving anything. These labels would be comical if they weren't so politically debilitating.

Yet people still demanded to know … are you conservative or liberal, right or left, Republican or Democrat?

My honest answer to that question is that I am a mutt like most normal people. Only in the political world do people claim to be purebreds—100 percent this or that. Normal people are mutts, conservative about some things, liberal about other things, and middle of the road about the rest. Given how messed up politics is at the moment, not too many among us feel good about calling ourselves Republicans or Democrats, liberals or conservatives. We deserve better and need something new.

But Wisconsin election law, as elsewhere, requires candidates to choose to run as either a Republican, Democrat, independent, or third-party candidate. I had to decide that first.

The most comfortable but least practical option for me was to run as an independent. The most probable way to have the greatest impact on the race was to run under a major party banner. I spent several weeks listening to those who had urged me to run, seeking their advice. Some said they would only support my candidacy if I ran free of the major parties, but more said, don't you dare run independent or third party and split the anti-Walker vote.

What I was hearing summed up how American democracy is caught on the horns of a dilemma. Most Americans are feeling fed up with the Republicans and let down by the Democrats—with good reason—as both major parties are failing the country. Yet a third party isn't the answer, at least not for now in our system. Like it or not, for better or worse, America has a two-party framework. Ours was not set up as a parliamentary democracy, where competing factions can join forces and form coalition governments. We don't have fusion voting, ranked-choice or instant runoff voting, proportional representation, or any of the mechanisms that would allow third parties or independent candidates to successfully compete in our elections and hold power in our government. This is why third-party or independent bids for office—whether it's Ross Perot one time or Ralph Nader another—regularly lead to dead ends.

So how do we get regular people back in the driver's seat of our government when both major parties are catering to a privileged few at the expense of everyone else, but our system is structured to enforce a two-party arrangement? We have to start with two articles of faith. First, it hasn't always been like it is now, and it doesn't have to be like this. Second, there is a way out of the trap we're in.

We need to make the major parties—or at least one of them for starters—better. They won't change unless forced. It's like the basic law of physics: An object at rest will remain at rest unless some force makes it move. A corrupt political establishment will stay corrupt, and failing parties will keep failing us unless we make them change their ways.

When past generations freed themselves from similar traps, they started by shedding old labels and fashioning themselves a new identity. They attached that newly minted brand to breathtakingly ambitious agendas. They were not bashful, in the least, about stating their aspirations for the future. And then they effectively forced those aspirations down the throats of the parties. When the smoke cleared, there were not three parties or four or five. There were two. But the parties were transformed. They were reconnected to the masses.[1]

Current conditions dictate that this must be done again, with so many Americans feeling politically homeless, feeling unable in good conscience to call themselves Republicans or Democrats, liberals or conservatives. Labels like those are now little more than the political equivalent of ethnic slurs.

When I speak of people feeling politically homeless, and when I say I am a commoner, I emphasize that the royals of our society made it so. When faced with economic and political threats eerily similar to today's conditions, past generations straightened things out on more than one occasion. I refuse to believe there is something so different about us or wrong with us that renders us less capable of making change than those who came before us. In so many ways, we have more going for us now than they did then. Political reboots have happened before. Another one is desperately needed.

Being neither elephant nor ass, but also recognizing that our country is stuck with a two-party system, I concluded that the best of the flawed options was to try to work subversively within that two-party setup in hopes of getting that system truly working for all of us and not just the politically connected few.

So I swallowed hard and chose to run as a Democrat.

I also committed to running free of big money influences, refusing to accept any single donation over $200 and no more than a total of $1,000 from any individual over the course of the campaign even though state law allows candidates for governor to take as much as $20,000 from a single contributor and up to $86,000 from a political action committee. I made it known that as governor I would not live in the mansion known as the Executive Residence and would not accept the full salary of the governor once elected but instead would be paid one dollar less than the average Wisconsin worker makes (about $45,000 annually).

My campaign's website was governorbluejeans.com, reflecting my intentions to barnstorm the state in blue jeans. Time and again, I was asked if I really was going to run the whole way in jeans. Again and again, I insisted I would and doubled down on the answer by vowing to be inaugurated in jeans and govern in them as well. I've never owned a matching suit—you know, where the pants are made of the same material as the jacket—and wasn't even married in a suit. It felt phony to put on that costume now, remembering the way the people of Mali described the importance of being yourself. No matter how long a log floats on the river, it will never be a crocodile. Besides, as I told a news reporter who pressed me on the matter, "Why is it assumed that it's wrong for an elected representative of the people to dress the way regular people dress?"[2]

With all those things decided, the hard part started. I started assembling a team and mapping out a campaign plan from scratch. While most of the contenders taking on Walker announced they were jumping in the race from the Democratic strongholds of Milwaukee or Madison, I wanted to return to my roots and declare my candidacy from the farm where I grew up in Clark County … if the current owners would have me. They were Trump voters and had a "Veterans for Bush" sign displayed conspicuously on the barn. Turns out they were honored to host my coming-out party and stood with me as I officially entered the race. Standing in front of the barn on a sunny September morning, I told a small gathering of family, friends, supporters, and journalists, "I am running for one reason and one reason only—to get our government working as well for the commoners as it does for the royals."

Capitol insiders thought little of my candidacy and even less of my chances. Veteran political observer Bill Kraus, who had helped mastermind Lee Sherman Dreyfus's dark horse populist bid for governor in 1978 and stunning upset victory, made Scott Walker the favorite in the 2018 race and put me down as a hundred-to-one longshot.[3] My odds were twice as steep as Kraus gave recent Stanford graduate Bob Harlow, who wound up being one of the first to drop out of the race after failing to qualify to have his name appear on the ballot.

The Democratic field was crowded, to put it mildly. There were two current state legislators, a former state representative, a former state party chair, the elected state school superintendent, Madison's "mayor for life,"[4] a union president, a wealthy businessman, and a liberal talk radio host, among others including a hair salon owner, a social worker, and some hundred-to-one shot lacking the standard political pedigree. A flavor for nearly every taste.

The state party outwardly remained neutral but did plenty behind the scenes to put a thumb on the scale. When my campaign sought to purchase access to the party's voter and member lists, we were given no answer for close to six weeks. Finally, our request was denied. The reason given was that I was not a party member. Never mind that I registered my candidacy as a Democrat. Never mind that I was traveling the length and breadth of the state bringing a Democratic message to places Wisconsin Democrats rarely, if ever, visited. Never mind that some non-members were granted access to the party voter database, and some were given the lists free of charge. We could not get a straight answer about what makes someone a party member. The word out of state party headquarters was that membership depended on paying dues of $25 annually. But national party rules explicitly prohibited basing membership on a requirement to pay dues. The state party's constitution and its bylaws were in conflict on the question. On paper, there was no clear answer. In practice, the party was all over the board. Some non-members got access, while others like me were denied. Even some dues-paying members running for office had been denied the lists if they were challenging Democratic incumbents. We got tired of waiting for clarity and sought voter information elsewhere. Well after we had done so, the state party chair informed us we could purchase the lists after all if we still wanted them. We did not.

While the runaround on voter and party member lists was an annoyance that held up our campaign planning, the more significant impediments thrown up by party insiders came in the form of a steady stream of rumors and innuendoes. The first was that I was supposedly anti-union. Supporters of mine were incredulous, pointing to my very public and very pointed opposition to Scott Walker's union-busting actions and wage suppression policies for the better part of a decade. They held up the fact that no one in the race had gone farther out on a limb on increasing pay for low-wage workers, and that I had even gone so far as to say years earlier that the ability to unionize should be cemented in place as a civil right. I also stood alone among the candidates in proposing a statewide experiment with a universal basic income program to create security and stability for vulnerable workers who were watching their employment automated out of existence. John Nichols of *The Nation* magazine singled that out as one of the best ideas put forward in the governor's race and said, "McCabe is on the cutting edge here."[5]

Yet everywhere I went, I faced questions about being anti-labor. When enough people had heard my answers and grew familiar with my stances on labor issues, that whisper campaign lost steam. Party operatives then spread a second false rumor, namely that I was not a real Democrat and was only in the race to be a spoiler and help Walker get re-elected. They told party members if I didn't get the Democratic nomination by winning the primary election I would then run as an independent in the general election to split the anti-Walker vote. They knew this to be untrue. They were well aware that longstanding Wisconsin election laws do not allow candidates who lose in a party primary election to nevertheless advance and have their names appear on the general election ballot. They spread the rumor anyway, and I was questioned about it at nearly every campaign stop.

I didn't see it as such at the time, but they were really paying me a compliment. They wouldn't have bothered with these efforts to muddy the waters if I hadn't been gaining traction as a candidate. Everywhere I went, I talked about ways to make health care affordable for everyone. Almost a year before the August 14 primary election, I participated in a health care forum in Milwaukee sponsored by a senior citizen group. Forum organizers' aim was to get Democratic candidates on the record in favor of accepting federal funds to expand the state's Medicaid program for the poor, elderly, and disabled, something Scott Walker steadfastly refused to do. All of the other candidates took the pledge, as did I. But I was the only candidate who didn't stop there. I said Medicaid—known in Wisconsin as BadgerCare—should be made a public option that anyone in the state could buy into regardless of income. By the end of the campaign, nearly every candidate in the race had embraced BadgerCare for All.

I also was first in the race to call for full legalization of marijuana in Wisconsin. Everywhere I went, I made the case that drug laws had proven ineffective, counterproductive, and racially discriminatory. Those who use marijuana made it abundantly clear they would use whether it's legal or illegal. Drug laws making a second marijuana possession charge a felony in Wisconsin were not making communities safer or improving public health but were filling jail cells with nonviolent offenders. That drove mass incarceration and is a key reason why Wisconsin spends more of its state budget on prisons than on the entire university system.

Everywhere I went, I called for cutting Wisconsin's prison population in half by emphasizing sentencing alternatives to imprisonment and focusing more on mental health and drug addiction treatment, pointing out that imprisoning twice as many people in Wisconsin than in neighboring Minnesota hadn't resulted in less crime in Wisconsin.[6] The two states have virtually identical crime rates. But because Wisconsin spends so much more on prisons than Minnesota, we are far less able to invest in empowering young people with higher education. By the end of the campaign, most of the candidates had joined me in calling for at least decriminalization, if not full legalization, of marijuana and were echoing my call for halving the prison population.

I told anyone who would listen that if you work you shouldn't be poor, and to erase the phrase "working poor" from our vocabulary, the minimum wage should be turned into a living wage by boosting the wage floor to $15 an hour. Some of the other candidates balked at first,

MIKE McCABE

arguing that low-wage workers should get a pay raise, but $15 was too high. By the end of the campaign, the entire field had publicly embraced a $15 hourly minimum.

Everywhere I went, I said there should be a rule for government: If a program works, keep it and fund it. If it doesn't, get rid of it. By that standard, I said the state's corporate welfare office should be closed, and taxpayer-subsidized private schooling should end. The Wisconsin Economic Development Corporation (WEDC) was created in 2011 to promote new business start-ups. A 2015 audit of WEDC was harshly critical of the agency's financial management and internal operations.[7] A follow-up 2017 audit concluded that WEDC couldn't account for the number of jobs its assistance programs had helped create or retain,[8] and another in 2019 showed the problems still weren't fixed.[9] More damning was the fact that Wisconsin ranked last in the nation in new business start-ups for three straight years.[10] WEDC was a waste of money. Handing out state-funded subsidies that make taxpayers pick up the tab for more than 33,000 Wisconsin students to attend private schools had been no more fruitful. When Wisconsin's school voucher program was started in 1990, it was pitched as a way to boost student achievement, improve school quality, and give families more educational choices. Test scores and other indicators mostly show voucher students are not doing any better than those attending public schools and by some measures are doing worse. Overall school quality in Wisconsin has slipped. Most families receiving vouchers already were privately schooling their children without state assistance, shooting a hole in the argument that the program provides choices that didn't previously exist.[11] After more than a quarter-century, this private school subsidy program has failed to deliver the promised results. Student achievement hasn't increased. Wisconsin's education system has not been made better. It's gotten worse. Families aren't getting more choices. Taxpayers are mostly just subsidizing the decisions some families already were making and previously were paying for themselves. Resources are being siphoned away from community schools, badly weakening them, especially in rural areas. After all these years, it's clear the voucher experiment hasn't worked in Wisconsin.

Everywhere I went, I said stop throwing good money after bad.

Everywhere I went, I talked about using close to a billion dollars in savings gleaned from closing the corporate welfare office and ending private school subsidies to fund a plan to bring high-speed internet to every part of the state within five years. To every audience, I said it should be Wisconsin's goal to be the first state in the nation fully powered by renewable energy and spelled out a plan to get there. At every stop, I crusaded for restoring local democracy[12] by repealing recently enacted state laws that took away decision-making authority from local communities in Wisconsin.[13] People at the local level have had governing power systematically taken away from them. Since 2011, more than 130 laws were made in Wisconsin limiting or prohibiting local decisions on subjects ranging from building codes and rental property inspection to school budgets and shoreline development. Elected representatives chosen by the people in local communities have had their hands tied with respect to the bidding process for local road projects, siting of animal feedlots, and approval of mining projects or the construction of oil and gas pipelines. Communities are not allowed to set their own workplace standards for wages, benefits, and working conditions. They can't have a minimum wage higher than the state's. They can't establish their own sick leave policies. They can't have residency requirements for local public employees. They can't join with other communities to set up regional transit authorities. They aren't free to put rules in place for sport shooting ranges. They don't have a say on the weight of vehicles using their streets and roads. The list of recently imposed state restrictions goes on and on. Communities should be free to decide what's best for them. State government should support their ability to govern themselves the way they could in 2010 in Wisconsin.

I told people that if elected, I'd periodically take the governor's office on the road, bringing cabinet secretaries and other agency officials with me to give people in urban and rural areas of the state alike greater access and more of a voice in state government. People shouldn't have to travel to the state capitol to be heard and served by their state government. It should come to them. My thought was that having state government set up shop from time to time for even a week in inner-city neighborhoods and rural communities gives residents more opportunity to voice their concerns and learn about state programs and services they may not know about. It also gives state officials greater insight into people's struggles.

I punctuated every stump speech, every media interview, every one-on-one encounter the same way. We have to deal with the reality that there is a cancer growing in the body of democracy that must be cut out. We have allowed cronyism and corruption and what amounts to legal bribery to take root in our country, and these weeds must be uprooted. I reminded every audience that we will never get living wages from a dying democracy, we will never get good health care from a sick political system, we will never get clean air and water from dirty politics, and we will never get anything more than thoughts and prayers after each new mass shooting as long as elected officials are paid to take no other action.[14]

The message was making an impression and creating a buzz. An early *Wisconsin Public Radio* listener poll showed me leading the Democratic field, amazingly enough. A few months later, the liberal group One Wisconsin Now, a party mouthpiece closely tied to the Democratic establishment, ran an online poll of its members and followers. Returns were being tweeted out and posted online until, much to the group's surprise and chagrin, I was leading the pack. Voting in the poll was extended for a few more days beyond the original deadline, and then was extended a second time. When voting eventually ended, the group decided against making the final results public, dismissing its own poll as unscientific. OWN's leader at the time, Scot Ross, had been a capitol staffer years earlier and was caught up in the corruption scandal described in chapter 2.[15]

In Wisconsin, the poll of choice for media organizations and election watchers is conducted by Marquette University. Marquette's first polling on the governor's race showed me running ahead of three of the five candidates who had raised the most money and within one percentage point of a fourth. The second Marquette poll in June of the election year featured head-to-head matchups between Governor Walker and the leading Democratic candidates. Journalists are drawn to polling data like insects to light but apparently were dumbfounded by who appeared to be running strongest against Walker and ignored the finding. A newspaper reporter for the small-town *Sauk Prairie Eagle* was one of only a few to highlight this needle in the haystack of Marquette's poll results, tweeting, "Mike McCabe is closest to Walker with only a two-point difference. All other candidates trail Walker by four or more points."[16]

Campaign finance reports are right up there with poll numbers on the list of things the media can't resist. And that's where I wasn't keeping up with the other candidates. The first reporting period in the governor's race covered the last quarter of 2017. My campaign's fundraising broke six figures, but only barely. We raised just under $104,000 in this earliest stage, with the money coming from individuals giving an average of $72. Some of the Democratic hopefuls raised three, four, even five times as much. The wealthy businessman in the race put almost a half-million dollars of his own money into his campaign's treasury. The union president got three-quarters of his money from union PACs, including more than half of his total haul from a handful of out-of-state labor committees. I tried with little or no success to make the point that the governor couldn't be beaten with money. Indeed, Walker had far much more than everyone else. He had out-fundraised all of his potential rivals combined by more than two-and-a-half times in 2017 and was sitting on nearly four times as much money as the entire Democratic field as 2018 dawned.[17]

In past elections Democrats spent ever-larger amounts—$33 million in 2014,[18] $22 million in 2012,[19] and $12 million in 2010[20]—in hopes of defeating Walker only to see Republican forces vastly outspend them and Walker win by virtually identical margins all three times. He had never faced a genuinely people-powered grassroots crusade creating a vivid contrast between the governor's campaign bankrolled by billionaire tycoons and one that is truly of, by, and for the people. In three straight elections, Democrats looked for and found a Goliath, but their Goliath was beaten to a pulp by the far-larger Republican Goliath.

I tried reminding Democratic operatives and voters alike that it was David who defeated Goliath. It was David who brought down the giant. Mine was a voice in the wilderness.

These days candidates for office are told they have no choice but to spend four or five hours every single day raising money. We spent ten, twelve, fourteen hours a day raising a citizen army instead. By the end, we had more than 3,000 volunteers pounding the pavement statewide. Neighbors talking to neighbors. We tried making our campaign a twenty-first-century version of how Bill Proxmire won statewide elections in Wisconsin for thirty years. His spending never reached $300 in any of his statewide campaigns. In his last run in 1982, Prox spent $145.10 and won in a landslide.[21]

The ghost of Bill Proxmire was on John Nichols' mind as he dissected my candidacy's prospects for his readers: "Mike McCabe does not go in for lockstep party loyalty. He's campaigning for the Democratic nomination for governor as a critic of the failings of both major parties. As such, he's running in the tradition of some of the state's most successful political figures. Former U.S. Senator Bill Proxmire frequently clashed with—and constantly frustrated—the leaders of his own Democratic Party. Former Governor Lee Sherman Dreyfus upended the Republican Party in the late 1970s with an insurgent gubernatorial campaign that objected to politics as practiced by more conventional Democrats and Republicans. So McCabe's maverick candidacy is in tune with the Wisconsin that was. The question of the moment—not just for McCabe but for all of us—is whether the Wisconsin that was still is."[22]

The answer to that question would come soon enough. ✪

CHAPTER FOUR
CRUEL AND UNUSUAL

As we ushered in 2018, our campaign kept traveling and attracting more volunteers while trying to raise money, of course, no more than $200 at a time. By election day, we had raised a little more than $300,000 to compete in a $93 million race.[1]

When you reflect on what's gone haywire in American politics, you can almost sum it up in one word. Hell, I can pare it down to two letters: TV.

That's an oversimplification, of course, but not that much of one.

In my lifetime, it was once possible to run successfully for statewide public office in Wisconsin for hundreds of dollars. The reason Bill Proxmire could run and win so inexpensively was that television had not yet become king of American politics. In Proxmire's day, most people learned about politics and government and elections and candidates by reading the newspaper, and Proxmire had a knack for getting his name in the paper with his everyman persona and his Golden Fleece Awards showcasing wasteful government spending.

Today, relatively few read newspapers. Many increasingly rely on online sources and glean suspect information from social media. But to this day, television is where most people get most of their news.[2] And with television news providing scant coverage of those running for office, candidates have to pay handsomely to get their messages to voters. The biggest campaign expense—by a long shot—is television advertising, and TV airtime costs a fortune. That's why more than $93 million was spent in Wisconsin's 2018 governor's race trying to sway voters, and why total spending in the previous two elections for governor was in the neighborhood of $80 million.

Some money goes for radio advertising, and a little goes to print ads. Online political advertising is growing fast but still pales in comparison to the spending on TV ads, and most of that advertising is misleading at best and character assassination at worst. Put another way, most of those tens of millions of dollars pay for poison. All those thirty-second attack ads poison the well from which public participation is drawn. They make would-be voters hate politics and politicians a little more than they did before. They poison democracy.

In this television age, a vast industry has grown up around the business of election campaigning. And every element of this industry works to sell candidates for public office the way laundry detergent or hair care products are sold. Every component of this industry works to make candidates less authentic. In exchange for exorbitant fees, consulting firms take care of every detail of campaign management. Candidates are told what to think and where to stand by pollsters. Speechwriters put words in their mouths, and ad agencies craft slick marketing campaigns. It all culminates in outrageous sums of money going to media ad buys.

The highly paid operatives who place the ads and very few others know a dirty little secret. They have to buy an increasingly large number of spots for their clients' ads at an ever-increasing cost to get the same audience reach that they used to get at a far lower cost. That's because viewers are more eager and more technologically equipped to avoid ads. This is another reality driving the cost of the political arms race.

Democracy's salvation depends on two related things. First, we've all been trained to accept that there is only one political currency that matters, namely money. Past generations understood that other currencies, like organized people and provocative ideas, had great power as well. And on more than one occasion, some of these other currencies were blended to make a concoction potent enough to overcome money's influence. In our day and age, these other political currencies have, for the most part, been taken out of circulation.

Second, the political addiction to television and the industry that caters to TV-driven campaigning must be broken. We need to challenge the acceptance that it is okay for those seeking public office to be peddled like consumer goods. We need to challenge an industry that makes candidates more fake at every turn. Candidates don't need pollsters to tell them where to stand. They don't need speechwriters to put words in their mouths. They don't need image consultants, and they don't need ad agencies to sell them to us. This industry is where the lion's share of political campaign resources go. It is why there are $90 million elections for governor in out-of-the-way places like Wisconsin and why billions of dollars are spent on electioneering nationally.

One of the worst things about modern politics is how it's been professionalized. As the paid consultants and career political operatives are selling candidates the way cars, mobile phones, and breakfast cereal are sold, they also are coaching their candidates on how to duck and cover, keep their guard up, and pull punches. A few of their puppets get elected and keep right on playing it safe, not proposing or voting for anything politically risky for fear of putting reelection in peril, and big problems keep going unsolved.

Amateurs—regular citizens with lives outside of politics—have been pushed out. Actual democracy requires their involvement. Our country needs amateurs involved. We need people running for office who don't obsess over what they could say or do to get elected but rather focus entirely on what needs to be said and done to rescue our society. The job that needs doing is not to win an office. It's to push the conversation, alter the debate, provoke thought, and make change. The aim of regular citizens brave enough to enter the fray should be to succeed even if they are not victorious, to bring about the greatest possible change in people's thinking even if they don't receive the most votes.

Sometimes lightning strikes and unconventional candidates running with purposeful abandon win, as happened in New York with the election of twenty-something Alexandria Ocasio-Cortez to Congress. A *Time* magazine profile of the rock star of the House observes that AOC "threatens the status quo, bringing a youthful impatience to a set of policies ... like Medicare for All and tuition-free public college. ... [S]he seems more concerned with movements than elections; she doesn't talk about flipping seats and votes, but rather of winning hearts and minds. Hers is the politics of the possible, not the practical."[3]

For every one who rocks the boat and wins, many more will see their efforts fall short. The emotionally charged documentary film *Knock Down the House* profiled four boat-rockers. Three of the four did not win their elections. But all of them set powerful, inspirational examples. The one who did win an office—Ocasio-Cortez—immediately started leading the push in Congress for a Green New Deal. I've heard it said the Green New Deal is like a watermelon, green on the outside but deep communist red on the inside. Critics—and there are many—call it radical. It better be. Drastic action is required to ward off climate catastrophe. As AOC rightly pointed out at a congressional hearing in early 2019, "We're going to pay for this whether we pass a Green New Deal or not. Because as towns and cities go underwater, as wildfires ravage our communities, we are going to pay. And we're either going to decide if we're going to pay to react, or if we're going to pay to be proactive."

Drastic action is required to deal with hate and violence that are growing like a cancer in our society. There needs to be an awakening to how financial insecurity and economic instability and inequality produce anxiety that easily morphs into hate. When jobs that pay a living wage are hard to come by, racial minorities and immigrants get scapegoated even when the primary culprits are automation and globalization, not immigration. Robots don't become the target of hate; people do. Current economic conditions in America are a breeding ground for hate. The gap between rich and poor is wider in America than in any other major developed country,[4] and economic indicators foreshadow further deterioration of the economic status of blue-collar workers.[5] Just as we can pretend not to notice global overheating, we can pretend not to notice the signs of emotional distress caused by growing economic insecurity. We can act now to search for ways to relieve the anxiety that comes with watching employment automated out of existence, or we invite growing unrest and more violence and continued eruptions of hatred.

We can't afford to pretend. Our country will circle the drain if we do. Preventing that fate depends on enough of us being willing to run for office or help someone else run to challenge all the pretending. It depends on enough of us being impractical and throwing caution to the wind. It depends on us breaking the consulting industry's stranglehold on our elections so we can get our democracy back. Perhaps candidates won't be able to seek office as cheaply as Bill Proxmire did, but they can and must find ways to run—and win—for millions less. They will then be that much less beholden to big-money interests and that much more able to truly represent the will of the people.

While running for governor, I took part in close to fifty candidate forums leading up to Wisconsin's August 2018 primary election. Interest groups sponsored some, while the media or a party organization sponsored others. Some focused on a single issue. Education. Economic development. Environmental protection. Criminal justice. Agriculture. Racial equality. Transportation. Energy policy. Other forums covered the waterfront, with questions on a variety of subjects. Audiences were as small as a few dozen people and as large as 700. One debate was televised.

These forums tested the candidates' ability to think on their feet, almost to the point of cruelty. We usually were not shown the questions in advance and were typically given a minute or two to answer, sometimes as little as thirty seconds. On one occasion, we were asked a three-part question about economics that took more time to ask than we were given to answer. At one of the earliest debates, the candidate on whom the media bestowed front-runner status—state school superintendent Tony Evers—was mangling an answer before throwing up his hands in frustration as his time was running out and blurting, "Oh, I give up." None of the press reported his stumble.

At a forum on labor issues held in a union hall in Milwaukee, candidates were given four-foot-high placards with a checklist of promises the sponsors hoped to get from each of us. One of the pledges was to fully veto any state budget that did not include language repealing Walker's signature actions stripping public employees of collective bargaining rights and discouraging unionization by making Wisconsin a so-called "right to work" state. The union president in the race proudly displayed to the crowd his placard with every box checked. The former state party chair said he'd gladly force a state government shutdown over these matters of principle. When my turn came, I showed the audience my placard with all but one box checked. I said I could not in good conscience promise to veto a budget in its entirety over the absence of a single provision, explaining that in Wisconsin vetoing a budget does not shut down the government. When a new budget is not approved, the state government continues to operate under the terms of the old budget, in this case, one written by a Republican governor and Republican-controlled legislature. I said I could not promise to take any action that would merely keep Republican budget policies in place for up to another two years. As I made this point, several candidates could be seen erasing, as discreetly as possible, the checkmarks they had made next to that one promise. Two candidates who spoke after me agreed that with Wisconsin's budgeting system vetoing an entire budget would be irresponsible and only extend the lifespan of Republican budget policies, not bring them to an end. That wasn't reported, either.

In all the forums combined, participating candidates were asked well over 200 questions. Never was there a forum devoted to money in politics or the multitude of other threats to democracy. At something like four dozen forums that spanned ten months in every part of the state, the candidates for governor were questioned about money in politics a grand total of three times.

Most Americans see widespread government corruption[6] and are deeply worried about it.[7] Most think politicians are listening to rich people and ignoring the rest of us. Scientific research shows there's good reason to think that way. A 2014 study by political scientists Martin Gilens of

Princeton University and Benjamin Page of Northwestern University concluded that the U.S. does not qualify as a democracy but rather is basically a corrupt oligarchy where voters barely matter. Or, as they put it, "Economic elites and organized interest groups play a substantial part in affecting public policy, but the general public has little or no independent influence."[8] In other words, average citizens only get what they want if economic elites or interest groups also want it. Most Americans want something done about the problem.[9] Most who are running for office, on the other hand, don't want to talk about it. The media and interest groups rarely, if ever, ask them to. The candidates are addicted to money because just about every play in their campaign playbook depends on nonstop fundraising. The media—especially the TV stations—also are addicted because selling advertising time to candidates is so lucrative.[10]

Money in politics corrupts our elections and our government in ways big and small.[11] It distorts and corrupts our economy and hurts the working class.[12] It might not be our country's biggest problem, but it is the problem underneath all other problems. In our elections, candidates are questioned about every conceivable problem more times than they can count. But they rarely, if ever, are asked about the problem beneath those problems. That's why it's so common to hear elected officials say no one cares about campaign finance reform. They reach that conclusion because they are almost never asked about it on the campaign trail. That needs to change. The curtain needs to be pulled back, and the way levers are pulled and buttons are pushed needs to be made plainly visible. It starts with repeatedly and persistently questioning those seeking public office about how the money fueling political campaigns corrupts our government, hurts our economy, and ruins our democracy.

When the curtain is pulled back, some fundamental truths become clear: clean air and water don't come from dirty politics; good health care isn't the natural offspring of a sick political system; and living wages are hard to come by in a dying democracy. It's so important to pay attention to that problem behind the curtain. Trouble is, few in the media who were covering the governor's race were questioning what was back there. Other things had a way of being top of mind.

Like traffic circles. For the record, I have nothing against roundabouts. Roundabouts are good things. They make intersections safer than stop signs do. Yet I was pegged as an anti-roundabouts candidate in my run for governor. Goes to show, you run for office and silliness inevitably ensues.

Now, as Paul Harvey always put it, the rest of the story...

I'm from farm country, and it breaks my heart to see rural communities going backward, digging up pavement and replacing it with gravel because they can't afford to keep filling their potholes.[13] Wisconsin once had some of the nation's finest roads. But by 2017, Wisconsin's roads were second-worst in the country by one measure.[14] This leads nowhere good. You can't have bad roads and a good economy. I pushed a "pay as we pave" policy to wean Wisconsin from heavy reliance on borrowing to pay for road projects. I also called for our state to embrace a "fix 'em first" policy reversing the emphasis on new construction and highway expansion at the expense of basic upkeep, making the case that with limited resources the top priority should be maintaining the roads we've already got and preventing their further deterioration.

As part of that fix 'em first approach, I told one news reporter that I would even be open to a temporary moratorium on new cloverleaf freeway interchanges and roundabouts to free up funds for needed repairs of existing roads. The reporter wrote that I support banning roundabouts. The story took on a life of its own. In a profile of candidates seeking the Democratic nomination for governor that appeared in newspapers throughout the state shortly before the August 14 primary election, the short write-up listed only three or four bullet points about my candidacy. One of them was "Favors a ban on roundabouts."

I lost count of the number of times I had to explain to voters that I didn't want roundabouts banned. Run for office. Silliness ensues.

At the same time, running for office is an unusually cruel thing to do to a family, especially one that hasn't lived and breathed politics. Nothing can quite prepare you—or loved ones—for the emotional rollercoaster you ride in an election campaign. For the candidate, there are the rigors of all the travel and the challenge of being "on" for every encounter at every stop. The intensity of the experience but also the monotony of it result in psychological wear and tear. Answering the same questions hundreds, if not thousands, of times. Listening and graciously accepting the same advice offered over and over and over again. At one gathering, a woman earnestly suggested that I grow a beard, thinking it would give me more gravitas. A different day, after I spoke off the cuff for close to thirty minutes and then answered questions afterward for nearly as long without notes, a lengthy line formed for one-on-one conversations. A woman told me I should write my speeches and read from prepared text. A man and woman standing right behind her both shook their heads vigorously, and the man silently mouthed "No! Don't!" It was hard keeping a straight face. Later that same day, a man lectured me about how unwise it is for someone with my rosy skin tone to wear clothes with any red in them. Stick with earth tones, he advised. Good grief.

On a daily basis, you are pulled in one direction and then the opposite. You are told to be yourself, only different. Day after day, well-meaning people tell you how you should look, dress, speak, and act differently. Sometimes the critiques of physical appearance or fashion sense get so personal that it makes you wonder if they would ever say such things to a spouse or sibling or friend. It's as if they don't see political candidates as people but rather as products on a shelf to be examined and rated. Candidates—successful or not—come in any number of different complexions, but all must have thick skin. But no matter how durable your hide, it's hard to sweep all of this into an emotional broom closet when you get home. You might crave some alone time after all the human interaction on the campaign trail, but you know you need to be as "on" with family as you are with would-be voters.

As trying as it is for the candidate, it has to be much worse for those at home. Relationships are starved, strained, and stressed. Bonds are ruthlessly tested. Loved ones with already full lives are further burdened with added household chores and called on to carry out responsibilities you should rightfully be there to handle. My wife, Marilyn, and I have been together for close to forty years. We're best friends. We've lived life as a team, serving overseas in the Peace Corps together and parenting together. During the campaign for governor, it felt like we were torn apart. I was on the road constantly. Marilyn still was working full-time to keep us financially solvent and had to do the work of two people at home, so she could rarely travel with me. Still, she was actively engaged in the campaign, putting in long hours nearly every evening and on the weekends. She also needed to be there for our son, Casey, who was a senior in high school for most of the campaign. Casey picked up some of my slack at home but had a heavy workload with schoolwork, hockey practice and games after school, a part-time job at a nearby fast-food joint, and a volunteer gig at a community radio station. More often than not, the campaign work Marilyn did was separate from my campaigning, so it was nothing like Peace Corps or parenting. She felt abandoned and rightly so. From time to time, almost like clockwork, those feelings boiled over. The anger was vented. It was warranted and needed and understandable. But it still left me feeling like an absentee husband and deadbeat dad. That took a heavy toll on all of us and left me wondering if public service was too costly.

It is not. Its value does exceed the price paid. For years, those who run Peace Corps have been telling recruits it's the toughest job they'll ever love. Running for office is sort of like that. It's stressful and exhausting, yet energizing. It's deeply painful for you and those close to you and can be terribly frustrating, yet it's uniquely rewarding. It's draining, yet it fills you up. And, in the end, as with the Peace Corps, you feel like you learn far more than you teach and get much more than you give.

We all live in bubbles. Running for office, you get invited into other people's bubbles. I can't think of many endeavors that afford as much opportunity to travel from bubble to bubble as I did while campaigning. It's a tremendous blessing, a true gift. I had the chance to travel to every nook and cranny of my home state of Wisconsin and listen to and share thoughts with those I met along the way. Here's what I found: We have a lot more in common than we think we do, but we're quicker to see each other as enemies than we used to be. We judge each other more harshly than we did not so very long ago. Folks in one part of Wisconsin feel misunderstood by people in other parts of the state but also are quite willing to jump to conclusions about the personal shortcomings or moral failings of the people in those other places. I can only imagine how these impulses intensify across a land as vast and diverse as America.

I found empathy to be in short supply. As a society, we seem to have forgotten the wisdom of not judging others until you've walked a mile in their shoes. I lost count of the number of times I heard someone in an urban setting say rural people are stupid and are voting against their own interests. My stock answer was that neither is true; it's just that people in the cities see rural interests differently than those living in the country see their own interests. Want to know how rural residents see their interests? Ask them for crying out loud. But truly understanding their answer requires a sincere effort to relate to their sense of place and way of life and unique challenges.

After I spoke to one of those urban audiences, a woman told me point-blank that rural people vote the way they do because they are all racists. If that's true, I responded, then how do you explain the election results in 2008? Dozens of rural Wisconsin counties helped elect the nation's first black president.[15] And if bigotry is why rural voters choose as they do, how do you explain the 2012 elections? Not only did large swaths of rural Wisconsin vote to re-elect President Obama, they also helped elect an open lesbian to the U.S. Senate.[16] Not many white male heterosexual Democrats were chosen to represent rural areas in the state legislature or other offices, but these communities were okay with the black guy and the lesbian.

Bigotry exists in rural America and every other part of the country. As a child, I saw literature for the white supremacist group Posse Comitatus regularly distributed in my area, but voters there were electing Democrats to Congress and the state legislature. Today it's a different story. In the 2014 election for governor, my hometown had the distinction of giving Republican incumbent Scott Walker his biggest percentage margin of victory of any community in the state.[17]

Something more than race or wedge issues like guns or abortion has to be behind this political realignment. People were just as socially conservative and just as fond of guns and hunting when they were electing Democrats in my youth as they are now. Making sense of changing party allegiances requires getting beyond stereotypes.

When I visited small towns, I ran into more stereotypes. I regularly heard that people in the cities are elitist, economically privileged, and morally decadent. I heard bitter complaints about how the politicians are catering to the cities at the expense of small towns and the rural way of life. What I heard made it seem like the rural-urban divide is wider than it's ever been in my lifetime.

Politicians have undeniably played a big role in making this so. They've fanned the flames of mistrust and sowed the seeds of hostility as part of a cynical and self-serving strategy of divide and conquer. But we don't need to go where they want to lead us. We can choose to tear down the walls between us and replace them with bridges. We can choose to promote understanding and thereby break down stubborn stereotypes. It starts with holding off on judging others until we've taken a good long walk in their shoes. A little empathy could go a long way.

Though I'm sure it won me few votes, I saw it as my responsibility as a candidate to do what I could to bridge the divides in our society. That meant talking about rural problems in urban settings and talking about inner-city challenges in rural and suburban communities. Speaking to an audience of more than 500 people at a candidate forum in an upscale hotel in the wealthy, nearly all-white Milwaukee suburb of Pewaukee, my message started this way: "We've got to deal with the fact that we live in a country that started with a constitution that said people could be property. And once that constitution was amended and slavery was abolished, those who sought that kind of economic and social control weren't about to embrace equality. They went about constructing Jim Crow. They went about building segregation laws that would allow them to continue to exercise that control. And once Jim Crow was swept away by the civil rights legislation of the 1960s, they didn't embrace equality. They went about building a new structure, and that structure stands on some pretty sturdy legs. It stands on voter suppression policies that have been created. It stands on mass incarceration. It stands on an evolution of policing philosophy. Every squad car in America used to say 'protect and serve.' Now the philosophy of policing has become 'intimidate and control.' That is the new Jim Crow. ... We have to commit ourselves to cutting the legs out from underneath that new Jim Crow."[18]

I went on to call for an end to crimeless parole revocation and made my pitch for cutting Wisconsin's prison population in half so the state can stop spending more locking people up than we spend unlocking human potential through higher education. The next candidate to speak was African American union leader Mahlon Mitchell. "It's hard to follow Mike, I ain't gonna lie to you. So everything he just said, I agree with. ... Mike, you had me clapping for you for a minute there," he said to an eruption of laughter.[19]

I ain't gonna lie to you. I had only recently become aware of crimeless parole revocation. I had not known that you could be convicted of a crime and sentenced to prison, do your time, be released to get on with your life, and then be imprisoned again without committing a new offense, sometimes for something as innocent as missing a meeting with a parole officer. I learned about this feature of our criminal justice system from people like Carl Fields. I first met Carl at an earlier campaign stop. He was in Pewaukee for the candidate forum that evening. Our paths crossed several more times, both before and after the election.

Carl is a black man in his late thirties living in Racine, a city in the far southeastern corner of Wisconsin with close to 80,000 people. His mother was killed in 2000 in a random shooting, throwing Carl for a loop and spinning his life out of control. Lashing out in pain and anger, he wound up in a confrontation with local police during which he fired shots in their direction. He was convicted of reckless endangerment and spent sixteen years in prison. He makes no excuses for his behavior, owning up to being a "knucklehead" in his youth and making horrible choices. Spending time with Carl, you'd never guess he had done hard time. There is a gentleness about him; he carries himself with a quiet serenity. He speaks softly, thoughtfully, carefully choosing his words. Bespectacled with horn-rimmed glasses, he comes across as bookish and exudes a burning intellectual passion.

Carl put his life back together. Having the stain of a felony conviction on your record makes it next to impossible to find a job. After struggling to find any employer willing to take a chance on him, Carl admits he thought about whether it might be easier just to reoffend. But he persevered and eventually found his niche as a program manager at a drop-in center for the homeless in an Episcopal church in Racine. He also became an organizer for a group called EXPO (Ex-Incarcerated People Organizing) and another initiative called Congregations United to Serve Humanity. He became chairman of the Racine Interfaith Coalition's Restoring Our Communities (ROC) task force. ROC and EXPO are projects of the social justice organization WISDOM, which advocates for ending mass incarceration and solitary confinement and for policies making it easier for those released from prison to reenter society, such as ban-the-box laws barring employers from asking job applicants about criminal convictions. Carl also is active in the Poor People's Campaign started in 2017 by the Reverend William Barber II of North Carolina.

In a society where so many who have the right to vote don't exercise that right, Carl Fields is someone who desperately wants to make a difference in his community and would dearly love to be able to vote but cannot. He remains on extended supervision until 2033 and, under Wisconsin law, won't have his voting rights restored until then. In the meantime, he lives in fear that even the most trivial slip-up could put him back behind bars, even with no new criminal offense. To know Carl and so many like him who've paid their debts to society but live under an ominous cloud is to know how unjust this is. Knowing Carl puts a face on some horrifying statistics, a black male incarceration rate in the U.S. that's nearly three times as high as for black men in South Africa in 1993 under apartheid. Wisconsin has a black male incarceration rate that not only is the highest in the nation but is eight times that of apartheid South Africa in 1993.[20]

Drive through the part of Racine known as Uptown and you see block after block of boarded-up storefronts and abandoned buildings. Once a thriving factory town, most of the plants in Racine now stand empty, leaving the whole community struggling. In another place on the other side of the state to the west, the 400-some residents of the rural Crawford County village of Gays Mills are dealing with chronic misfortune of their own. After devastating floods in 2007 and 2008 left homes uninhabitable and local businesses ruined, townsfolk started planning in 2009 to move the village hall and other pillars of the community to higher ground. By 2012, much of the new part of Gays Mills had been built. Then more flooding came in 2016 and 2017. In 2018, yet another flood—one of historic proportions, even bigger than in 2007 and 2008—hammered the beleaguered community. What some call hundred-year floods are coming just about every year now.

Not far outside of Gays Mills is a farm that's belonged to the Schwert family for over one hundred years. During my campaign, I spent the better part of a day with that family, something any self-respecting political consultant would frown upon. I could imagine the consultants' disapproval as John Schwert and his son Brent showed me around the farm. John's wife, Lois, wasn't there. She was working as she does nearly every day at a nearby apple orchard to bring in a paycheck to supplement the family's income. For his part, John not only milks the cows and works the fields but also repairs neighbors' machinery on the side to earn a few extra bucks. What this family was doing to survive overwhelmed me. Growing up on a dairy farm, I milked my share of cows and did my share of farm chores. The day's work started at 5 a.m. and wasn't finished until at least 8 p.m., seven days a week. And that was just to keep up with the farm work. To do all that and then have one family member also working as a mechanic and another toiling in an orchard was hard to fathom. John's voice was weary, his body hobbled, his spirit by all indications broken. He looked and sounded defeated.

Brent had left a promising career that had taken him to Europe only to return home to help his parents try to keep their heads above water, which is not easy to do nowadays in Gays Mills. Talking to Brent, you could tell he was worried not only about his parents' physical well-being but also their emotional state. My travel companion that day, as was usually the case, was our campaign's event coordinator, Beth Hartung, who also grew up on a family dairy farm. The Schwerts seemed honored by our visit and enjoyed talking farming with us. This campaign stop seemed to lighten the mood for people carrying a heavy weight, which is why we stayed so long. The political consultants would say lifting people's spirits is not a candidate's job. But that is exactly what's wrong with our politics and those political professionals. They are so busy selling a product that they've grown oblivious and insensitive to all the forgotten people in forgotten places. If the choice has to be made, I'd rather be humane than be governor.

When the political consultants don't have their candidates dialing for dollars, they have them pressing the flesh where the largest numbers of voters can be found. Meaning they'd never plan a stop in Minong, Wisconsin. Minong is one of those places you could miss by blinking, deep in the Northwoods. The population was 527 as of the 2010 census. There's not much work to be found, except for one factory that makes Jack Link's meat snacks. Our campaign stopped through Minong for a meet and greet at a local tavern. Before that event, Beth and I were approached by a young woman with two small children. She told us her father had heard about the gathering we were having and very much wanted to meet me. But he's wheelchair-bound, she told us, and the hydraulic lift on his van was broken, so he was stuck at home. She asked if we would consider stopping by his house and seemed taken aback when I said we had a couple of hours before our event and would be happy to.

Jeff Fox lives in a house about the length and width of a small mobile trailer home that sits on a concrete slab. Chickens scratch and peck at the bare ground outside the front door. Out back under a tree sits his van, looking to be in substantial disrepair. Outside, the house is run-down and shabby. The front door opens to a single room. The walls and ceiling are unfinished, lacking even plaster or drywall. Furnishings are limited to a bed, one chair, and a metal rack for hanging clothes. A gas stove for cooking is in the corner. Jeff greets Beth and me in his wheelchair. His beard is bushy and unkempt, his clothes soiled and tattered, with a blanket draped over his legs. His eyes lit up as soon as he saw us. His cheerful, lighthearted tone of voice was unexpected as I looked around at how little he had and how vulnerable he was living out in the middle of nowhere with a significant disability and without reliable transportation. He was talkative but also hungry for information about where I stood on a wide range of issues and what I would do for communities like his if elected governor. He told us of his involvement with ADAPT, a national grassroots effort to organize disability rights activists to engage in nonviolent direct action, including civil disobedience, to protect the civil and human rights of people with disabilities. He regaled us with stories of trips to Washington, D.C. and the times he was harassed or arrested for protesting.

Jeff's daughter and her two young children came to our meet and greet later that evening. She approached me as the gathering was breaking up to thank me for paying her dad a visit and to let me know how much that had meant to him. When I think back on that encounter, I always wish I could have brought people from Pewaukee or other such well-to-do places to meet Jeff and his daughter and granddaughters and see for themselves how they are making do in Minong. It's only about 325 miles from Minong to Pewaukee. It might as well be a million.

I think again about those two men who approached me at campaign events, each holding out a hand to greet me and each introducing himself as a deplorable. When we parted company, I couldn't help but feel exasperation about this moment we are living through and the toxic political environment we've created, where we are convinced "our side" is right and good and the "other side" is wrong and evil. But I also was more convinced than ever that the solution to the extremism that has taken hold of our country is what Martin Luther King Jr. called "radical empathy." The way to fight radicalism that breeds hate and violence is with a different kind of radicalism. As Dr. King said: "Here is the true meaning and value of compassion and nonviolence, when it helps us to see the enemy's point of view ... for from his view we may indeed see the basic weaknesses of our own condition, and if we are mature, we may learn and grow and profit from the wisdom of the brothers who are called the opposition."

With only enough money left to pay for some online ads and to bump up the number of views of some of our campaign videos on social media, I continued to trudge around the state, breaking seemingly every rule in the political consultants' playbook. Our campaign's six paid staffers and more than 3,000 unpaid volunteers sprinted for the finish line. It amazed me that they still had any fuel left in their tanks. For the better part of a year, rain or shine, through snowstorms and heatwaves, they had stood with signs and banners they dubbed "people-powered billboards" at busy intersections and highway overpasses, smiling and waving at passing motorists. They had canvassed neighborhood after neighborhood, knocking on doors, handing out literature, and planting signs in yards. They had given our campaign a ubiquitous presence at community festivals, county fairs, and local farmers' markets. They had worked night and day, going so far as to form teams in places like Racine—"light brigades" they called themselves—brandishing illuminated signs that could be seen after sunset. Their efforts were noticed.

The other candidates in the race often remarked privately to me about my "army." Others made note publicly. As the day of reckoning drew near, former state senator and UW Milwaukee professor Mordecai Lee predicted an election day surprise, telling Wisconsin Public Television's audience that there is a "grassroots prairie fire" that polls maybe didn't detect. "If I had to take a bet, I'd bet that they are unpredictable," Lee said of Wisconsin voters.[21] My campaign team was sure he was talking about us. In the end, he was wrong. Candidates who entered the race with more name recognition and stockpiled enough money to saturate the broadcast airwaves with thirty-second promos surged down the stretch. The safest bet—school chief Tony Evers—won the nomination. I was left in the dust.

But I had done my duty. I was convinced Wisconsin was on the wrong track and needed new leadership. I didn't want to see a repeat of the previous three elections for governor. An intensely competitive primary election with the crowded field of candidates pushed Evers not only to be a stronger campaigner but also forced him to embrace a far bolder campaign platform. The previous Democratic nominees for governor were able to get away with playing it safe and standing for very little. Each lost to Walker. Evers moved over the course of the campaign to increasingly ambitious positions on living wages and health care access. He embraced the goal of cutting Wisconsin's prison population in half, legalizing marijuana, and closing down the state's corporate welfare office. He not only won his party's nomination, but he also defeated Walker.

It was over. I felt like I should have no regrets. I had run an impactful race, though not victorious. Still, watching the documentary *Knock Down the House* about the four women who ran for Congress against all odds in 2018 hit me like a ton of bricks. Much of what they were saying and shown doing in the film mirrored my own experience as a candidate the same year. I felt a kinship with the three whose efforts came up short. I marveled at Ocasio-Cortez's shocking upset win. The last poll in that race showed her trailing her opponent Joe Crowley, one of the top-ranking Democrats in the House, by 35 percentage points. A particularly poignant moment in the film shows an anguished Ocasio-Cortez coming to terms with her likely fate on the eve of the election, wondering aloud if she had let down all the people who had done so much on her behalf. I tried my best to fight back tears, but they streamed down my cheeks. Her pain was mine too.

As I watched AOC sort through her emotions, I thought about the more than 3,000 people who worked so incredibly hard to get me elected governor. They were my voice, my surrogates in neighborhoods up and down the state. They were my TV ads. I thought about one in particular from the La Crosse area who volunteered his evenings and weekends even as he was working more than forty hours a week at his paying job to make ends meet. As the election approached, he donated his two weeks of paid vacation for the year to work full-time on the campaign. Like Ocasio-Cortez, the feeling that I had let him and so many others down tormented me. I thought I had worked through those emotions, but watching the film made me realize I had just stuffed them in some psychological sock drawer. The movie forced that drawer open.

I thought about the promises I made to myself when I was being pushed to run. I promised myself I would do it the right way, win or lose. I wouldn't sell out to big-money interests. I wouldn't get down in the gutter and throw mud on opponents. I would focus on what I'm for. I could handle losing an election but didn't want to lose myself. I did stay true to myself throughout the experience. But given the outcome, the movie made me ponder whether those promises had been principled or selfish.

Before Trump was even a presidential candidate, it was hard not to notice that conditions were ripe in Wisconsin—and across the country—for the rise of the kind of ultra-nationalist, fear mongering, immigrant scapegoating politics of division and exclusion he embodies. A big part of the reason why I let myself get talked into running for office was that I sensed our country was headed toward a dark and dangerous place. The *Wisconsin State Journal*'s profile of my candidacy, mentioned at the beginning of chapter 2, ended with a recounting of stories about how a neighbor of mine who committed suicide and a bullied brother had led me to understand that "we are all in this together and we've got to look out for each other, and our politics need to reflect that."

Everywhere I traveled, I brought ideas about how we might change the way we think and talk about politics and act as citizens to help us avert disaster. My campaign was one meager attempt to offer an antidote for the rural versus urban and left versus right divides that are ripping America apart. In today's political environment, few seem to be looking for antidotes. Most hunger for more righteous indignation and condemnation of the other side. Choosing not to feed that beast and satisfy these appetites means swimming against some powerful currents.

My upbringing and life experiences have led me to believe—and to say over and over as a candidate for office—that we are all in this together, and we've got to look out for each other, and our politics need to reflect that. My candidacy did not prove to be a sufficient antidote to the political poisons so many Americans have ingested. The search for an effective remedy must continue. And if that involves swimming upstream, so be it. Only dead fish go with the flow. ⊙

CHAPTER FIVE
OUR THROW-AWAY ECONOMY

The American economy is on a tear. In April 2019, the nation's unemployment rate fell to its lowest level in five decades.[1] That sent the stock market soaring again to new record heights.[2] Which begs the question: With the economy booming, why is trust collapsing in America?[3]

Trust in government, down. Trust in business and nongovernmental organizations, down. Trust in the media, down. For nearly two decades, the communications marketing firm Edelman has been asking people around the world about their level of trust in various institutions. In its 2019 Edelman Trust Barometer, the firm said it had never before recorded such steep drops in trust in the United States.

What the hell is going on?

Abe Voelker can tell you. At Christmastime, he and his wife and children travel to northern Wisconsin to celebrate the holiday with his parents and siblings on the dairy farm he grew up on near Rice Lake. Shortly before I met Abe, he had made this annual pilgrimage and learned it would be his final Christmas coming home and milking cows because the family was going to be throwing in the towel and selling off their herd. They just couldn't make a go of it anymore. Every month they were losing money and couldn't see any sense in continuing to go deeper in debt just to continue operating.

A few months after getting that jolting news, Abe wrote a poignant story, "On the death of my family's dairy farm," that he published on his blog. About a month after Abe's article was brought to my attention, I shared a stage with him, his mother, Jamie, and younger brother Noah at a public forum in downtown La Crosse. The idea was to give city folk a chance to get to know what farm life is like these days.

Every time he went home for a visit, Abe helped his dad and Noah with the barn chores. The cows need milking twice a day, seven days a week. On the Voelker farm, the first milking starts at about 4 a.m., with the second beginning at around four in the afternoon and continuing well into the evening. Abe says he never had the work ethic to be a farmer. Ever since he was little playing video games, he was fascinated by electronics. He went off to college and became a computer programmer but was thankful that his kid brother loved farming and stepped up to help his dad and mom keep the family business going. Two older brothers had already left the farm—neither of them "got the farming gene," Abe says.

Years later, as he mourned the coming loss of his family's way of life, Abe wrote: "This probably shouldn't be a huge shock. Ever since I can remember, there has always been a steady drumbeat of family farms going bust. ... Our family farm was subjected to the same ups and downs as every other farm but had always managed to weather every storm." He recalled a time in the late 1990s when he was in elementary school, and milk prices were so low that some farmers were dumping their milk down the drain in protest.[4] His mom, Jamie, tried to organize area farmers. They went to their state representative to plead for his intervention, only to be told they were a negligible part of his constituency and should come back when they had more support.[5] They tried rallying fellow farmers to close off their land to recreational activities such as hunting, fishing, snowmobiling, and trail riding by all-terrain vehicle enthusiasts. They even tried blockading a creamery's weighing scales to protest the low prices. In 1997, they started an organization called Save Our Family Farms to push for Canadian-style commodity supply management in hopes that could reduce market volatility, and by late 1998 their group had morphed into a fledgling union. They had some success in raising awareness, but in the end, their efforts didn't have any discernible effect on government policy or milk prices or their bottom line. Dairy farmers once again had to either hold on tight and ride it out, or go bust. Many went under.[6]

The Voelker farm survived that time, but barely. The dismal milk prices, combined with Abe's dad needing knee surgery after years of kneeling on concrete to milk cows, put the family in the position of having to sell off most of the herd. Bottomed-out milk prices lowered the value of the cows, and the family got less money than they had hoped for. Abe vividly remembers the day the cows his family loved so much were auctioned off. "To a kid it felt like vultures were paying a pittance to carry away a piece of my identity. By the end of the day ... that anger turned to sadness and a sense of loss," he wrote over twenty years later.

By his early teens, with his dad recovered from his surgery and his older brothers graduated from high school and moved out, the family's herd had been regrown to near-previous levels. Fast forward a couple of decades, and Abe is programming computers, married with kids, while his dad is in his seventies and still working seven days a week from before sunrise to well after sunset with Abe's kid brother Noah at his side. The economics of dairy farming have grown cruel again. As recently as 2014, farmers were paid more than twenty-three dollars for one hundred pounds of milk—about twelve gallons and about what a good cow gives in a day—but by 2018, the price had plummeted to just over fourteen dollars. It rebounded to between fifteen and sixteen dollars in 2019, but for typical family farmers in Wisconsin these days, the cost of producing one hundred pounds of milk hovers around seventeen or eighteen dollars. Families like the Voelkers are losing a buck or two on the milk each one of their cows produces every day.[7]

Contrast that with the massive industrial operations taking over in America's Dairyland and elsewhere around the country, officially known as Concentrated Animal Feeding Operations (CAFOs), defined as having at least 1,000 beef cattle, 700 dairy cows, 2,500 swine, 125,000 broiler chickens, or 82,000 laying hens kept in confinement, with feed brought to the animals rather than the animals grazing in pastures or free-ranging. In the dairy business, operating in such a way at such a scale is one of the reasons these factories can cut the cost of production to somewhere in the neighborhood of twelve dollars per hundred pounds of milk, allowing them to operate in the black. Another big reason CAFOs can produce milk so cheaply is what economists call *negative externalities*. In plain English, they shift significant costs—such as proper waste management and pollution clean-up—to neighbors and the broader society. If they had to pay the full cost of their method of production, it would cost them a hell of a lot more than twelve dollars to make twelve gallons of milk.

Looking at government statistics on dairy farm profitability, the trend lines are unmistakable. Only operations with many hundreds, if not thousands, of cows can survive. Tragically, for people like the Voelkers, despite their love for the land and their animals, the demise of the family farm has been by design. The farming landscape started changing in earnest in the 1970s when President Richard Nixon made agribusiness lobbyist Earl Butz his secretary of agriculture. Before Butz was nominated for the post, he was a director of three large agribusiness corporations. His reputation for favoring a "get big or get out" philosophy dated back to at least the 1950s, when he was already lobbying for industrialization of agriculture at the expense of small farms. In 1955, Butz wrote: "Adapt or die; resist and perish. ... Agriculture is now big business. Too many people are trying to stay in agriculture that would do better someplace else."[8]

Before Butz, when memories of the Dust Bowl and destruction of the land through overproduction were still vivid, farming practices were ruled by New Deal-era controls. Grain farmers were even paid to keep fields fallow in times of overproduction. Farming production was kept in line with American consumption. The farmer got a price they could live with, and consumers got abundant and inexpensive food. Nixon brought Butz in to get rid of the New Deal policies. He steered the food economy toward consolidation and concentration of production into fewer hands, with no sympathy for "inefficient" small farmers, around whose necks he placed a noose in the form of continually shrinking profit margins.[9]

The push to giganticize agriculture continued to intensify, especially during the Reagan years, and carries on with a vengeance today despite the destruction of a way of life for countless families and the residual devastation this has caused small towns across the rural landscape. My family left farming, but not before we buried a neighbor who took his own life when the bank was foreclosing. For their part, American consumers, in general, and urban dwellers, in particular, mostly shrug. All do so at their own peril.

Family farmers produce the kind of food you want to eat, and they do it in greater harmony with their surroundings than mammoth animal factories that produce so much manure that huge pits must be dug, forming artificial lakes made of animal waste. These are open-air manure lagoons that emit toxic fumes known to elevate rates of asthma in children living nearby. The liquid itself is laced with toxic chemicals, pathogens, and bacteria. When the lagoons leak, and they do leak, say during heavy rainfalls, local well water is contaminated, as are lakes and rivers where wildlife live and people recreate.

By 2010, the alarm was being sounded for those willing to listen. A report that year by the National Association of Local Boards of Health warned that the "agriculture sector, including CAFOs, is the leading contributor of pollutants to lakes, rivers, and reservoirs. It has been found that states with high concentrations of CAFOs experience, on average, twenty to thirty serious water quality problems per year as a result of manure management problems." The report went on to describe the harm from even a single manure spill: "When groundwater is contaminated by pathogenic organisms, a serious threat to drinking water can occur. Pathogens survive longer in groundwater than surface water due to lower temperatures and protection from the sun. ... Even if the contamination appears to be a single episode, viruses could become attached to sediment near groundwater and continue to leach slowly into groundwater. One pollution event by a CAFO could become a lingering source of viral contamination for groundwater. Groundwater can still be at risk for contamination after a CAFO has closed and its lagoons are empty. When given increased air exposure, ammonia in soil transforms into nitrates. Nitrates are highly mobile in soil and will reach groundwater quicker than ammonia. It can be dangerous to ignore contaminated soil. ... If a CAFO has contaminated a water system, community members should be concerned about nitrates and nitrate poisoning. Elevated nitrates in drinking water can be especially harmful to infants, leading to blue baby syndrome and possible death."[10]

The possibility of death became all too real in Wisconsin in 2017 when an infant died from blue baby syndrome in the rural Juneau County community of Armenia, which had experienced a spike in private well nitrate levels after a 6,000-cow CAFO set up shop there. A Juneau County man was forced to sell the home he had lived in for twenty years after a CAFO began repurposing water irrigation systems to spray manure, and the liquid soaked into the walls of his home. "It was an ammonia smell. It hurt so bad even to breathe," the man said at the time.[11]

In 2017, a family living not far from Green Bay in Kewaunee County filmed the shower in their home, showing the water running brown after a rainfall and circling the drain of the bathtub.[12] As long ago as 2004, a six-month-old became violently ill in the county after taking a bath in water poisoned by manure runoff, prompting a state representative from the area to call the situation a public health crisis. The crisis led to no substantive action. A decade later, more than a third of wells tested in Kewaunee County were found to be unsafe to use due to unsafe levels of coliform bacteria or nitrates.[13] The problem was not isolated. Testing done in April 2019 in Grant, Iowa, and Lafayette counties in the southwestern part of Wisconsin showed more than 90 percent of private wells were contaminated with fecal matter, and many of the wells contained illness-causing pathogens such as salmonella, rotavirus, and cryptosporidium.[14]

Just a mile down the road from the Voelker farm is the largest CAFO in Barron County with over 5,000 cattle. The operation has been cited for four Safe Drinking Water Act violations due to elevated coliform bacteria counts, as well as a Clean Water Act violation for discharging waste into a wetland. That citation served as no meaningful deterrent, as Abe's mom, Jamie, later made a video recording of waste streaming down into a creek that runs through the Voelkers' property.[15]

In addition to contamination from manure and fertilizer spills, the high-capacity wells these industrial livestock operations rely on to draw over 100,000 gallons of water per day disrupt the water table and sometimes even dry up the wells neighbors depend on for drinking water. In the Central Sands region of Wisconsin, rivers such as the Little Plover, which was known as a first-rate trout stream, have nearly dried up entirely because so much water has been sucked out of the ground by high-capacity wells.

What's unfolding now for the Voelkers and so many other dairy farm families has hit other food and livestock industries across the country. The vast majority of chicken farmers are now under contract with—and controlled by—industry giants like Tyson.[16] The largest hog producer in the country, Smithfield Foods, is based in Virginia, owned by a Chinese company, and has operations in Mexico, Poland, Romania, and elsewhere. Three court verdicts went against Smithfield in 2018 alone, for nearly $100 million in total damages, for the company's irresponsible manure handling practices.[17] Smithfield called them "nuisance" lawsuits that were "an outrageous attack on animal agriculture, rural North Carolina, and thousands of independent family farmers who own and operate contract farms. From the beginning, the lawsuits have been nothing more than a money grab by a big litigation machine."[18]

This is the environment in which the food Americans eat is being produced. As Abe Voelker puts it: "In the name of efficiency, profits will be concentrated in fewer and fewer hands while waste gets concentrated into more and more toxic forms to be dumped on rural communities." As Wisconsin Farmers Union president and Vernon County dairy farmer Darin Von Ruden put it at the urban-rural summit in La Crosse: "Everyone wants inexpensive food, I want affordable food, but we need consumers who want good food, produced by farmers who do it the right way. That costs a little more. If you want something for nothing, eventually you end up with nothing."

As Abe reflected on what his family had and what is being lost, he wrote: "The farm was woven through all aspects of our family's life, and the success of our family depended on everyone's contribution to the farm. It saddens me that my brother Noah won't be able to pass that legacy on to his daughter, and I can't give my own kids a glimmer of it by having them work on the farm over the summers ... It's also a loss for Wisconsin's culture—America's Dairyland—that we aren't going to have farm kids coming up anymore, and our rural pastoral landscape that was dotted with barns, silos, and pastures with grazing cattle is being replaced by an industrial one with huge buildings, heavy machine traffic, and artificial lakes made of animal waste. Those of us who grew up in these rural areas and moved out but longed to return can't even bear to do so any longer because the land has been blighted. While the future is still uncertain for my kid brother, Noah, I have no doubt he will succeed at whatever he puts his mind to. ... If there's anything good to come of the situation, I am glad at least that he'll be freed from the burden of having cows, which require one to be out in the barn every single day without end. It will also be a relief to my dad, who ... is now in his seventies and still has to work out in the barn every day. ... Whatever happens, these family bonds that were forged on the farm remain, and we will take care of each other."[19]

These are the promises of the forsaken. They look out for one another because they know no one else will. They know that despite an economy that appears on the surface to be booming, deeper examination reveals that Americans used to grow together and now are growing apart.[20] For three decades after World War II, every income class got ahead. The poor, middle class, and rich all experienced income growth that outpaced inflation. Since then, the rich have gotten astronomically richer, the poor have become poorer, and the middle class is slowly but surely being exterminated.

Growing economic inequality produces political inequality. That intensified political inequality breeds even more economic inequality. The two feed off each other. The youngest in our society are victimized most by this vicious cycle. They are being buried under a mountain of debt to get the education and training they need, only to find a scarcity of decent job opportunities when they go out in the work world. No wonder the millennials are the only American generation showing signs of favoring socialism to capitalism.[21]

Generational discontent is not the greatest threat to American capitalism, however. Crony capitalism is an even bigger enemy of a free market economy. Our government spends substantially more on corporate welfare than it does on the social welfare programs that make up the proverbial safety net.[22] We do not have a free market economy. We have a politically manipulated economy. Those with the capacity to buy politicians and own our government are able to make the public bear their economic risk while keeping the profits of their enterprises to themselves.

Against this backdrop, Democrats continue to gamely defend welfare for the less fortunate. Republicans and Democrats alike continue to fill the public trough to feed the rich. Maybe we should focus instead on creating an economy where both kinds of welfare are unnecessary and can be eliminated. To unscrew America, we need one economy benefiting us all, with a free and fair market for everyone, not crony capitalism for a favored few. At the heart of one-for-all economics are two bedrock principles. The first is that if you do an honest day's work, you should not live in poverty. In today's economy, growing numbers of people work every day and often hold down more than one job but still cannot earn enough to lift themselves above the poverty line. That is both morally wrong and intolerable. The second principle is that demand, not supply, is the primary driver of economic growth. Feeding the rich in hopes of stoking supply has been a miserable failure, never producing more than a trickle for the masses and causing the grotesque economic inequality we are experiencing today. Putting money in the pockets of consumers and thereby stimulating demand does far more to prime the economy's pump.

America is growing apart. It's easy to overlook the phenomenon when the overall economy is growing, with unemployment low and the stock market booming. It comes into sharp focus when you witness the struggles of people like the Voelkers, the Schwerts, Jeff Fox, Carl

Fields, and so many others. Those who rule places like Wisconsin want everyone to focus on the state's unemployment rate, which today is quite low. They are equally eager to have everyone look past other troubling facts, such as wage and job growth that is lagging behind the national average, a poverty rate that recently reached its highest level in thirty years,[23] and a middle class that's disappearing faster than anywhere else in the country. They pay no attention to rising economic inequality and hope no one notices that the income gap has been widening faster in Wisconsin than in other states.[24]

As unwilling as they are to acknowledge, much less do something about these politically inconvenient realities, they are even more reluctant to engage the public in any discussion about even greater challenges that lie ahead. There is a reason why, as Americans were fixing to elect a new president in 2016, more than half were believing our kids will be worse off than their parents.[25] The U.S. is hurtling toward an increasingly jobless economy, and most everyone sees it coming. Even the politicians can see it but don't want to deal with what is plainly visible on the horizon. Instead, they look for scapegoats, telling frightened workers that immigrants are stealing their jobs. Or they offer empty promises that closed factories can be reopened, and lost assembly line jobs will somehow magically reappear. This is the cruelest kind of hoax.

Today's immigrants aren't replacing yesterday's factory workers on the assembly lines, robots are. Even if new factories replace the old shuttered ones, how many people will work in those plants? Driverless vehicles are coming. When they arrive, what happens to the millions of Americans who drive trucks and buses and taxi cabs for a living? Workers have every reason to feel vulnerable, and those feelings are only going to intensify. Fewer and fewer workers have union representation. There was a time when virtually every American household included at least one union member. Today, less than 11 percent of all Americans and only 6 percent of private sector workers belong to a union.[26] Labor unions were an outgrowth of the Industrial Revolution. That revolution came and went. In what came after, unions struggled to adapt and steadily lost membership. Workers lost bargaining power.

An economy has grown around us where just about everything is made to be thrown away. There are disposable eating utensils, cups, and plates. Disposable towels and disposable diapers. Disposable razors. Disposable gloves. Disposable cameras and disposable batteries. The list goes on and on. When so much of what is made and sold in this country is designed to be discarded after a single use, it was only a matter of time before the workers who make the products are seen as disposable too, especially since those doing the selling are increasingly located half a state or half a country or half a world away. With industry leaders less rooted in the communities where their companies do business, they don't think twice about relocating countless factories to far-flung places in search of cheaper labor. In the few factories that remain, workers surrender their jobs to automation.

Those in power in our government at the moment are proving remarkably insensitive to the uncertainty and anxiety and feelings of betrayal and abandonment that always accompany major economic transitions and dislocations. When the country was going through an industrial revolution more than a century ago and large numbers of people left the land and went to work in factories and offices, the political system responded by providing vocational training, workers' compensation for those injured in the workplace, unemployment insurance, retirement security, and much more. With a global, technology-driven, increasingly jobless economy now emerging that is leaving so many working people exposed and vulnerable, the government so far is doing next to nothing to cushion the blow.

Those presently in charge of government passively watch as economic markets grow increasingly monopolized, and more workers get discarded, causing inequality to expand rapidly. They give the monopolists free rein, which is no surprise considering how they've joined forces with those economic monopolists to engineer monopolies on political power. They add injury to insecurity in places like Wisconsin, a state once known for its pristine environment, by looking the other way when industry actions lay waste to natural resources[27] and even inviting industries to write their own pollution permits.[28] Health and safety protections have been stripped away,[29] and the state is seizing power from local communities that want to do better by their residents.[30] It's as if the powers-that-be figure that since people are disposable, there's no reason to worry too much about them being poisoned.

Antitrust laws that are supposed to promote competition by guarding against the formation of monopolies, keep markets free, and protect consumers are no longer doing any of those things. If antitrust laws were worth a damn, if they still worked, we would never be in a position of having no choice but to bail out gigantic banks because they are too big to fail. Walmart wouldn't have put just about every Main Street five-and-dime, grocery, lumberyard, and hardware store across America out of business. We wouldn't have six mega-corporations controlling most of what we read, see, and hear every day.[31]

American antitrust laws date back to the late 1800s. They are so named because as the Industrial Revolution was unfolding, state laws didn't allow companies to own stock in other companies, and mergers were tightly controlled. The captains of nineteenth-century industry got around those laws by forming trusts in which one corporation was created to oversee the management of stocks of cooperating corporations. Through the trusts, supposed competitors colluded to fix prices, control production, and drive out new competition through price wars.

Business consolidations in the oil, sugar, tobacco, beef, and whiskey industries, among others, led to concentrations of capital and put control of commerce in fewer and fewer hands. Eventually, trust became synonymous with national monopolies. The nation's first antitrust law—the Sherman Antitrust Act of 1890—outlawed any "monopolization, attempted monopolization, or conspiracy or combination to monopolize." The old antitrust laws are still on the books but are not enforced the way they once were. If they were worth a damn, if they still worked today, maybe America would not be experiencing such rapid growth in the concentration of wealth in the hands of a few at the top[32] and would not be the most unequal nation among all the industrialized countries of the world.[33] The way antitrust laws are being applied and enforced today actually undermines trust in free markets.

If antitrust laws were worth a damn, maybe billionaires and corporate conglomerates wouldn't have taken ownership of our government and wouldn't be calling the tune on Capitol Hill and in statehouses across the country. Maybe there would be more trust in government. It's safe to say that if antitrust laws with any teeth applied to politics, we'd have more than two major parties. In the 2016 presidential election, voters were given the choice of the two most unpopular major party nominees in the history of polling. Donald Trump became one of the choices by getting fourteen million votes in the Republican primaries and caucuses. With more than 230 million Americans eligible to vote at the time, the support of 6 percent of eligible voters was all it took to secure the Republican nomination for president. Just under seventeen million Democratic voters in party primaries and caucuses—about 7 percent of all eligible voters—made Hillary Clinton their nominee.

After Trump's election, public approval of the Republican Party fell to an all-time low.[34] The Republicans' loss was not the Democrats' gain. Favorable opinions of Democrats dropped to their lowest level in more than a quarter-century.[35] Now that's antitrust in the truest sense of the term. Public dissatisfaction with the major parties and discontent with the current workings of the political system are causing increasing numbers of Americans to lose faith in democracy and begin to warm up to alternatives like military rule, according to the World Values Survey conducted by a global network of social scientists.[36]

If that's not a wake-up call, what will be? ✪

CHAPTER SIX
GROWING TOGETHER AGAIN

Unscrewing America will take nerve. The courage of conviction is required.

In this regard, once again Wisconsin is to the nation what canaries are to coal miners. America faces radical threats that call for a revolutionary response. In Wisconsin, it's been the friends of the filthy rich and uber-powerful, the ones who are more than happy to screw over the poor and powerless, who've behaved radically, who've shown the most political nerve in recent years, namely politicians like Scott Walker.

From 2010 to 2014, multibillionaire oilmen Charles and David Koch spent close to $6 million putting Walker in the governor's office and keeping him there and at least $3 million more to make sure Walker allies were in charge of Wisconsin's legislature and highest court.[1] That's just what was detectable. Surely, millions more flowed through "dark money" channels. And they were just getting warmed up. The Koch group Americans for Prosperity threw more than eight million dollars behind Walker for the 2018 election.[2]

The Koch brothers were hardly alone in bankrolling Walker's rise to power. The lengthy list of his benefactors reads like a who's who of corporate bigwigs—Las Vegas casino tycoon Sheldon Adelson, Amway Corporation founders Dick and Betsy DeVos, Ameritrade's Joe Ricketts, to name just a few.[3] Many other powerful interests joined them. Long before the 2018 election was anywhere in sight, the National Rifle Association had bought $3.5 million worth of Walker stock.[4]

Did Walker ever come through for the plutocrats. Within weeks of taking office, Walker set an example that other right-wing governors around the country would follow by dropping a bomb in the form of a "budget repair bill" that stripped some 170,000 public sector workers of their right to collectively bargain and effectively eviscerated their unions. The action provoked massive protests. Crowds swelling to 100,000 people or more swarmed the state capitol grounds. A 24/7 sit-in lasted for weeks in the rotunda. Walker and his legislative allies were unfazed. They acted swiftly to ram through the crippling legislation, and Walker brazenly signed the bill into law.[5]

Walker convinced some private-sector labor leaders to hold their fire by assuring them he planned to confine his union busting to what he derisively called the "big government unions." Then he later screwed them over, too, pushing through the "right to work" legislation so coveted by the Koch brothers and their ilk and thereby turning Wisconsin into an anti-union state.

The fury of the historic 2011 protests morphed into an effort to remove Walker, his lieutenant governor, Rebecca Kleefisch, and several of his Republican allies in the state senate from office through recall elections. It's no small task in Wisconsin to recall a statewide officeholder. More than 540,000 voters' signatures are needed on a petition to trigger a recall election. More than a million signatures were gathered, forcing an election in 2012.[6] But with the help of the Koch brothers and so many others like them, pro-Walker forces spent nearly sixty million dollars to pull him through.[7] He survived the recall attempt and held on to his office. He stood for reelection in 2014 and won again.

As the 2018 election approached, many groups had big hopes to finally bring down Walker and big plans to move Wisconsin politics in a distinctly different direction. One of them was Our Wisconsin Revolution (OWR), which grew out of Bernie Sanders' 2016 presidential campaign. OWR had signed up legions of activists across the state— well over 10,000 of them—with the aim of recruiting and supporting candidates at the state and local levels to challenge the status quo and shake up the system. The group set its sights on influencing the 2018 governor's race and joined forces with another progressive organization to establish Wisconsin's Choice, a plan to host candidate forums all over the state and then hold three rounds of voting, culminating in the endorsement of a "people's champion."

The first round of online voting was to narrow the number of candidates under consideration for an endorsement to nine. I made that cut. The second round was to identify a final four. I made that cut as well. Another forum was held featuring only the four finalists. Videos were made and shared highlighting the finalists' positions on key issues. The final round of voting was to choose the people's champion. The vote was held, but the initiative's leaders announced a change of plans. The results of the voting were not going to be publicly shared, and no endorsement was going to be made. Several activists who had been hired as program staff told our campaign that I had finished first in the voting, but could say no more.

With Wisconsin's Choice not choosing, Our Wisconsin Revolution's leaders made it known that the group could hold its own vote and make an endorsement independently. OWR members were invited to vote. This time, the results were made public. I got 57 percent of the vote. The second-place candidate received 14 percent. But no endorsement was made in the August party primary election. OWR's ruling structure had established a 60 percent membership support threshold to get the endorsement.

Our Wisconsin Revolution ended up waiting until after the primary election to endorse the Democratic nominee—centrist Tony Evers—who had not made the final four in the Wisconsin's Choice endorsement derby and was easily the least revolutionary candidate in the Democratic field.

After groups like Our Wisconsin Revolution chose not to try to influence the direction of the race before the August 14 primary and instead rubber-stamped the establishment's favored candidate, they had to watch with anguish as Evers later backed away from stances he took to win the nomination. His budget proposal offered nothing on prison reform, leading to sharp criticism from the social justice group WISDOM. "The Governor's campaign promise of reducing the prison population seems to have been moved to the back burner— or maybe completely off the stove," WISDOM state director David Liners fumed.[8] Evers also backtracked on his campaign promise to dissolve the state's corporate welfare office, the Wisconsin Economic Development Corporation,[9] and warmed up to the controversial deal Walker made through the WEDC with the Taiwanese multinational electronics manufacturer Foxconn after condemning the arrangement as a candidate and pledging more than once to undo it.

All this should be a cautionary tale for the rest of the country. America worships at the altar of free markets. Except we don't actually have free markets. We have politically manipulated markets. We have crony capitalism. Corporate titans schmooze politicians and play the elected representatives of the American people for chumps. They play states off against others. They pit communities against each other, promising investments and jobs in exchange for tax breaks, outright subsidy payments, and exemptions from environmental regulations. Whoever is the highest bidder, whoever serves up the juiciest cuts of corporate welfare, is declared the winner. The real winners are the big corporations who game the political system to pad their own bottom lines.[10] Small businesses can't compete with the subsidized giants and end up closing their doors.[11] Main Streets wither and die. Downtowns become ghost towns. In place after place, big promises are made.[12] Promises are bent, if not broken. Communities pay a hefty price and have little or nothing to show for it when all is said and done.

Still, there is no shortage of willing chumps. Wisconsin is one of the latest to fall under the spell. Former governor Walker, with the president of the United States cheering him on, handed over one of the largest corporate welfare packages in U.S. history to Foxconn, a global conglomerate with a lengthy track record of broken promises.[13] A technology columnist for *Bloomberg News* saw all the markings of a sham in Foxconn's expressed desire to invest $10 billion in Wisconsin to manufacture large LCD panels mostly for televisions.[14] For starters, he said, making these screens in Wisconsin, or anywhere in the U.S., is too expensive to make business sense to Foxconn. Besides, he'd seen this

MIKE McCABE

movie before and suggested that "$10 billion figure should have been the first warning sign for the people of Wisconsin—including those responsible for looking after the interests of its citizens—because it's more than Foxconn spends in five years worldwide."

Sure enough, Foxconn's plans for Wisconsin kept changing. The company backed away from its original intentions and started sending mixed signals about what it planned to do in Wisconsin. First came news that Foxconn was rethinking its commitment to making large LCD screens for TVs and was considering making smaller displays for cars, personal computers, tablets, mobile devices, and niche products instead.[15] Then came word that plans were being scaled back, and the Wisconsin factory would be smaller than originally planned.[16] Next, there were rumblings Foxconn would import workers from China rather than rely on Wisconsin labor.[17]

Eventually, the company hinted it might not build an assembly plant at all and would have no need for many blue-collar assembly line workers, but rather was looking to develop a research and development facility employing mostly white-collar engineers and researchers.[18] The next day, Foxconn reversed course again in response to negative news coverage and political blowback, claiming it still had every intention to build a factory in Wisconsin, but it would be what's known as a Generation 6 facility, a downgrade from the Generation 10.5 plant the company initially set out to build.[19]

Despite Foxconn's dubious track record, despite the bleak history of these kinds of corporate welfare deals proving beyond a shadow of a doubt that government and business generally do not make good bedfellows, Evers' new administration suddenly had its hopes up, with a top cabinet official saying Foxconn is "at the front of the governor's agenda, and it's part of Wisconsin's agenda moving forward."[20]

In true capitalism, where there are real free markets, there are no guaranteed profits. Corporate welfare makes this uncomfortable reality disappear for those receiving it. It allows corporations to hedge their bets in the marketplace. It lets them shift their risk to the public while keeping the rewards to themselves.[21] They win even when they make bad business moves. They win because they have us to cover any losses. They count on us being chumps.

And while politicians are tripping over each other to turn over the keys to the public treasury to captains of industry—domestic or foreign—they do next to nothing to provide shelter from the storm to those being ravaged by globalization and automation and get-big-or-get-out market concentration. Farm families like the Voelkers and the Schwerts and former factory workers who've seen their standard of living cut in half are left to their own devices.

Working Americans have good reason to question whether there's anyone really working for them on Capitol Hill. And they are rightly wondering if there's a place for us all in this emerging economy, or if a bunch of us are going to be thrown away. As we all try to gain our footing with the ground shifting beneath us, adjusting to new economic realities that can be cruel and capricious would be so much easier if we had the government on our side. One of these realities is that workers now have to change jobs much more frequently than in the past. Guaranteeing access to medical care with health insurance coverage that follows workers wherever they are employed would create much-needed stability and security while also freeing people to leave dead-end jobs to start new businesses. The political system has so far failed to meet this glaring need.

Virtually every day while traveling across Wisconsin as a candidate for governor, I encountered people stressed out over health care. Some didn't have insurance. Those who did were no less anxiety-ridden. Even if they had good insurance, they lived in fear knowing they were a pink slip away from not being able to afford medical care. Much more frequently, I heard people tell of substandard or even useless insurance coverage. They were afraid of getting sick because they would have to pay out of pocket for any medical attention they received, and they didn't have the money. They told of insurance plans with annual deductibles of $4,000 or $5,000 or more. One woman claimed all she could afford was a plan with a $10,000 annual deductible. She asked rhetorically how sick she would have to be to land in the hospital for a long enough stay for her insurance to kick in and start paying any of the bills.

Many of the people I talked to had obtained insurance through the Affordable Care Act (ACA). Their stories made clear to me that the ACA is misnamed. It provided them with affordable insurance, not affordable care. With their insurance coverage and the sky-high deductibles that came with those plans, they could not afford to fall ill. Perversely, for some, the stress this caused was actually making them sick.

Republicans have tried repeatedly but unsuccessfully to repeal and replace the Affordable Care Act, more commonly known as Obamacare. The ACA erred on the side of getting more people insured and requiring insurance to cover the health conditions people have, but in doing so, keeping insurance premiums affordable was next to impossible to achieve over the long haul. What President Trump and congressional Republicans pushed erred on the side of lowering premiums for most people in the long run, but doing so by jacking up costs for the sickest among us and taking insurance coverage away from large numbers of people.

Neither approach meaningfully addresses the biggest single failing of the U.S. health care system. Health care administrative costs in America are twice as high as the global average.[22] Compared to the rest of the world, more of our health care dollars pay for paperwork, and less of the spending goes for patient care. That's because we have a multi-payer system that forces health care providers to submit claims for payment to dozens of different insurance companies. That means dozens of different forms to fill out and dozens of different systems to navigate and different procedures to follow to get medical treatment paid for. This is why the U.S. has the least efficient health care system among eleven developed nations.[23] Solutions to this problem are not being developed in Washington. The problem is not even discussed on Capitol Hill. Neither party's favored approach addresses it.

Since the Affordable Care Act's approval in 2010, Congressional Republicans voted more than sixty times to repeal and replace the law.

They have the repeal part down. It's the replace part that has them stumped. They haven't figured out what to put in its place and have settled on no alternative. If they are bound and determined to repeal and replace Obamacare, then do it right. Do it in a way that makes health care more accessible and affordable. Do it in a way that makes the health care system less bureaucratic and brings down administrative overhead costs. Go ahead and repeal the ACA, then fold the existing Medicare and Medicaid programs and the VA system for military veterans into one and call it Americare. Make every American eligible. No one would be forced to enroll. If you want to continue to buy private insurance, you should be free to do so. But Americare would be there for anyone who wants it.

Three federal programs and their accompanying bureaucracies, as well as the federal and state infrastructures devoted to administering the Affordable Care Act and its insurance exchanges, would be brought under a single roof, making the nation's health care system more streamlined and efficient. Medicare provides a sturdy foundation upon which to build Americare. Medicare is well established and widely supported by the seniors it serves, so popular that one of the signs most commonly seen at Tea Party rallies carried the message "Keep Government Out of My Medicare" or some variation on that theme.

Any program that has earned that kind of loyalty from Tea Partiers, and is so highly valued by the nation's elderly,[24] should be made available to Americans of all ages. All Americans should be allowed to benefit from the fact that Medicare does a far better job of controlling costs and is much more administratively efficient than the rest of the U.S. health care system.[25] Our country is ranked at or near the bottom in the developed world in the efficiency and effectiveness of health care.[26] We spend more and get less.[27] Regardless of what kind of health care delivery system we have in place, well over thirty trillion dollars is going to be spent on medical care in the next decade in America. But if we replace the multi-payer system we have now with a single-payer system like Medicare for all, the cost will be two trillion dollars less over ten years, according to one study.[28] Another analysis says the savings would be more like five trillion dollars.[29] Goes to show we can do better. Much better. Out with Obamacare. In with Americare.

As much sense as I think this makes, when I was talking to stressed-out Wisconsinites I still had mixed feelings about describing the long-range goal of a national single-payer health care system or even my short-term aim of making Wisconsin's version of Medicaid—BadgerCare—a public option that anyone in the state could choose to enroll in. It is high-quality insurance. There are no deductibles, and the insurance kicks in immediately and pays medical expenses from the first visit to a doctor's office. On the one hand, I dearly wanted to showcase what our society's approach to health security could and should be, but on the other hand, I didn't want to fill them with false hope. I knew what my chances of winning the election were.

With the emergence of an increasingly jobless economy and disposable workers, new approaches to maintaining social cohesion are going to have to be considered. If our society is going to hold together, we have to renegotiate the social contract. The old social contract in America was that if you were willing to work hard, you could hold a job at one company for all your working years. You were paid a middle-class wage, had good health insurance, and a full pension for your retirement. There was unemployment compensation in case you were thrown out of work for a period of time and workers' compensation in case you were injured in the workplace.

We are still operating under that old social contract, even though job security has evaporated. Working for the same employer for thirty, forty, or even fifty years is a thing of the past. Finding—and keeping—decent health insurance is now a losing battle for many workers. Pensions have largely gone the way of the dinosaur. More and more American workers feel they are being screwed over. The country sits on a powder keg as a result.

If our minds are open to a new social contract, we can steer clear of the social, political, and economic turmoil and upheaval this new economy has the capacity to create. If heads are buried in the sand, chaos will reign. For years now, the fate of our economy has rested on a business development strategy rooted in lavishing riches on the wealthiest among us in hopes that some of what they have will trickle down to tens of millions of others. Not enough has trickled. An about-face is in order. Instead of enriching a few and then praying they work some magic for the rest of the population, the focus should be on empowering the masses.

For close to forty years now, the American economy has been under the spell of supply-side theory, better known on the streets as trickle-down economics. The theory is that expanding the economy's capacity to produce more goods is the best way to stimulate economic growth. In practice, that theory produces feed-the-rich policies—such as steep cuts in the income taxes corporations and the wealthiest Americans pay—aimed at encouraging private investment in businesses, production facilities, and equipment.

Those policies have worked like a charm in one regard. They have made the rich vastly richer. With everyone else's earnings stagnating, the gap between America's rich and the rest has grown dramatically by every statistical measure since trickle-down took hold of our economy.[30] Trickle-down economics has been a colossal failure when it comes to producing shared prosperity. George H.W. Bush called it "voodoo economics" for supercharging the accumulation of national debt, but its biggest sin is that America was growing together before the supply-siders took over and has been growing apart ever since.[31]

There are conspicuous reasons why the only thing trickle-down economics does well is produce income and wealth inequality. Feed the rich and they don't eat much of what they are fed. They store it away. They amass more wealth. Every dollar added to their net worth is a dollar out of circulation that creates no multiplier effect in the economy. Put more money in the pockets of everyday workers and consumers, and they spend it. That creates demand. When someone wants to buy, someone else is eager to sell. The economy is stimulated.

That's the fundamental flaw in supply-side theory. You can shower incentives on corporations and the super-wealthy to supply more goods, but if no one is buying what they are making, the new factories will be shuttered in no time. Demand drives economic growth, not supply. Shared prosperity doesn't trickle down; it springs up from the ground like a geyser.

Shifting from divisive trickle-down economics to geyser economics means concentrating on stoking demand rather than trying to manipulate supply politically. Boosting wages is a good place to start. The federal minimum wage has been increased twenty-two different times, and every time supply-siders screamed that increasing it would be a jobs killer. Never worked out that way. The national gross domestic product (GDP) steadily grew through every minimum wage increase,[32] and states that increased their own minimum wages have seen faster job growth than those that didn't.[33] That's because workers who earn more spend more. Good capitalists figure out how to supply what consumers are demanding. They scale up their operations to meet the increased demand, and that means hiring rather than laying off.

Another key to geyser economics is overhauling our tax system. America effectively has two tax systems, one for the rich and another for the rest. Federal and state taxation devalues and disincentivizes work by taxing earned income at a steeper rate than unearned income, such as capital gains on investments. State and local tax systems across the country are grotesquely unfair to working- class Americans, allowing the wealthiest one percent to pay the lowest overall tax rate.[34] That needs to change. We don't need new taxes. We do need to make sure everyone pays the ones we already have. That will reduce the share of total taxes paid by low-income and middle-class Americans, leaving them with more to spend on other things. Demand will be further stoked.

Big business handouts are a favorite recipe in the trickle-down cookbook. Funny how so many of the handouts wind up hidden in shell companies and tax havens overseas[35] and don't actually create any additional supply—or jobs—here at home. States have fallen in love with this recipe too. Here in Wisconsin, corporate welfare costs hundreds of millions of dollars a year yet creates no noticeable economic stimulation and hardly any jobs, and those doling it out can't even reliably account for how the taxpayers' money is spent.[36]

For the sake of free-market capitalism and shared prosperity, geyser economics is predicated on doing away with crony capitalism. We're better off taking the money wasted on handouts to corporations and the ultra-wealthy and investing it instead in things like affordable, debt-free education. An entire generation of young Americans is buried under a mountain of college debt. With them spending twenty, thirty, even forty years paying off student loans, think of how many are putting off purchases of cars and houses and other such goods. Imagine what it would do for auto manufacturers, car dealers, home builders, and realtors if we made education as affordable for today's youth as it was for us older folks. They'd gladly supply what legions of young Americans would suddenly be able to buy.

There's a geyser ready to blow, for the benefit of every income class, if we're smart enough to shift our attention from supply to demand. In the short term, this turnabout can be started with five initial steps.

STEP ONE is to substantially boost wages. That means raising the wage floor and turning the minimum wage into a living wage. That will have a ripple effect up the income ladder. As mentioned, the federal minimum wage has been boosted more than twenty different times, and jobs didn't disappear. In fact, new ones materialized. The national economy grew steadily through every minimum wage increase, and states that increased their minimum wages had the fastest job growth. Makes perfect sense. Put more money in workers' pockets, and they don't pad their net worth with it or stash it in tax havens in Bermuda or the Cayman Islands; they spend it. That stimulates the economy.

STEP TWO is health care stability and security. All Americans should have affordable and high-quality health coverage, whether we are between jobs or have no choice but to change occupations or have fallen on hard times. That coverage should follow us wherever we go.

STEP THREE is to make education and job training as affordable for our kids and grandkids as it was for us and our parents and grandparents. Debt-free education and training have to be part of the new social contract. There was a time when a high school diploma was a pathway to the American Dream, but it no longer is. More advanced education and training are needed, and our society needs to clear a path that does not leave young people or workers of any age buried under a mountain of debt.

STEP FOUR is equipping every last person living in America with indispensable twenty-first-century tools such as high-speed internet and access to mobile phone service. It is not possible to fully participate in the global economy and twenty-first-century American life without these tools. There are too many dead zones in too many places in America—some in remote rural areas and some in heavily populated inner cities—a recipe for economic stagnation and greater inequality.

STEP FIVE pays for these essential investments in every American. The new social contract depends on restructuring the tax system. Achieving one-for-all taxation involves systematically identifying and closing loopholes, tax shelters, and other features of the tax code that facilitate tax avoidance. Also required is a commitment to taxation based on ability to pay and elimination of current policies that doom low- and middle-income folks to pay a larger share of their incomes in total state and local taxes than high-income tax dodgers.

Over the longer haul, as automation, globalization, and evolving family structures wreak further havoc in American workplaces, other innovations will be needed. Maybe part of the answer is moving to the 30-hour workweek, which Amazon and other companies are trying out.[37] That would make work available to more people and better accommodate stressed two-earner households. Maybe the time will soon come for serious consideration of a universal basic income program or federal jobs guarantee to provide vulnerable workers with more stability and financial security. That would require all of us to see the value in making sure no one is left behind. Maybe making union representation a civil right could be a piece to the puzzle.[38] Or perhaps the evolution of workplaces in the U.S. cries out for reinvention of how worker rights are advanced and labor laws are written.

America is growing apart, but once we recognize the relationship between political inequality and economic inequality and break the vicious cycle, we can grow together again. Sustainable growth and prosperity gush up; they do not trickle down. We will grow together again when we recognize that the times demand a new social contract in America. A national conversation is needed about the short-term and long-range elements of that compact. It's not happening in the halls of government in America. That fact alone speaks volumes about the current disconnect between the government and the governed. ✪

CHAPTER SEVEN
DÉJÀ VU

It's Bacon's Rebellion all over again.

In January 2011, Wisconsin Governor Scott Walker met with Beloit billionaire Diane Hendricks at the headquarters of a company Hendricks owns. After Walker gave Hendricks a hug and a kiss, she asked, "Any chance we'll ever get to be a completely red state and work on these unions?"

Without missing a beat, Walker said, "Oh, yeah."

Hendricks probed further. "And become a right-to-work [state]? What can we do to help you?"

Walker answered: "Well, we're going to start in a couple weeks with our budget adjustment bill. The first step is we're going to deal with collective bargaining for all public employee unions, because you use divide and conquer ... ."[1]

If Scott Walker is anything, he's well aware of history. As noted in chapter 6, Walker skillfully pitted one group of working people against others and stripped employees of their rights and crippled labor unions in Wisconsin. He used the oldest trick in the book. It's a trick that shaped America well before the formation of the republic.

It's not often taught in school, at least not in predominantly white communities, but in the earliest days of the American colonies in the 1600s, African Americans had a legal status similar to that of

European American indentured servants.[2] That changed abruptly and dramatically in the aftermath of what came to be known as Bacon's Rebellion. This uprising in 1676 by settlers in the coastal Tidewater region of Virginia led by Nathaniel Bacon challenged the heavy-handed rule of colonial Governor Sir William Berkeley, who was dismissive of the conditions and political challenges faced by settlers in the colony's western frontier in the Blue Ridge Mountains.

Those voyaging to the new world to escape economic hardship, physical deprivation, and religious persecution in Europe had two choices. If they had the means to secure a place on a transport ship, upon arriving they were given land to farm in a colonial outpost. If they couldn't pay, they entered into indentured servitude, usually for about seven years, before obtaining land to settle. That unpaid labor was the foundation upon which the plantation system was built.

By 1676, laboring-class workers, both free and indentured, of both European and African descent, were growing discontented. The land given to those freed from servitude was on the outer reaches of the territory and far from the colonial capital of Jamestown. They felt unjustly taxed and faced restrictions on their right to vote and to have a voice in colonial affairs. They were increasingly concerned for their safety and felt vulnerable in the wilderness, as clashes between settlers and Native Americans were becoming commonplace.

Bacon pulled together a collection of frontier settlers who had recently been freed from servitude and granted land along with still-indentured laborers to protest their treatment by the Tidewater aristocrats. On July 30, 1676, Bacon and his army issued a "Declaration in the Name of the People" accusing Berkeley of unjust taxation, installing favorites in high public offices, and monopolizing the beaver trade with Native Americans, among other grievances.[3] Bacon, himself a plantation owner in the inland backcountry, had his own ulterior motives. He felt snubbed by Berkeley, who had left Bacon out of his inner circle and refused to allow Bacon to take part in his fur trade. After months of conflict, Bacon and several hundred of his followers marched to Jamestown on September 19 and burned the colonial capital to the ground. Berkeley fled. Even before an English naval fleet could arrive to aid Berkeley and restore his rule, Bacon died of dysentery in late October. Berkeley returned to the burned capital and a looted home in January 1677. John Ingram stepped into the rebellion's leadership vacuum caused by Bacon's death, but many rebels parted company with Ingram, and the insurgency lost steam.[4] Some of Bacon's landowning followers returned their loyalty to the Berkeley government. Others had their property seized, and twenty-three men were executed by hanging.[5]

While Bacon's Rebellion did not overthrow Berkeley's regime, the sight of free and indentured laborers from both Europe and Africa united and fighting side by side did throw a mighty scare into the wealthy, landowning aristocracy. These workers came together to upend the plantation system that concentrated wealth in the hands of the colonial elite. Those fighting sought an end to unpaid labor and second-class citizenship. In short, they wanted opportunity and upward mobility. Recognizing the threat this posed to their economic system that depended on indentured servitude, alarmed ruling elites saw the need to drive a wedge between the united laborers. They established a new birthright for laborers of European descent, both free and indentured, setting them apart from their brethren of African descent and enlisting them as supporters of lifetime hereditary slavery. This identity was "white." Soon after Bacon's Rebellion, a series of white-skin privilege laws were enacted using this new terminology, breeding discord between free whites and African Americans and Native Americans.[6] White supremacy was invented to divide and conquer, to maintain the aristocracy's grip on political and economic power. The result of this maneuver was that the African slave trade started in earnest in the colonies to replace the old system of trans-race indentured servitude.

It's anyone's guess what would have happened if European and African laborers had stuck together in the 1600s. Maybe if indentured servants from Europe had not sold out their counterparts from Africa for a slightly elevated social standing and a few economic crumbs, the African slave trade would not have taken root in America. If the aristocrats' divide-and-conquer maneuver had not worked, maybe the coming revolution could have produced a truly democratic republic. Maybe the Three-Fifths Compromise never would have been struck, and maybe the original sin of slavery would not have been embedded in the new nation's constitution and remained there for nearly all of America's first century.

But poor and powerless American settlers did turn on each other. Some did sell out others, and rulers kept right on using this oldest of tricks. Irish immigrants coming to America were not granted legal status as white in their new country until the mid-1800s and only after they aligned with pro-slavery forces in opposing abolition. Russians, Jews, and Italians were not considered white under the law until well into the twentieth century.

Think about that. People with my complexion and my ethnic heritage were not "white" according to the law for more than two centuries after the first American settlers arrived in places like the Tidewater coastal region of Virginia and established settlements like Jamestown. For other ethnic groups with my same skin tone, it was more than 300 years after the colonies started springing up before they were granted legal status as white. That is the history that is rarely, if ever, taught in school, the hidden story of how white-skin privilege was invented by the wealthy and well-placed out of desperation to keep people under their thumb.

To this day, we fall for the trick that Sir William Berkeley and his fellow plantation owners skillfully employed so very long ago. We still allow ourselves to be pitted against others with whom we share so much in common socially, economically, and politically. We still are put at each other's throats by ruling elites who divide and conquer us to enrich themselves. Unscrewing America depends greatly on learning history's lessons and seeing the modern-day aristocrats' manipulations for what they are.

Like nearly all Americans, I am the offspring of immigrants. The peasant farmers whose family name I inherited came from Ireland. They left a homeland savaged by famine, trading a grim reality of financial ruin and starvation for the promise of a new and better life. They were part of what might be described today as a massive caravan that took incalculable risks to make its way across a vast ocean seeking refuge, comfort, and opportunity. My immigrant ancestors settled first in New Jersey before journeying to northern Illinois and eventually Wisconsin. They made this land their home and passed down a way of life from generation to generation. A big part of that way of life was a welcome mat and an unlocked door. Throughout my childhood, there was always a pot of coffee and a fresh-baked cake or pie at the ready just in case visitors came calling, be they acquaintances or strangers.

Because of my ancestry and upbringing, it felt so—how should I say it?—foreign to me when U.S. Citizenship and Immigration Services changed its mission statement in early 2018, deleting the longstanding reference to America as a "nation of immigrants" and scrubbing language describing the agency's purpose as "providing accurate and useful information to our customers, granting immigration and citizenship benefits, promoting an awareness and understanding of citizenship."[7] The agency's mission now speaks antiseptically of "protecting Americans, securing the homeland, and honoring our values."

Undefining America as a nation of immigrants does not honor our values; it abandons them. Some will say it's only a mission statement; it's just words. But these words have been acted out. A country known for lifting a lamp beside a golden door has been firing tear gas over a barrier of razor wire.[8] Our government was shut down over one man's insistence on making that barrier even more impenetrable.

My dad fought in some of World War II's bloodiest battles. He risked his life to defeat the Nazis, not to pave the way for his country to embrace their master race mindset. He made it out of the horrors of war alive and vowed not to pick up a gun ever again. He never did. When awakened in the middle of the night by the sounds of a suspected intruder or other disturbance, he'd grab a baseball bat and disappear into the darkness to restore order. I marveled at his fearlessness.

When our country is at its best, America is just as fearless. When we are at our best, we don't spend billions of dollars building monuments to paranoia. We sure don't allow fixation on the erection of such a monument—call it a wall, call it a fence—to bring useful functions of government to a grinding halt. When we are at our best, ours is an open-minded and big-hearted country, a compassionate nation. At our best, we have a strong sense of national purpose and an indomitable spirit. At our best, there's no need to obsess over being great. When America is at its best, greatness takes care of itself.

> Not like the brazen giant of Greek fame,
> With conquering limbs astride from land to land;
> Here at our sea-washed, sunset gates shall stand
> A mighty woman with a torch, whose flame
> Is the imprisoned lightning, and her name
> Mother of Exiles. From her beacon-hand
> Glows world-wide welcome; her mild eyes command
> The air-bridged harbor that twin cities frame.
> "Keep, ancient lands, your storied pomp!" cries she
> With silent lips. "Give me your tired, your poor,
> Your huddled masses yearning to breathe free,
> The wretched refuse of your teeming shore.
> Send these, the homeless, tempest-tost to me,
> I lift my lamp beside the golden door!"
>
> —Emma Lazarus, *The New Colossus*,
> inscribed on the Statue of Liberty

There was a time when efforts to keep people in their place were easily recognizable. Bondage is hard to miss. Women were chattel and blacks were slaves. The nation's royals eventually lost their moral and legal justification for employing such crude and brutal means to keep people down, but not their desire for race, class, and gender superiority. So slavery was out, and Jim Crow was in. Poll taxes and literacy tests and other such tactics were put to use. Give them rights, but make sure they are not equal rights.

The civil rights legislation of the 1960s and early 1970s ended the old Jim Crow but not the royals' discriminatory impulses. The ink was barely dry on the series of laws addressing race and sex discrimination, and a new Jim Crow was promptly fashioned that makes discrimination more disguised than ever. As I said at that candidate forum in the wealthy, nearly all-white Milwaukee suburb mentioned in chapter 4, the new Jim Crow stands on sturdy legs. I didn't mention that day the discriminatory punch that was packed by the demolition of longstanding restrictions on money in politics. The U.S. Supreme Court's money-equals-speech ruling in 1976 gave the mightiest in America new ways to thwart the will of the masses generally and people of color in particular. At first glance, political donations don't appear racially discriminatory, and their power as instruments of social and economic control is masked because, in theory, anyone can make them. But the difference between theory and practice in campaign giving is as distinct as race and class divisions themselves. Almost all of the money flowing to elected officials comes from an elite cadre of overwhelmingly wealthy and white individuals.[9] Control over the levers of power is preserved by making political expression and participation prohibitively expensive for all but a few.

Monopolizing political speech has been done in the name of protecting the First Amendment. That's the evil elegance of the 1976 Supreme Court edict that limiting money in politics by its very nature infringes the exercise of free speech. The 2010 decision in the *Citizens United* case built on that platform. *Citizens United* effectively married two court doctrines: the money-is-speech ruling and a much older precedent holding that corporations have rights as citizens under the Fourteenth Amendment. If money is speech and corporations are people, then no limits can be placed on corporate spending to influence elections. *Citizens United* opened the floodgates, and corporate money washed over the American political landscape as never before.[10] The barely visible hand of organized money has robbed voters in most parts of the country of their ability to control their own political destiny. Long before voters ever cast a ballot, whoever is most successful in attracting money wins what amounts to a wealth primary that weeds out any meaningful competition, leaving the people with a vote but little, if any, choice. The wealth primary works hand in hand with the practice of gerrymandering political boundaries to strip elections of competitiveness and render them pale imitations of democratic contests.

Having secured the means to keep people down by allowing them to freely vote in elections whose results are preordained, America's royalty nevertheless took no chances. Discriminatory drug policies and the practice of racial profiling by law enforcement authorities and the resulting mass incarceration of African American males became another pillar of the new Jim Crow. This was largely done in the name of fighting the scourge of drug abuse. America's five-decade-long war on drugs never put much of a dent in drug use, but it has been a remarkably efficient tool of racial discrimination.[11] Voter suppression policies powerfully complement it. Since the 2010 election, nearly half of the states made laws restricting the right to vote in one way or another.[12] These laws have been sold as election integrity measures. The public has been repeatedly told such laws are needed to prevent rampant voter fraud. In reality, voter fraud in the U.S. is nearly non-existent.[13] But in Wisconsin[14] and elsewhere in the country,[15] new laws restricting voting in the name of preventing fraud have proven remarkably effective in preventing racial minorities, the poor, and the young from casting ballots.

Monopolized political speech, mass incarceration, and voter suppression together form a potent discriminatory force. Overcoming the new Jim Crow starts with recognizing it and calling it what it is and seeing through the false justifications.

Gender politics provides another glaring illustration of how America's white male power structure divides and conquers. There is no more sensitive topic than abortion and no more effective wedge for the powerful to use to drive us apart. Here's a truth about American politics that never seems to get acknowledged much less discussed: No major party in this country actually wants to outlaw abortion. One says it does, but its actions tell a different story. In recent years, Republicans have at times controlled both houses of Congress and the White House, so they had plenty of opportunities to make a law banning abortion across the nation. Such a law surely would be challenged in court, but the ideologically conservative Republican appointees who have made up the majority on the U.S. Supreme Court since 1971 would have the final say. You'd expect them to uphold the law because Republican presidents have consistently considered an anti-abortion judicial record a key litmus test of the fitness of any judge to serve on the nation's highest court. For that matter, those Republican-appointed Supreme Court justices needn't have waited for an act of Congress. At any time during the better part of the past five decades, the court could have taken up any number of abortion cases and outlawed abortion. They have had that power. Year after year, they chose not to use it.

Recently in Wisconsin, Republicans have more often than not controlled both houses of the state legislature as well as the governor's office. Nothing was stopping them from making a state law prohibiting abortion. A state supreme court controlled by Republican-backed justices would presumably bless such a law. Like their national counterparts, Wisconsin Republicans have had the power to outlaw abortion. They repeatedly chose not to do so.

Perhaps they realize that outlawing abortion won't make the procedure disappear. It will only make it more dangerous and even deadly. In any case, instead of pursuing a ban, they've concentrated on obstructing and inconveniencing the women who seek abortions and the medical professionals who perform them. But most of all, they focus on using this deeply personal and intensely emotional issue as a political football, which they have kicked around for close to fifty years. They have used it to divide people and then harvest the votes these divisions produce. They have shown over an extended period of time that they have every intention of keeping this game going indefinitely.

The glaring irony and hypocrisy are stunning. The Republican Party has gone to the greatest lengths to market itself as the party of limited government and personal freedom. But when it comes to the private lives of Americans, Republicans favor a very intrusive and meddlesome government. They don't trust the choices Americans make in the bedroom and the doctor's office. They want the government to have a looming presence in those places. More than anything, they want to keep people at each other's throats. They want to keep us arguing about whether abortion should be legal or illegal. For a half-century, we've kept kicking their football. We've screamed at each other. We've harassed and attacked each other. Sometimes it's led to unspeakable acts of violence. All done to try to settle a matter that those in power have proven to be keenly interested in keeping unresolved.

Imagine where we would be on this issue if we had instead spent all this time looking for common ground on how to make abortion unnecessary. We would have talked so much more about how best to deal with sex education, how best to promote birth control and family planning, how best to combat poverty. We might have even hashed out some differences by now. Think about what might be possible if we chose to stop kicking the political football and focused on starting a conversation on this incredibly sensitive topic that the ruling elites clearly do not want us to have.

Add this to the list of things we need to see clearly and understand to unscrew America. But the way the world works today, really seeing is easier said than done. In case anyone still doubted that social media have become interwoven into the fabric of American life, raging Twitter wars over which lives matter should put those doubts to rest once and for all. The #BlackLivesMatter hashtag started as a marker for social media comments pleading for America to come to terms with the racism that is so deeply embedded in our society and became the name of a national movement protesting repeated deaths of black men at the hands of police and agitating for racial justice.

Then came the backlash. An #AllLivesMatter hashtag became all the rage on Twitter and other social media, and the slogan was even snuck into the Canadian national anthem by one member of a singing quartet performing at the Major League Baseball All-Star Game in 2016.[16] Prominent political figures ranging from the former mayor of New York[17] to then-Republican nominee for president Donald Trump[18] proclaimed Black Lives Matter to be "inherently racist." A Wisconsin legislator proposed a Blue Lives Matter bill in response to a deadly sniper attack on police officers in Dallas.[19]

Next, there was a backlash against the backlash. Black Lives Matter supporters took to the internet to pronounce All Lives Matter racist, likening it to crashing a funeral to remind mourners that others have lost loved ones or showing up at a cancer fundraiser and yammering about how many other diseases need curing.[20] Others rightly made the point that those in the All Lives Matter camp were falsely suggesting Black Lives Matter means *only* black lives matter when it is intended to convey the idea that black lives matter *too*.[21]

Heaven help us.

All these hashtags have now become hashtraps. As *The Daily Show*'s Trevor Noah aptly explained in July 2016: "It always feels like in America, it's like if you take a stand for something, you automatically are against something else." He went on to say, "For instance, if you're pro-Black Lives Matter, you're assumed to be anti-police, and if you're pro-police, then you surely hate black people."

If it is possible to find common ground on the subject of race, the search has to start in a shared place. We all have had life experiences that give us some insight into matters of race relations, but those experiences are by their nature limited and do not enable any of us to see the whole picture. We all have blind spots. We can't even see how much we don't know and don't understand about each other. That is something every one of us has in common.

I once had the great blessing of being able to live for more than two years in West Africa. It was my first opportunity to experience being a racial minority. It allowed me to see things I couldn't see before. But I still couldn't see what it's like to be a black man in America. I could only see what it was like to be a white male American in an all-black country. I gained valuable insight from the experience but undoubtedly was left with pronounced blind spots. If we are ever going to get to a better place when it comes to race, the journey has to start with all of us acknowledging and accepting how much we can't see and how little we know. Maybe we can even come up with a hashtag for it— #BlindSpotsMatter.

Ordinary Americans of every stripe—I call them commoners—have been divided and conquered in innumerable ways. They have been taught to resent each other, to see each other as enemies. They've been brainwashed to think this way by the Sir William Berkeleys of today, by wolves who present themselves as fellow sheep. These wolves have persuaded them to vote for different political parties. Those parties harvest their votes but do next to nothing to help them. United, the commoners could have a seat at the table. Divided, they are on the menu.

The wolves have always acted cleverly enough to lure sheep out of their flock with a little enticement here and a small inducement there. And then they feast on the very sheep they befriend. This routine is older than the republic, and it continues to work today, keeping both our political system and our economy at work enriching the aristocracy at the expense of the indentured and leaving us with the gruesome economic inequality seen in our country today. There's no unscrewing America without seeing what's been hidden from our view. ✪

CHAPTER EIGHT
THE NEXT MOONSHOT

When at our best, ours is a country of builders, doers, go-getters, dreamers. It's what put a man on the moon.

Today, as we wall ourselves off, it's hard to put a finger on a common aim Americans are united in pursuing. Preventing the ecological, economic, and social calamity sure to be brought on by global overheating could and should be such an aim. America, at its best, would set an example for the rest of the world to follow. At our best, we would shoot for the moon and put our ingenuity to the task of making the United States the first nation on Earth fully powered by renewable energy.

The clock is ticking. The science has been crystal clear for a very long time.[1] The stakes are extraordinarily high for our country and all of Earth's creatures.

What *The New York Times* described as a landmark report in late 2018 by the United Nations Intergovernmental Panel on Climate Change warned that unless drastic action is taken to get carbon emissions under control by the year 2030, the global ecosystem will begin an irreversible slide toward breakdown.[2] In the U.S., this will devastate agriculture, worsen food shortages, and overwhelm the public health system. There will be widespread flooding. Mass migration will follow, with climate refugees fleeing for higher ground, putting strains on border security as never before. A mass die-off of coral reefs will occur as soon as 2040. Uncontrollable wildfires will rage. Storms will continue to intensify and become ever more destructive. The UN's scientific panel on climate change painted a far more dire picture of the consequences of rising global temperatures than previously thought and said in no uncertain terms that avoiding the damage requires transforming the world economy at a speed and scale that has "no documented historic precedent."[3]

That is a tall order. But then so was landing on the lunar surface. America's weather vane is not pointing to the moon. Wisconsin was once a national leader in protecting the land, air, and water but has lowered its defenses when it comes to safeguarding the environment. With Scott Walker as governor, the jobs of dozens of resource management scientists in the state Department of Natural Resources were eliminated, and the agency scrubbed any mention of climate change from its website.[4]

While sending scientists packing and officially denying the existence of any climate crisis, state officials busied themselves granting the oil industry's every wish. In 2014, the DNR gave Enbridge Energy Company the go-ahead to triple the volume of tar sands crude flowing in its oil pipeline from Canada and North Dakota through Wisconsin to Chicago-area refineries to more than a million gallons a day. That's more volume than the controversial Keystone XL pipeline linking western Canada to the Gulf Coast.[5]

Based in Canada, Enbridge has a spotty safety record, guilty of more than one hundred environmental violations in over a dozen Wisconsin counties.[6] In 2010, one of the company's pipelines in Michigan burst and spilled close to a million gallons of tar sands crude into thirty-five miles of the Kalamazoo River. Because the thick tar-like substance has to be diluted with hazardous chemicals to move it through a pipeline, nearby homes had to be evacuated. It took Enbridge seventeen hours to discover the spill, and the cost to clean it up surpassed one billion dollars.[7] Citizen groups like the Wisconsin Safe Energy Alliance and Brave Wisconsin based in rural Lake Mills did their best to organize opposition to Enbridge's expansion plans but were steamrolled by state officials. Even minimal protection for communities in the form of a $25 million spill cleanup insurance requirement was nixed when an eleventh-hour amendment was added to the state budget in July 2015 prohibiting counties from requiring extra insurance from pipeline companies.[8]

Another last-minute budget amendment, shown to have been written by Enbridge's attorneys, gave the state's Public Service Commission the authority to approve any eminent domain claim made by a "business entity."[9] Eminent domain—commonly called condemnation—is the power of the government to take private property for public use, provided that just compensation is paid to the owner. Eminent domain authority was meant to clear the way for public works projects benefiting the citizenry, such as widening roads, building schools, and constructing parks. The authority has been expanded over the years to include such things as improvement of "blighted" neighborhoods. In 2006, Wisconsin was one of many states that enacted protective legislation to ensure that eminent domain served the public interest, "prohibiting the use of eminent domain to condemn non-blighted properties to be transferred to another private entity." Those protections were wiped out by the 2015 state budget amendment. The maneuver was designed to give Enbridge the power to condemn private property for oil pipeline construction and operations. The power was later abused by authorities in the village of Mount Pleasant to force homeowners and farmers off land coveted by the Taiwanese manufacturer Foxconn as part of the package of inducements described in chapter 6.[10]

Mount Pleasant's population is just 26,000 people, but it's home to some of America's largest cabbage farms. Village officials designated farms and homes in the 2,800-acre, four-square-mile territory sought by Foxconn as "blighted," a term long reserved for properties considered run-down or unsafe. Kim and James Mahoney had just built what they described as their "dream home" less than a year before being notified their property was condemned as "blighted" and would be bulldozed to make way for the Foxconn development.[11]

Since 2005, a dozen states have amended their constitutions to ban eminent domain for private gain and provide more protections for property owners. But not Wisconsin. The Enbridge pipeline passing through communities like Lake Mills is transporting a product as thick and sticky as peanut butter that produces more greenhouse gas than conventional forms of gasoline and heating oil.[12] It is not destined for Lake Mills or any other Wisconsin community. It is headed to Illinois for refinement and then to markets elsewhere. Wisconsin does not stand to gain—Enbridge does.

Others misused eminent domain with the government's blessing on the other side of the state, namely companies involved in mining sand to ship to other states to facilitate what's known as "fracking"—short for hydraulic fracturing—to extract oil and gas from previously hard-to-reach shale deposits. Wisconsin's sand is mixed with large quantities of water and toxic chemicals and injected into the shale, where it opens cracks allowing the trapped oil or gas to escape.

With political donations from natural gas and sand mining interests to Wisconsin officials ballooning 2,100 percent in just five years, this industry grabbed land for mines and processing operations that now pepper northwestern Wisconsin. The industry got another assist in 2017 in the form of one of those state budget amendments, taking away community control over the mining and sand processing plants by prohibiting local governments from setting air and water quality standards tougher than state rules and also forbidding any local regulation of blasting at mine sites and truck traffic.[13]

While traveling as a candidate for governor, I visited families living near sand mines. I saw pitchers of water drawn from their faucets the color of weak tea. I saw people wearing masks to avoid breathing the fine dust that hangs in the air. I heard the story of a farmer whose business was devastated when dozens of his beef cattle mysteriously died. His land was within a few hundred yards of a sand mine. Authorities pinpointed no cause of death, but the farmer figured it had to be either the air the cattle were breathing or the water they drank. Another story brought to my attention was that of Brenda Tabor-Adams, a small business owner living with her husband and young son between the small towns of New Auburn and Chetek. They are surrounded by mines, two within a third of a mile and three more within a mile of her once-quiet rural property. With trucks running twelve hours a day, six days a week, her customers were competing with 1,000 sand trucks a day to reach her business. She feared for the health of her family and neighbors, and for the future of her business, but those concerns were dismissed as "collateral damage" by local officials. "Our government has failed us miserably," she said.[14]

At the same time Wisconsin was bending over backwards to green-light every imaginable effort to boost petroleum production, the state was not lifting a finger to promote the development of clean energy alternatives to fossil fuel use. With the climate crisis creating an urgent need to step on the clean energy accelerator, Wisconsin hit the brakes instead. In 2016, a $7 million cut was made to state funding for the Focus on Energy program that promotes energy conservation and renewable energy investment. With that kind of leadership, it comes as no surprise that Wisconsin found itself dead last among twelve Midwest states in the percentage of the private sector workforce employed in the clean energy sector.[15]

If Wisconsin could just reach the regional average for producing clean energy jobs, that would put roughly 30,000 more people in the state to work in that sector. For a governor who came to office promising to create 250,000 new jobs in his first four-year term but still was woefully short of that mark by the end of two terms, the backward thinking about climate science and renewable energy development might just have cost him his job in the end. He chose to ignore the sector of the economy with the greatest growth potential. Evidently, he overlooked the headlines in 2017 about renewable energy creating jobs twelve times faster than the rest of the economy.[16] He failed to grasp what we all must grasp if America is to be unscrewed: Environmental protection is not the enemy of economic development. A healthy economy and healthy planet must go hand in hand. There are three bottom lines in business, not just one. A truly productive and successful business is one that is financially profitable, one whose workers and customers are treated right, and one that is a responsible steward of natural resources.

Committing Wisconsin—and all of America—to a climate action plan to achieve 100 percent renewable energy by 2050 or sooner, a 50 percent reduction in overall energy use by 2030 or sooner, and zero climate-disrupting air pollution emissions by 2050 or sooner is essential if we are going to transform the economy at a speed and scale that has no documented historic precedent. The good news is that such a moonshot could be a savior for the planet and a godsend for the economy.

The clock is ticking. The science is clear. The stakes are exceptionally high.

Another United Nations report issued in early 2019, the UN's first comprehensive examination of biodiversity on the planet, concluded that humans are putting nature under more stress than at any other time in history, dooming over a million species of plants and animals to extinction unless their habitats are restored. More than 1,000 pages long, the assessment included the findings of more than 450 researchers and cited 15,000 scientific and government reports, and had to be approved by representatives of all 109 member nations. Some nations experiencing the most intense effects of climate alteration and biodiversity loss, like small island countries, wanted more in the report. Others, like the United States, insisted on more cautious language. Still, the report tells a frightening story. About three-quarters of Earth's land, two-thirds of its oceans, and 85 percent of crucial wetlands have been severely altered or lost, making it harder for species to survive. Almost half of the world's land mammals and nearly a quarter of the birds have already had their habitats hit hard by global overheating. Every year, 300 to 400 million tons of heavy metals, solvents, and toxic sludge are dumped into the world's waters. A third of the world's fish stocks are overfished. If the planet warms another 0.9 degrees, which other reports say is likely, coral reefs will likely dwindle by 70 percent to 90 percent. At 1.8 degrees of additional warming, 99 percent of the world's coral will be in trouble.[17]

The earth has undergone five mass extinctions, like the one that killed the dinosaurs. The UN report was careful not to call what's going on now a sixth die-off in the making. After examining the findings, one

University of California ecologist begged to differ, saying we are "in the middle of the sixth great extinction crisis, but it's happening in slow motion." One of the report's co-authors tried to strike a more hopeful note. "The key to remember is, it's not a terminal diagnosis." The report does emphasize that many of the worst effects spelled out in the assessment can be prevented by changing what we eat and how we grow food, how we dispose of waste, how we produce and use energy, and by dealing with climate change.[18]

All of this makes the lengths officials in places like Wisconsin have gone to feed the continued addiction to fossil fuels by promoting the extraction and transport of previously hard-to-reach forms of petroleum almost comically shortsighted. Plenty of old skirmishes—both political and military—broke out around the world over oil. Tomorrow's conflicts will be over human migration due to displacement caused by climate change and over resources like water. Pressure to divert water from the Great Lakes is intensifying. The Great Lakes hold six quadrillion gallons of water, 20 percent of the world's fresh surface water. As this precious resource becomes increasingly scarce elsewhere, more and more people are eying that water.[19] The mighty Colorado River has been siphoned to irrigate cropland and supply thirsty cities from Denver to Phoenix to the point where it now runs dry at its end, no longer reaching the ocean at the Gulf of California as it did for millions of years.[20]

Toxic tap water produced human tragedy and a white-hot media spotlight on Flint, Michigan.[21] Far less attention has been paid to the fact that excessive lead levels are found in almost 2,000 water systems across America, including more than eighty communities in Wisconsin.[22] Not many people know that the incidence of lead poisoning of children in Wisconsin is almost exactly the same as the rate found in Flint, and Milwaukee's lead poisoning rate is nearly double Flint's.[23]

Wisconsin is one of the most water-rich states in the nation. Yet the state's groundwater is imperiled.[24] Lakes and streams are drying up because of an unchecked proliferation of high-capacity wells for massive animal feedlots and large-scale crop irrigation.[25] Water quality protections have been stripped away due to politicized resource management,[26] resulting in indiscriminate manure spreading by industrial agriculture operations that produces contaminated drinking water in places like Kewaunee County.[27]

It boggles the mind that lawmakers here responded to all of this with efforts to further weaken water protections and make it even easier to get permission to drill high-capacity wells.[28] And it was hard not to notice that the wealthy interests who wanted to do all the drilling were showering large political donations on the governor[29] and state legislators.[30] Here we have a privileged few being allowed to take as much water as they want, even if it makes lakes and streams and neighbors' wells dry up. We have a politically connected few being allowed to pollute as much as they want, even if it makes others sick. That our government is no longer adequately protecting everyone's right to clean drinking water is a telltale sign of how government has been captured by powerful interests. That politicians are allowing a few big industries to hog all the water or to poison it for others is a measure of how sick our democracy has become. I got my start in life milking cows and working the land with my family. As family farmers, our job was to feed people, not poison them. It breaks my heart to see agriculture increasingly practiced in a way that is not sustainable over the long haul for the land, air, water, animals, or people. No one anywhere should turn on a water faucet and be afraid to drink what comes out.

Oil and water don't mix, but they do have a lot in common. Both are precious natural resources, and both have a way of bringing out the worst in us. Both inspire greed, and both can corrupt. As water becomes the new oil, and the water wars escalate, the question is whether greed will govern us, or will we summon the wisdom and resolve to make sure what government does when it comes to water and other natural resources is done for the good of the entire planet and all of its inhabitants. Democracy's survival depends on it, and so does the survival of our species. ✚

CHAPTER NINE
FEELING LIKE POTTERSVILLE

Transforming the economy at a speed and scale unprecedented in history requires a renewed sense of national purpose and a reimagined social contract between us. Also needed is a different way of thinking about how best to make our economy grow sustainably.

In Wisconsin, the lobbying group that passes itself off as the voice of Wisconsin business is backward. Wisconsin is home to some truly innovative, forward-thinking business leaders who are finding ways to successfully compete in the twenty-first-century economy. But they aren't being heard in the state capitol. The state chamber of commerce—known as Wisconsin Manufacturers and Commerce (WMC)—is supposed to be their voice, but it's not. WMC's thinking is stuck in the twentieth century. In some ways, it's still in the nineteenth century.

WMC's philosophy is that the key to economic development is lowering the cost of doing business. Lower wages. Lower taxes. Lower environmental standards. This recipe is dangerous to our future, but it also hasn't been working for years. If low costs are the secret to stimulating the economy, then why did one of Wisconsin's seventy-two counties create nearly half of all new private sector jobs in the state in 2016 when some of the state's highest wages, taxes, and cost of land are found in that county?[1] Why did the number of private sector jobs in that one high-cost county grow at four times the rate of the state as a whole?[2] If Wisconsin Manufacturers and Commerce knows how to make the economy better, why has Wisconsin been losing manufacturing jobs? WMC gives answers to questions that aren't even being asked anymore. The state chamber of commerce is inhibiting commerce. WMC's outdated philosophy is holding Wisconsin back.

One of Wisconsin's greatest business success stories in many a year has to be the electronic health records software pioneer Epic Systems. The company is fairly young, having started in 1979, and is growing by leaps and bounds, continually expanding its campus and adding about 1,000 employees or more every year.[3] Epic's home base, the Madison suburb of Verona, recently passed one of the largest school referendums in the history of the state for construction of a new high school and other costly upgrades, almost entirely paid for by the community's largest private employer, namely Epic.[4]

Epic's success isn't owed to WMC's agenda of lower taxes, lower wages, and lower environmental standards. Epic's leadership is not at all on the same wavelength as WMC's leadership. In fact, Epic wants nothing to do with WMC. A statement the company issued in June 2008 said, "Epic has never belonged to Wisconsin Manufacturers and Commerce (WMC)," and went on to say, "We made a decision to try to work only with vendors that do not support WMC with its current management. This was not a decision we made lightly, but believe it is the right thing to do." The memo took aim, in particular, at WMC's meddling in Wisconsin's Supreme Court elections, which Epic's top management saw as a "travesty of ethics." The memo explained the company's posture: "We believe business exists to support society. When instead business undermines society's basic principles, then we each choose whether or not to tolerate it. The process of selecting judges for the Wisconsin Supreme Court should be of the highest integrity. ... We believe that what we tolerate is what we stand for, and as corporate citizens, we stand for the preservation of the foundation of the judicial system."

Yet, at the state capitol today, WMC continues to be recognized as the voice of Wisconsin business. But it represents what business was. Epic is what business is. Those renewable energy equipment manufacturers and installers that are creating jobs twelve times faster than the rest of the economy, as noted in chapter 8, are what business will be. To thrive in the twenty-first century, Wisconsin needs to do an about-face and fundamentally change its approach to economic development. My state and my country need to watch and listen more to the Epics and the green energy entrepreneurs and take to heart the formulas for success in the twenty-first century they are coming up with, and pay far less attention to the likes of WMC and their backward thinking.

To the greatest extent possible, government should stick to doing those things private businesses can't or won't do. This rule gets broken all the time, almost always with less than favorable results. Take Wisconsin's approach to promoting job growth, for example. What you have in the Wisconsin Economic Development Corporation is a bunch of state bureaucrats pretending to be investment bankers. Wannabe entrepreneurs who've sought private financing and had their projects turned down by investment banks, venture capitalists, and angel investors are able to make a few well-placed political donations, get some strings pulled, and get financing from WEDC courtesy of state taxpayers.[5] Here we have the public sector acting as the investor of last resort for enterprises that private sector financiers won't touch. That's not only proven to be a waste of taxpayer money and a breeding ground for corruption, but a prime example of government getting involved where it does not belong. Politicians are fond of saying government should be run like a business. Wisconsin's corporate welfare office is proof of the folly in that philosophy. Business and government are different creatures, and they have separate purposes.

Successful private businesses have to be able to turn a profit. But not everything that is profitable has social value or promotes the common good. And not everything that is socially valuable or advances the public interest is profitable. Pornography is undeniably lucrative and thrives in the private sector but has questionable social value and is often associated with social ills. Likewise, it is hard to see how gambling makes us better people or strengthens our society, but it is a profitable business for sure. On the other hand, it can't be plausibly disputed that such things as schools, libraries, parks, police and fire departments, sanitation crews, and military forces are valuable or even indispensable to our society. Still, none of them would exist—or at least all would be vastly diminished—if they had to be profitable.

Here is another place where Wisconsin has strayed from common sense. Educating all of our children, regardless of need or disability, is not profitable. The private sector can't do it. The only sure way to run a school *and* turn a profit is to cherry-pick students who are easiest to teach and steer clear of those whose needs make them considerably more costly to educate. Wisconsin has chosen to favor schools that are not required to take all comers, rapidly expanding its private school voucher program and sharply increasing funding for voucher schools while cutting state aid for public schools that are mandated to accommodate all students no matter how expensive they are to serve.[6]

Business and government are different creatures that serve separate purposes. The government cannot be run like a business because the public sector's role in our society is so fundamentally different than the private sector's. And businesses surely should not be expected to operate like the government. The private sector has its place and its rules. So does the public sector. To each its own.

A central challenge for education is to figure out how to make a college degree or other advanced training as affordable and obtainable for our kids and grandkids as a high school diploma has been. Given the way the economy is evolving, the future of the American Dream depends on it. But something predictable happens when it is suggested that the promise of free public education be extended through college. Hardcore right-wingers grumble about handing out "free stuff," which seems to be their preferred way of balking at helping to pay for anything that helps someone else. But something else happens too. Many liberals instinctively call for means testing—targeting any public benefit to the poor or near-poor—arguing that only those who could not otherwise afford to pay should get society's assistance. This liberal impulse is

MIKE McCABE

understandable. It is also self-defeating. It ends up undermining the very kind of public investments liberals think are so critically important. It does so by stigmatizing public investments and sowing the seeds of resentment and hostility toward the beneficiaries.

Means testing inevitably pits those who qualify against those who don't. Means tests also are prone to creating poverty traps. You have to be needy enough to qualify for a public benefit, and you have to stay needy enough to keep receiving it. It is no accident that the most successful and enduring government programs—like Social Security—are not means tested. Everyone pays, everyone benefits.

For as long as there have been politicians, there have been whipping boys. No one was better with the whip than Wisconsin's Scott Walker. As previously discussed, he was highly skilled in the use of divide-and-conquer tactics, a master at pitting one group of struggling and vulnerable people against another. It's his favorite play, the governor's political equivalent of legendary Green Bay Packers coach Vince Lombardi's power sweep or Southern Cal's famed "student body right." Walker turned to this page in his playbook repeatedly, whenever he was feeling the least bit threatened politically. One such time was in early 2017 when he proposed stricter work requirements for those receiving food stamps in Wisconsin.[7] He counted on Democrats to rush to the defense of food stamp recipients and accuse him of beating up on the poor. That expected response was critical to the successful execution of the governor's play.

Once they did what they always do, Walker could paint the Democrats as the party of handouts, the party devoted to taking from those who work and giving to those who don't. He could pit those who are having a hard time making ends meet but don't qualify for food stamps against those who rely on them to eat. And did he ever. His play also diverted attention from the dismal failure of his feed-the-rich economic policies, which, as mentioned in chapter 1, had left Wisconsin leading the nation in shrinkage of the middle class and dead last in new business start-ups and entrepreneurial activity.

When Walker did what he always does, and the Democrats responded how they always respond, the questions that most needed asking didn't get asked. The debate most needed was never had. Wisconsin should have been debating how to create an economy where if you work, you won't be poor and won't go hungry. It is undeniable that we don't have such an economy today. We should be aspiring to an economy where food stamps and other forms of welfare become unnecessary. We should have been talking about the fact that government spends more on corporate welfare than it does on social welfare that makes up the proverbial safety net.[8] Wisconsin was becoming a shadow of its former self economically, which left Walker in need of a whipping boy, a scapegoat, someone to bear the blame for his administration's failings. That's where food stamp recipients came in handy to him, as long as the Democrats played into his hands and did their part to help him isolate and stigmatize them.

To have a just and decent society, we need to be there for each other. And we need our government to reflect that spirit of interdependence. Arriving there depends on us being smart enough to resist impulses like means testing that makes government programs vulnerable to divide-and-conquer tactics. To the greatest extent humanly possible, what government does needs to be done for our whole society. Everyone pays, everyone benefits.

I've lost count of the number of times I've watched Frank Capra's beloved 1946 film *It's a Wonderful Life*. It must be north of forty. Yet it has a way of hitting closer to home with each passing year. The movie's battle of wills between public-spirited George Bailey and greedy Mr. Potter has always symbolized conspicuous social and economic tensions between America's privileged rich and struggling working class. But with the gap between the rich and the rest widening and the country's middle class losing ground, and with hate on the rise[9] and the nation's political system so thoroughly corrupted, the classic storyline of one man's absence causing idyllic Bedford Falls to transform into the nightmarish Pottersville resonates more than ever. America feels more and more like Pottersville.

Mr. Potter's consuming greed has abundant real-life parallels. The depiction of the common good giving way to cold, self-centered individualism has a ring of familiarity to it too. The powerful forces Capra put up on the big screen for public inspection are stronger and more dangerous now than they were in his time. It's hard to see *It's a Wonderful Life* as anything but an indictment of warped values putting commercialism above community. Those values are much more deeply embedded in today's America than they were in Capra's day and age. The film's depiction of government and politics is ambiguous. The story plays out against a backdrop of the nation and its federal government winning World War II, an accomplishment Capra treats with pride and respect. But then there's that scene where Mr. Potter is fuming about how George Bailey's business practices are besting his own. His secretary interrupts to remind him of an appointment with a congressman, and he angrily sputters, "Tell the congressman to wait." Capra's viewpoint is unmistakable: The richest man in town has more access to and control over his elected representative than others in the community have. Conditions in this regard are much worse now. Compared to 1946, government is far less trusted[10] and is seen as far more corrupt in today's America.[11]

There is plenty in Capra's vision of Bedford Falls and Pottersville to make both liberals and conservatives squirm. The movie's religious themes are not subtle, even though George Bailey admits—in a prayer, ironically enough—that he is not a praying man. *It's a Wonderful Life* tells a story of divine intervention prompted by the prayers of friends, family, and admirers of George's as he considers taking his own life. Such piety causes indigestion for some modern liberals. At the same time, Mr. Potter is the film's villain. He is a vile, soulless money-grubber but is a tame caricature of today's crony capitalists who have done such violence to small family-owned businesses like the Bailey Building and Loan and who hold such sway over today's Republican Party. Mr. Potter's antisocial self-absorption pales in comparison to the trendsetter of modern American conservatism and current inhabitant of the nation's highest office.

Capra warned the American people in 1946 about what he saw coming. It came. Unless there's divine intervention, it's up to us to channel our inner George Bailey and preserve Bedford Falls. It's up to us because the political consultants aren't teaching the Bailey family's ethics to the elected officials they steer. They teach them to read from a script. They call it values-based messaging. Whenever a bill becomes law or a budget is adopted, or any muscle is moved at the capitol, one side says it's just what the people need. The other side says it doesn't reflect our shared values. A few speak sparingly, but most go into great detail. Some zero in on one thing, while others recite lengthy lists. None of them ever do seem to say exactly which values were advanced or violated.

Still, it's clear from any vantage point outside the capitol that the values lawmakers put on display as they practice politics and pass bills and build budgets are not those we all were taught in kindergarten. Share. Take turns and play fair. Don't hit. Say you're sorry when you hurt someone. Don't take things that aren't yours. Clean up your mess. Stick together. The Golden Rule is hard to find, both in the actions and the behavior of those doing the acting.

What a better country America would be if our politics didn't so often scream, "You are on your own!" and instead reflected that we're all in this together and need to look out for each other. What a healthier planet we would have if governments and businesses and consumers alike picked up after themselves and put things back where they found them. How sane and just our society would be if public policies matched those sandbox values, if we stuck together, and shared and treated others as we like being treated.

Our country is in trouble. We have our work cut out for us. We need to change how we talk to each other so we can ultimately decide together what kind of society we want. We need to equip every American to be a full-fledged citizen in a democracy, so the many and not the money can decide the direction of our country. We need to challenge the political establishment to change its ways with the goal of transforming the parties and the political system so those who govern work for all of us instead of taking their cues from a privileged few.

We can't all build our own roads. There are some things we need to do together. If we don't apply that basic principle to every challenge we confront as a nation, then what some small rural communities in Wisconsin are doing—ripping up pavement and going back to dirt roads—will come to broadly symbolize America's fate. **☉**

CHAPTER TEN
THE FORTY-YEAR CLEANSE

To get a good read on the state of the union, just pull up a chair at the dinner table. More often than not in America these days, what you experience is not exactly a Norman Rockwell illustration.

Sharp political differences have some on pins and needles at holiday family gatherings. Some are at each other's throats and end up cutting their get-togethers short, especially those who are traveling to what feels to them like enemy territory. After analyzing location data from ten million smartphones and matching them to precinct-level voting data, researchers at two different major U.S. universities concluded that "partisan differences cost American families sixty-two million person-hours of Thanksgiving time."[1]

Democracy may be on America's menu, but at least three key ingredients needed to make the dish are increasingly hard to find. We can't have a stable society, much less a democracy, without dialogue, and the capacity for dialogue is vanishing in America. We scream at one another, we hurl insults back and forth, or at best we talk past each other. We stay in the friendly confines of our own side's echo chambers, hearing what we want to hear and what reinforces our own beliefs and filtering out the rest. We consume news tailored to our existing biases, leaving us with no common frame of reference on most any topic. This makes it next to impossible to have conversations that yield mutual understanding and make it possible to hash out differences.

We can't have a stable society much less a democracy without citizenship, and citizenship is vanishing in this country. Civics in not meaningfully taught in school. Concern for the common good is becoming downright uncommon. Selfishness reigns supreme in modern American life. We work. We shop. We mostly keep to ourselves. Keeping to ourselves is incompatible with citizenship. Being a citizen is inherently social. Governing a society is intrinsically public. Generally speaking, Americans nowadays prefer all things private. More so than at any time in memory, public matters make us squirm or even dread having dinner with extended family. Is it any wonder that a certifiable narcissist inhabits the nation's highest office?[2]

We can't have a stable society, much less a democracy, without trusted and legitimate political institutions. Americans are increasingly sour on the two major parties[3] and are longing for a viable alternative.[4] Trust in government is low and falling.[5] Americans are increasingly afraid, and concern about government corruption is not only on the rise but tops the list of fears.[6]

Some of the divisions in our society can be as confounding as the Russians were to Winston Churchill—a riddle wrapped in a mystery inside an enigma. As journalist Alec MacGillis incisively observed in *The New York Times*, some of the poorest parts of the country are inclined to support the politicians who are most hostile to any form of government assistance to the poor. Democrats may not want to hear it, but MacGillis was speaking directly to them when he said, "The temptation for coastal liberals is to shake their heads over those godforsaken white-working-class provincials who are voting against their own interests. But this reaction misses the complexity of the political dynamic that's taken hold in these parts of the country. It misdiagnoses the Democratic Party's growing conundrum with working-class white voters. And it also keeps us from fully grasping what's going on in communities where conditions have deteriorated to the point where researchers have detected alarming trends in their mortality rates."[7]

Democrats used to appeal to rural voters but don't anymore, and this fact makes it next to impossible for them to construct coalitions broad enough to produce governing majorities. If the Democrats are to avoid going the way of the dinosaur, they have to solve the rural riddle. Clues abound. MacGillis made the point about how many rural voters oppose programs they consider handouts aimed at helping what they regard as the undeserving poor. This is an incredibly important point for Democrats to ponder given the liberal impulse, mentioned in chapter 9, to target any government assistance to particular constituencies through means testing, making their programs highly vulnerable to the divide-and-conquer tactics of the Republicans. For decades, the Democrats have ignored the political law of universality: The most widely supported and successful government programs are ones where everyone pays and everyone benefits. When the Democrats won the hearts of a majority of people in the past, it was because the party had a big hand in creating things like Social Security and Medicare, the interstate highway system, rural electrification, and the GI Bill that tangibly benefited everyone, or at least directly touched every American family.

Think about how almost every major highway project done any time in recent or distant memory that reached into rural areas featured bypasses of small towns. Think about the impact this has on those communities. Their family-owned cafes and coffee shops and restaurants close. Their main streets die. Shaving a few minutes off your or my travel time can be a death sentence for a small town. Rural residents need only make one trip to the city, and resentment is bred as they see where all the gas taxes they pay are spent. Rural communities don't need multi-lane monstrosities with cloverleafs and traffic circles. They need high-quality, well-maintained paved roads. Most city folk have no idea how many country roads are still unpaved to this day and how many of the paved ones are rutted and chock full of potholes.

Think about how a local school is a rural community's bedrock, even to a greater degree than in urban or suburban areas. The rural school is a hub of community activity. Everyone goes to the school play or the high school football game. Lose the school and the community is lost. School district consolidation and school closings have hit many rural communities with the force of a bomb.[8] Look at a map showing which parts of the U.S. have access to broadband internet. The urban centers do, but the rural areas don't.[9] The telecommunications industry and its apologists in public office often are heard saying that programs are in place to address this disparity. A recent Microsoft study put the number of Americans lacking access to high-speed internet at 163 million—close to half the country's population.[10] And the digital divide is unquestionably a rural-urban divide.[11] Many living in rural areas can't get reliable mobile phone signals either. How can you start a business and compete in today's economy without access to these services? High-speed internet and mobile voice are to the twenty-first century what telephones were in the twentieth, namely essential communications technologies that remain out of the reach of most rural people.

Addressing these concerns would be immensely helpful to rural areas. But today's breed of Republican won't support massive infrastructure investment—the twenty-first century equivalent of rural electrification or constructing the interstate highway system—to bring high-speed internet and mobile phone service to every part of the country. Today's GOP won't rescue rural public schools because it is too busy trying to privatize education nationwide. Today's Republicans won't bite the tax bullet to significantly upgrade rural roads. They won't end means testing of government assistance because it is politically advantageous for them to pit the poor against the nearly-poor.

If any of these steps are to be taken, it'll have to be Democrats taking them, if enough of them wake up to the need and the opportunity. That's a big if. Especially considering what happened when the Democrats last controlled both the White House and Congress. That was when the country was dealing with the fallout of the Great Recession—the worst economic downturn in America since the Great Depression. Tens of millions suffered. More than eight million jobs were lost, and nearly four million homes were foreclosed each year. Family incomes dropped. Poverty spiked.[12] Millions more watched neighbors forsaken by their government as I had as a teenager when a neighbor took his own life after the bank notified his family it was foreclosing. The Obama administration's response to this new foreclosure epidemic was to bail out the nation's lenders, but not the borrowers.[13] I can't help but think this had a great deal to do with why Democrats lost more than 1,000 seats in Congress, state legislatures, and governor's offices across the nation during Obama's presidency.[14]

The traumas of the Great Recession brought millions of Americans to a fork in the road politically. Some went right at the fork, others went left, giving rise to two landscape-altering social movements. The Occupy movement on the left, with its "We are the 99 percent" catchphrase, changed the national conversation by bringing income and wealth inequality to the forefront of public consciousness. Democrats weren't focusing on it, nor were most liberal advocacy groups. Before Occupy, the term "one-percenter" wasn't part of our political vocabulary, and little attention was being paid to how the nation's rich were getting vastly wealthier, while the poor were growing poorer, and the middle class was disappearing. Occupy changed that. Occupy made talk of economic inequality commonplace. That's no small achievement.

The Tea Party movement on the right, with its "Don't tread on me" mindset, changed the Republican Party. In so doing, Tea Partiers changed Congress and state legislatures across the country. They put the fear of God into mainstream GOP politicians. Those politicians were given a choice. Either grant Tea Partiers their wishes or face their wrath on the campaign trail. A few, like House Republican leader Eric Cantor, took their chances at the ballot box. Most others fell in line, spooked by how the Tea Party made examples of the likes of Cantor.[15]

Other than obvious ideological differences, the big distinction between the Occupy and Tea Party movements was that one deliberately steered clear of involvement with elections, while the other jumped into elections with both feet. That says a lot about the right and left today. One side is dogged in its pursuit of political power and will go to any lengths to get it and keep it. The other prefers to protest and march and picket. Any honest assessment of the overall impact of these two movements has to conclude that the Tea Party has had a bigger influence on our country's direction, which suggests the ballot is mightier than the placard. This calls into question the strategic impulses of the forces gathering in America to resist the turn the nation has more recently taken.

After Donald Trump's election, a new strategic blueprint called "Indivisible" was cooked up by some former Democratic congressional staffers, suggesting those on the left could block Trump's agenda by copying tactics the Tea Party used to obstruct Obama's. They claimed to offer "best practices for making Congress listen" to the people. Such a claim begs an obvious question: If former Democratic staffers on Capitol Hill know the best ways to make Congress listen to us and have a fail-safe blueprint for resisting Trump, how did they manage to become so utterly powerless in Washington and why couldn't they prevent the Tea Party takeover of Congress? But more importantly, a part of the Tea Party's approach—the most important and effective part—was conspicuously missing from their strategy. Tea Partiers not only condemned Obama's every move, they contested Republican elections. In the end, they were unable to deny Obama a second term. But they did end Eric Cantor's career and the careers of a slew of his establishment Republican colleagues. They seized power in Congress to the point where they could dictate terms to House Speaker John Boehner as well as his successor Paul Ryan. Considering who concocted the Democrats' new recipe and what key ingredient they chose to omit, it looked less like an effort to engineer a Tea Party-style insurrection on the Democratic side and more like an attempt to head one off at the pass.

Conditions in 2016 were undeniably conducive to massive populist uprisings in our country and elsewhere in the world, most notably in Europe. Both England's Brexit vote and Donald Trump staking his claim to America's Republican Party were visible symptoms of the condition. The boiling discontent and anti-establishment fervor were the natural byproducts of political and economic inequality and the callous disregard that ruling elites have shown for the brutal effects of economic globalization. The anxiety and anger fueling raging populism can be steered in a constructive, forward-looking direction. Or it can just as easily be channeled in the opposite direction, toward barbarism or even fascism. This destructive path is likely to be taken if those with progressive values ignore or pooh-pooh the conditions, attempt to suppress or steer clear of the populist eruptions such conditions inevitably produce, or try to shoo away those wielding pitchforks.

Hungry people will eat wherever they are invited to the table. Here in the U.S., there is great danger in the Democratic establishment's current impulse to keep theirs a stay-the-course, steady-as-she-goes party that only occasionally supports a smidgen of incremental change when not defending the status quo. That impulse drives people with a powerful appetite for fundamentally rearranging the social order into the waiting arms of backward-looking demagogues promising to restore America's greatness by returning to some mythical simpler time, just as similar demagogues are promising to do in Europe. It is no accident or surprise that Marine Le Pen, leader of the far-right French National Front, calls working-class people who are raging against the machine "les invisibles et les oubliés."[16] The invisible and the forgotten are fascism's fuel.

Here at home, large numbers of people feel invisible and forgotten. They noticed when bankers and Wall Street financiers were bailed and not jailed when their reckless behavior cost so many of the invisible and forgotten their life savings and brought the nation's economy to its knees. They notice every time the rich get another tax cut, or big corporations get state handouts even as they are sending jobs overseas.[17] They see political, social, and economic systems that consistently favor an elite few at everyone else's expense. And they are pissed. All signs indicate the invisible and forgotten are unwilling to be ignored much longer. They are hungry, and they will find a place to eat. The only question is what will be on the menu. It could be economic and political elitism or inequality and injustice that get devoured. Or it could be freedom and democracy and civil society.

If you're a *Divergent* fan, you already know the book and film trilogies transport audiences to a time and place where the population is divided into factions, each with its own mindset and personality type. Loyalty and service to a faction produce harmony—until it doesn't. Then all

MIKE McCABE

hell breaks loose. That's imaginary. Now back to reality. University of North Carolina political scientists Marc Hetherington and Jonathan Weiler made a compelling case in their recent book *Prius or Pickup?* that American society is being torn apart, but it's not disagreements over the issues of the day or even differing political ideologies that are doing the ripping. Rather, the culprit lies far beneath the surface in the form of deeply ingrained worldviews that are reflected in our lifestyles—the vehicles we drive, where we choose to live, how we parent, even the pets we keep.[18]

Hetherington and Weiler zero in on two types of worldviews, which they label fixed and fluid. Fixed sorts see a world full of danger, where other people and nature are out to get them. They feel threatened, which the authors say makes them more likely to keep a gun close by with a growling dog at their side and a heavy-duty truck in the driveway. Fluid folks, on the other hand, find the world a less threatening and generally hospitable place. They tend to see others as basically good and the world as mostly safe—hence the hybrid car in the garage and the cat curled up on the living room sofa. By the authors' account, you need only ask four questions to tell whether someone has a fixed or fluid worldview. The questions have nothing to do with politics but rather are about child-rearing. Is it more important for children to be independent or to respect their elders? Is it better for children to be obedient or self-reliant? Is it preferable for them to be curious or to have good manners? Is it more important to be considerate or well-behaved? Those who want respectful, obedient, well-behaved kids who mind their manners are said to have fixed worldviews. Those who think it's best to have children who are independent, self-reliant, curious, and considerate fall on the fluid end of this worldview spectrum.

There are political implications aplenty because Hetherington and Weiler go on to point out there's been a "marriage of worldview and party" in American politics—a sharp departure from the mixed-worldview political parties of the past. We no longer have parties based on issue platforms. We now have factions based on personality types and ways of seeing the world—birds of a feather flocking together. This presents a mammoth challenge. When one faction senses danger and wants protection and security and order, and the other feels secure and wants to explore and be open to new experiences, how do the two relate to each other, much less hash out differences? On the outside looking in are the mutts. Most of us are not purebreds, not 100 percent this or 100 percent that. Some among us want a big dog but a small car. Some want their children to be strong-willed *and* well-behaved, curious *and* safe. Are the mutts among us doomed to be politically homeless? Hetherington and Weiler acknowledge there's a third type of worldview. They call it mixed. But they shed very little light on what might happen to the mutts in the emerging faction system.

As expected with fiction, *Divergent* does not leave that stone unturned. Those who don't blend into any faction are cast out. The factionless are treated as refuse. But those who fit in several factions—the divergent—are seen as dangerous threats and are hunted down. All hell breaks loose. That's imaginary. Now back to reality. Where will the marriage of worldview and party take us? One can only imagine. In the not-too-distant past, the major American political parties were big tents. They were broad-based coalitions, the idea being that the broader the coalition, the better the chance of winning elections. Starting in the 1970s and intensifying ever since, the parties have been purifying themselves.

We are continually being told how divided Americans are and how politically polarized our society has become. Go out and talk to people of every political stripe, and differences come to the surface for sure. But I've still been left with the clear impression that most Americans continue to have a great deal in common, much more than we've been led to believe. The political parties and their echo chambers have made us more tribal, not the other way around.

Hetherington and Weiler engage in a fair amount of exaggerated overgeneralization. Not all Republicans drive trucks, and not all Democrats drive hybrids. But their conclusion is nevertheless hard to dispute. Both major parties have undergone worldview cleansing. Republicans embraced what they call the fixed worldview and purged liberals, progressives, and moderates from their ranks. Democrats opted for the fluid worldview and parted company with conservatives, in general, and country folk, in particular.

Until the most recent decades, there were liberals like Nelson Rockefeller and Lowell Weicker in the GOP. In Wisconsin, Republican state lawmakers like John Manske were cut from this cloth. They are not found in the party's ranks anymore. Progressives like Teddy Roosevelt and Bob La Follette once had a home in the Republican Party. As recently as the early 1980s, Wisconsin still had state legislators from this lineage like Clifford "Tiny" Krueger—a 425-pound one-time circus "fat boy" with a heart to match his girth. No longer. There used to be Republican moderates. Today's GOP is a donut. No middle. As recently as the early 1980s, there was an abundance of centrist Wisconsin Republicans. Many were women who favored legal abortion and women's rights, like Mary Panzer, Barb Lorman and Peggy Rosenzweig. Many other middle-of-the-roaders were men like Dale Schultz and one-time Governor Lee Sherman Dreyfus. Moderates were exterminated from the Republican ranks. Panzer was challenged and defeated in a primary by right-wing zealot Glenn Grothman, whose colleagues nicknamed him Spooky for his extreme views. Lorman was taken out in another primary challenge by Scott Fitzgerald, who went on to lead the cleansed Republicans in the state senate. Rosenzweig lost to someone charitably described as quirky[19] and eccentric[20] who ran as a family-values conservative. The last centrist to go was Schultz, who opposed Scott Walker's union-busting legislation. He promptly faced a primary challenge, saw the writing on the wall, and in 2014 announced he was leaving the legislature.

Northern abolitionists started the GOP and it became known far and wide as the party of Lincoln. Republicans abandoned that legacy in the 1960s and 1970s with their southern strategy taking advantage of Democratic support for civil rights to court southern whites and flip the south from a Democratic stronghold to a rock-solid base of Republican support. This north-south political realignment pushed the GOP sharply to the right and set in motion the worldview cleansing within both major parties. What's evolved out of this is a Republican Party that's whiter,[21] righter,[22] older,[23] extremer,[24] and smaller.[25] The party is fixed and falling. Ordinarily, that would be great news for the Democrats, but it hasn't worked out that way. The Democratic Party is fluid and flailing, at its weakest point in a century.[26]

Not so long ago, there were conservative Democrats. The Dixiecrats switched sides and paved the way for Republican seizure of the south. The Blue Dogs are now an endangered species.[27] In Wisconsin, conservative Democrats lacked a clever nickname, but their numbers were significant. Rural conservatives like Gervase Hephner of Chilton and Dale Bolle of New Holstein populated the state legislature. Other small-town Democrats like Tom Harnisch of Neillsville, Harvey Stower of Amery, Bill Rogers of Kaukauna, and Bob Dueholm of Luck were more moderate or even liberal, and their numbers were substantial too. They're long gone. The Democratic Party used to appeal to rural voters, but it sure doesn't today.[28] It has become an urban party.

With an unpopular president, declining public approval for the Republican Party, GOP leaders coping with white supremacy in their ranks, and with support for Republicans starting to slip in the suburbs,[29] you'd think the Democrats would be the nation's majority party by default. That's not the case. Even after Democrats made significant gains in the 2018 midterm elections, Republicans still controlled most of the country's statehouses as well as the U.S. Senate and the White House.

Democrats have solid backing in the cities, but those are a few blue islands in a sea of red. The party has lost the support it once had in rural areas. The worldview cleansing that's been done on the Democratic side is a big reason why. It's created single-mindedness on social concerns but leaves the party without a coherent philosophy on pocketbook issues. There used to be Democrats on both sides of the abortion debate. No more. There used to be Democrats on both sides of civil rights questions. Not now. It is difficult, if not impossible, to get elected as a Democrat nowadays without being socially progressive. But it is entirely feasible to run as an economically elitist, pro-Wall Street, corporate Democrat. Today's political landscape is littered with Democrats who favor the economic status quo—a continuation of feed-the-rich, trickle-down economic policies—from the Clintons on the national stage to the likes of Ron Kind here in Wisconsin. Then there are economic boat-rockers, including democratic socialists like Bernie Sanders and Alexandria Ocasio-Cortez, who want Democrats to get serious about economic inequality in America. These two camps are more or less of one mind on social issues, creating a united front on lifestyle. But they are at odds on economics. For the most part, the economic status quo Democrats have had the upper hand. But you simply cannot be socially progressive *and* economically elitist and have any hope of winning in rural areas. This is why Democrats have fallen out of favor in socially conservative, economically distressed rural America.

I've never seen a time when our public institutions were more disrespected and distrusted, and with good reason. I've also never seen a time when government was less responsive to regular people. Over and over, our government is put to work for the privileged, wealthy, and well-connected. People notice this. They realize their voices aren't being heard, and their interests are not being served. That's a recipe for disrespect and distrust of public institutions. These conditions are especially poisonous to the Democratic Party. The Democrats are widely seen as the party of government. There is reality to that perception. Of the two major parties, the Democrats most strongly believe that government is essential to a civil society and can have a positive and constructive impact on people's lives.

But here's the problem for Democrats. It's next to impossible to be popular as the party of public institutions at a time when so many people have so little faith in those institutions. People see public officials climbing the ladder, advancing their careers, feathering their own nests. They see those officials exchanging favors, scratching the backs of those who scratch theirs. None of that looks much like public service. Being the party of disrespected and distrusted public institutions explains why Democrats have been on a decades-long losing streak, why they do not control either Congress or the White House, and why they are not calling the shots in two-thirds of state capitals.[30]

The current political culture celebrates greed and emphasizes self-advancement over the common good. It treats public service as just another opportunity for self-dealing. When such a culture flourishes, it's today's Republican Party that much more comfortably fits the role of the party of the times we live in. Democrats can say they are concerned for the common good and are acting in the public interest, but when they appear to be operating comfortably within the system as it works today, and when they cater to a few constituencies at everyone else's expense, voters inevitably see them as hypocrites. In a political culture where greed is triumphant and self-dealing the norm, Republicans are credited for at least being upfront about their intentions, and Democrats are punished for hypocrisy.

The Democrats have been in decline for more than forty years. That's not to say they haven't won an occasional battle in that time, but they've been losing the war for that long. It's been a downward spiral ever since the Great Society era drew to a close soon after the dawning of the 1970s. Forty years of losing argument after argument about which direction the country should head has had a profound cumulative effect. America is more walled off and more locked up.[31] We are more militaristic and armed to the teeth,[32] defended to the point of ridiculous overkill.[33] All largely because we are becoming more unequal by the day.[34] That's what forty years of trickle-down economics and crony capitalism and deregulation for deregulation's sake get you.

In its heyday, the Democratic Party was countrypolitan. A slang term most often associated with music, countrypolitan can apply to anything—or anyone—that's a mix of rural and metropolitan. That's what the Democratic Party used to be decades ago. It is not countrypolitan today and hasn't been for quite some time now. The Democrats started losing ground when they stopped appealing to people outside the cities. The Democrats' decline won't be reversed until they get serious about exploring why poor rural and rich suburban people are sticking together to support right-wing values and policies, how they could be persuaded to part company, and how rural and urban interests could be reunited. The Democratic Party has much to gain and little to lose from such exploration. But lower- and middle-class Americans in both rural and urban areas stand to gain the most. Policies benefiting them don't stand much of a chance of becoming the law of the land as long as the vast wealth of a few holds policymakers in such an iron grip. For there to be a chance of commoner-friendly thinking being reflected in government actions, a new countrypolitan coalition needs to emerge, one that packs enough punch to stagger the reigning political champion—the one percent's money. Legions of diligent campaign finance reformers are watching helplessly these days as old safeguards against government corruption have been stripped away, and the floodgates are opened ever wider, allowing more and more money to pour into elections and lobbying. They are powerless to stop political inequality from breeding still more political inequality. Growing political inequality then produces greater economic inequality and sustained social inequality. And the more government is seen working for just a few at everyone else's expense, the more the masses despise government. The more government is despised, the easier it is for a wealthy and well-connected few to control.

This vicious cycle is a quandary for the 99 percent and the Democratic Party. Preventing our nation from becoming more stratified, more walled off, and more fractured depends on breaking the vicious cycle of political and economic inequality. Today's Democratic Party appears to be at a loss about how to do it or even what to try. Democrats would do well to start by reacquainting themselves with the forgotten countrypolitan formula that worked so well for them from the 1930s through the 1960s. Democrats will win consistently again when they show genuine discomfort with the current political culture and the way the system presently functions. More importantly, the public interest will win when the political culture is changed, when all the ladder climbing and nest feathering and back- scratching gives way to actual public service and actual acts of sacrifice for the greater good. The public interest will prevail when today's "me politics" becomes tomorrow's "we politics."

American politics has changed immensely in the last generation or two. It used to be more of a hobby, something done on the side by people with lives outside of politics. When I got my first taste of the inner workings of Wisconsin's state capitol in the early 1980s, being a lawmaker was a part-time job. Now it's full-time. Not because there are so many more laws that need making, but rather largely because soliciting political donations has become a daily chore. Politics has been taken over by professionals, and most who are serious about it consider it a career. There has always been lobbying in the halls of government, but the primary currency of lobbyists used to be information. That was before lobbying was married to election fundraising. Petitioning government and supplying campaign cash have now become inseparable.

Abortion was a touchy subject in the '80s and remains so today, but back then there were Democrats and Republicans on both sides of the issue. Republicans who favor legal abortion are no longer welcome in the party's ranks, and Democrats who have qualms about abortion aren't tolerated by their party either. Two species of politicians have gone extinct in the last couple of generations. There used to be rural Democrats, and there used to be centrist Republicans. The fact that there are not modern counterparts for the rural Democrats or middle-of-the-road Republicans of yesteryear is a symptom of illness in our political system. The disappearance of these species is a warning signal that we ignore at our peril. So here we are, with two major parties, both of which have stopped trying to bring together people with differing worldviews, neither of which is remotely capable of uniting our country. Where do they go from here? Where do we go?

The more I talk with people on the "other side," the more I'm convinced we're not nearly as divided and polarized as we're told. What could bind us together is far more substantial than what drives us apart. Yet we have a political establishment that's working overtime to put us at each other's throats, more so than at any time in my life. We are constantly invited to fear one another, to hate, to see each other as enemies. The invitations are not going to stop, but we can decline them. The major parties are addicted to money, and they've discovered fear and hate of the "other side" move more people to open their wallets than understanding and compassion. The solicitations will continue, but we can stop mailing in checks in response to their appeals to our darkest impulses. So many of us have succumbed to double standards. When

MIKE McCABE

"our side" does it, it's right. When the "other side" does the same darn thing, it's wrong. We can call that what it is—hypocrisy—and hold ourselves to a higher standard. We've been taught to think and talk about politics horizontally, from right to left, which makes it easy for people with a great deal in common to nevertheless see each other as opposites. There are other ways to look at politics and define ourselves politically. We can stop thinking right and left and start thinking and talking up and down to better understand and describe those who are lording over us.[35]

America's major political parties used to be big tents, broad-based coalitions with a mix of worldviews. Both have engaged in worldview cleansing, purging themselves of those who don't fit the preferred personality type. But many, if not most, Americans have mixed worldviews themselves and feel like square pegs being pounded into round holes. That's why both parties are so unpopular right now. We can clamor for a return to political parties that are broad-based coalitions instead of single-worldview social clubs. And we can challenge party leaders to change their ways and open up their organizations instead of purging them of disparate personality types.

But the change that can make the biggest difference has to start from outside our political institutions. It has to start between us. Humans are complicated. No two of us are exactly alike. Our political beliefs come from our different upbringings and our different life experiences. Emerging brain science also suggests that 30 percent to 40 percent of political attitudes come from genetics.[36] We're hard-wired to feel the way we do about politics. This means we're often going to disagree. Not only won't we see eye to eye, we're not even going to be looking at the same things or seeing what we look at in the same ways. That's okay, as long as we have solid relationships with those who look and see and think and talk and act differently.

Our salvation is in relationships. My late brother and I were polar opposites. We fought like cats and dogs, as brothers do. He was short and stocky. I was tall and skinny. He loved to hunt. I liked playing baseball. When we both left the farm, he went to work in a factory, and I went off to college. But there was a brotherly bond that kept us close throughout life. We always looked out for each other. We needed each other. Republicans and Democrats were like that once and need to become like that again. A few years ago, I knew we were really in trouble when I ran into an old friend who'd worked for several Republican legislators. She told me she knew it was time to leave the capitol when she was called into the assembly speaker's office and scolded for having been seen taking a walk with a Democratic staffer. They hadn't been talking politics. They were just getting some fresh air and engaging in small talk. That got her formally reprimanded.

If America is to be unscrewed, such relationships can't be punished. They need to be nurtured. They are our salvation. ✪

CHAPTER ELEVEN
DAN'S SHADOW

When my brother Dan was born in April 1957, something went wrong. He was placed in an oxygen tent, and then there was some kind of malfunction. He had turned blue by the time a nurse came to check on him. The circumstances of Dan's birth caused some brain damage, which in the years to come manifested itself in a variety of neurological problems. Dan developed facial tics and involuntary muscular twitching. His eyelids blinked rapidly and repeatedly, and his eyes darted and rolled. A sizeable tumor growing in his mouth puffed out his cheek. After it was surgically removed, more growths appeared on his face. Cutting them off left unsightly scars, and then other lumps grew in their place.

Dan's outward appearance doomed him to unspeakable torment in his childhood. He was relentlessly bullied at school and endured constant name-calling. He was small for his age and was an easy target for thuggish classmates who seemed to be earning their stripes by beating up my brother. Three years younger than Dan and no match physically for his attackers, I nevertheless tried intervening on his behalf when I saw him being picked on. But far more often, it was Dan coming to the aid of his little brother when I found myself in a tough spot.

Of all the names Dan was called, he hated one most of all, one that stuck with him into his high school years. When I was probably ten or eleven years old, Dan and I were fighting about something or other, but whatever it was, he had a way of getting under my skin, and he had my blood boiling that day. In anger, I blurted out that name. That thoughtless act of cruelty badly hurt him and profoundly changed me.

He said nothing. In his eyes, though, was a mixture of surprise, sadness, pain, and desertion. Every contour of his face told me he felt utterly abandoned. It was as if he were saying, "Even my own brother? Is there anyone who won't do this to me?"

That day, Dan taught me the single most important lesson of my life without saying a word. Some years ago, I lost the only brother and most influential teacher I ever had to colon cancer shortly after his forty-seventh birthday. The mountainous betrayal I committed as a child was forgiven, if not forgotten. Dan and I were close as adults and saw each other frequently. We were nothing alike and took separate paths in life, yet there was an unbreakable bond between us. I was at his side as he lay on his deathbed and was the one he trusted to handle the affairs of his estate. Before he died, I told him how much he meant to me and what an enormous imprint he made on my life. I watched him take his last breath.

Dan was quite possibly the friendliest person I've ever met. His outgoing nature and openness to strangers always struck me as remarkable. Dan was given ample reasons to close himself off and shield himself from being hurt by others, but for reasons unknown to me, he chose not to. He was his own man and did not put on airs. What you saw is what you got with him. He could handle rejection, I guess, because he had so much practice.

More than anything, Dan's life taught me that none of us is self-made. We all stand on the shoulders of others. We all need a helping hand from time to time and are all called to lend one when needed. I am certain that I would never have done the kind of work I did for so many years if Dan had not been my brother. He was barely five-foot-five but cast a much longer shadow. Growing up in that shadow shaped my values and my politics. It's probably why I served in the Peace Corps and later ran for public office. He taught me everything I needed to know about compassion and service.

Dan loved to hunt and fish and didn't care much for ball sports. But he was unquestionably the reason this diehard Wisconsin Badgers fan was cheering so hard for the University of Virginia's men's basketball team in the 2019 NCAA tournament. Coach Tony Bennett's team going all the way to the Final Four and then winning the national championship was poetic justice after becoming the first top-seeded team to lose to a 16-seed in the tournament's history just one year earlier. Part of what had me rooting for the 'Hoos was their lack of a blueblood pedigree. There was not a single five-star recruit or McDonald's All-American on the roster. No one-and-done players making a quick stop in the college ranks for a single season before going pro. A bigger reason I was all in for Virginia was how Bennett handled the previous season's defeat in the tournament's first round at the hands of small conference underdog University of Maryland, Baltimore County. I marveled at how gracious and poised and classy Bennett was in defeat after his team made history losing to a 16-seed for the first time ever. In his own way, Tony Bennett reminded me of my brother.

Until 2018, the University of Wisconsin men's basketball team had made nineteen straight appearances in the NCAA tournament, including three trips to the Final Four and one run to the national championship game. That streak started under coach Dick Bennett, Tony's father. The Wisconsin program's success was built on a foundation of Bennett's five pillars: humility, passion, unity, servanthood, and thankfulness. In fact, those five words to live by are literally cemented in the foundation of the Kohl Center, the arena the Badgers call home. Before it opened in 1998, before the flooring even went in, Bennett placed a laminated card bearing his five pillars in the sand under the concrete that was poured.

These pillars are nowhere to be seen on Capitol Hill. They are conspicuously missing in the behavior of today's lawmakers. Three of the secrets to the Badgers' sustained success on the hardwood are most noticeably absent in the marble corridors of power—humility, unity, and servanthood. Authentic leadership requires humility. Good leaders give credit and take blame. In his D-Day message to the troops on June 6, 1944, General Dwight D. Eisenhower told them the "eyes of the world are upon you" and reflected on the extraordinary demands placed on the Allied force assembled for Operation Overlord. But Eisenhower also prepared a second message taking full responsibility in the event the invasion failed. "My decision to attack at this time and place was based upon the best information available," Eisenhower wrote. "The troops, the air and the Navy did all that Bravery and devotion to duty could do. If any blame or fault attaches to the attempt it is mine alone."[1] He gave credit and was prepared to take blame. Today's politicians routinely do the exact opposite. As with humility, unity is as scarce in politics as it is indispensable in any team endeavor. If you picture our government as a team, then it currently is a dysfunctional one. Instead of seeking unity, the team's captains consciously sow seeds of division. Perhaps the ingredient of success that is hardest to find in politics nowadays is servanthood. A true public service ethic has withered away, and the aims of those who govern mirror the greed and self-centeredness that dominate American life. Those who hold office are supposed to be servants but act like masters. More often than not, they rule, they don't serve. At least they don't serve the masses. They scratch the backs of a wealthy and privileged few and get their backs scratched in return.

The qualities that won Virginia a national championship and have made the Wisconsin men's basketball program a powerhouse are in terribly short supply in politics. What makes a successful team also makes a successful country. Coaches are fired for managing teams the way our nation is being managed.

My past work as a government watchdog and whistleblower led me to spend more time than I liked in the state capitol. With each passing day, I found the place increasingly unpleasant. Just setting foot in the building dampened my spirits. It's a beautiful setting, but there's growing ugliness in what goes on inside. Since 2015, I've set foot in the capitol only three or four times, and none of the visits were my idea. I made a point of staying away. I hit the road instead. I crisscrossed the countryside in my home state, attending community events and gatherings from Argyle to Appleton to Ashland, from Waukesha to

Waterloo to Wausau. Sometimes it was bigger towns like Eau Claire, Green Bay, Janesville, or La Crosse. Other towns were small, like Lake Mills, Darlington, Viroqua, Elkhorn, and Owen. For every trip to Milwaukee, there have been visits to Menasha and Menomonie, Hayward and Hudson, Brookfield and Baraboo, Portage and Prairie du Chien, and dozens of places in between.

I stopped to talk with people on street corners and met with residents in churches, coffee shops, cafes, bowling alleys, libraries, taverns, barns, feed mills, town halls, and community centers. I was invited into high school classrooms and to college campuses. What I heard varied from place to place but, at the same time, was strikingly similar. Distill all the stories down, and common themes emerge. People are reluctant to talk politics, but you can tell they want to. Political discussions have been too painful lately. The most commonly used word to describe both the economy and the political system has got to be *rigged*. It amazes me how often that word is chosen. Pessimism is rampant. People seem afraid of what the future holds. Many are beaten down. No matter how hard they work, they see themselves falling behind. They have a hard time imagining how that's going to change. This leads not only to intense frustration but also a strong suspicion that America's best days are behind her. Optimism is dormant but not dead. People want to believe things can get better and are on the lookout for signs we might be turning the corner. Leadership is craved. Few see themselves being the ones able to satisfy the craving. Most see leadership coming from someone else. Someone else isn't leading.

The word *Democrat* is toxic almost everywhere outside of Madison and Milwaukee. Most people living in small towns or out in the country are Republicans, but only because they despise Democrats. Few actually seem to like the Republicans deep down. Most people can tell you what Republicans believe in, whether they agree with it or not. Most struggle to put into words what Democrats stand for. What they do say isn't flattering. Young people are not nearly as apathetic as older people think they are. They know what's going on. They care. They may feel powerless, but that's different than not caring. People of every age tell you who's to blame for the mess that's been made, but then they say something that hints at understanding how all the resentment and scapegoating lead nowhere good.

There doesn't seem to be much room for truth anymore. It's been crowded out by false narratives born of tribal allegiance. The soap opera that is the American presidency is a vivid illustration. One side is certain Donald Trump won the White House by colluding with the Russians. The other side is equally convinced federal law enforcement authorities are corrupt. Facts be damned.

Nearly the entire U.S. intelligence community, as well as Special Counsel Robert Mueller, concluded that Russia meddled in the 2016 election and worked to get Trump elected president.[2] As a candidate, Trump himself asked the Russians to hack Hillary Clinton's emails.[3] Donald Trump Jr. and other top Trump campaign operatives got dirt on Clinton from emissaries of the Russian government and did so gleefully, with Donald Jr. squealing, "I love it."[4] It's dishonorable and disgraceful that they didn't tell the Russians to get lost and didn't immediately alert law enforcement officials and federal election authorities to the interference.

Of course, acting dishonorably and disgracefully is not proof of criminal conspiracy. As the president pounced on this reality to declare "complete and total exoneration," his personal lawyer Rudy Giuliani condemned Mueller's work as "the most corrupt investigation I have ever seen"[5] and called on Trump accusers to apologize for the probe.[6] These themes were dutifully repeated and amplified by right-wing pundits who insisted the probe was unnecessary and never should have been done. Apologize? For an investigation that produced more than three dozen indictments and close to 200 criminal charges?[7] None of that fact-finding and criminal prosecution should have been done? Has all regard for the rule of law evaporated?

While we shouted, "Trump colluded!" and "Mueller is corrupt!" at each other, nothing was being done about growing economic inequality in America. We weren't dealing with the coming climate catastrophe. We were neglecting serious deficiencies in our health care system, ignoring rising rates of depression, declining life expectancies, and other signs of America's mental health crisis,[8] and more or less trying to jail our way out of it.[9]

We're overlooking symptoms of social ills like the addiction epidemic that have Americans feeling unhappier than ever.[10] We're not addressing the crisis in farm country and its implications for our food supply. We're not coming to terms with the causes and effects of unsafe drinking water.[11] Our attention is diverted from the social and economic cost of increasingly unaffordable education[12] and crippling student debt.[13] We're not confronting the injustice of a homeless man getting life in prison because he was hungry and wanted to eat and tried selling $20 worth of marijuana,[14] while an adviser to four presidents was convicted of eight felonies for hiding $55 million overseas, defrauding banks that lent him money, and evading more than $6 million in taxes and was sentenced to a mere forty-seven months for his crimes.[15] And we're sure not responding in any meaningful way to democracy's decline throughout the world—including in America.

So here we are, leaving urgent matters unattended, screaming, "Collusion!" and "Witch Hunt!" at each other, certain that our side is right and their side is wrong. A recent study showed that more than 40 percent of people in each major party view the opposition as "downright evil."[16] That translates to close to 50 million voters who cast ballots in 2016 believe that those aligned with the opposition party are not only wrong but in league with the devil. All of this—putting tribe before truth, demonizing opponents, prioritizing the settling of scores over working together to solve problems that can bring down our country— is madness. This is how great nations fall and how democracies die.

But it's not the only way.

Henry Ford famously said his customers could get one of his cars in any color they wanted as long as it was black. American consumers have come a long way since the days of the Model T. American voters haven't. Ford's "They can have what I say they can have" philosophy is nowhere to be seen any more in commerce but still looms large in elections. Some 150 years ago, Boss Tweed quipped, "I don't care who does the electing, so long as I get to do the nominating." It's not so different today. As *The Daily Show* host Trevor Noah wisecracked in 2016: "When it comes to everything except presidential candidates, Americans have the most choices for more things than anyone else in the world. Like, I can walk into a supermarket—any supermarket in America—and choose from literally 400 different kinds of yogurt. ... And yet, when it comes to selecting America's leader for the next four years, you're stuck with two choices: Hillary Clinton and Donald Trump. Or to put that in yogurt terms: vanilla and Sriracha baboon anus."[17]

This is the truth, but not the whole truth. We see ourselves stuck with two choices alright, and not just in presidential elections but all partisan elections. We can vote for major party nominees who sometimes win but rarely do what we want once elected and regularly sell us out. Or we can vote for minor party candidates who seem less compromised and more likely to act in our interests but never win. It's an inadequate and profoundly unsatisfying choice. Here's what's amazing. As demanding as we are as consumers, that's how passively accepting we are as citizens. We don't have to be passive. We don't have to be accepting. We have more power than we know. And we have more choices than we realize. When major party establishments offer us bleak and bleaker, our choices are not limited to either holding our noses and selecting what we consider the lesser of evils or saying to hell with it and casting a protest vote for someone with no chance of winning. There is another option.

Roughly a century ago, farmers in North Dakota were at wit's end about the insensitivity of elected officials to their economic plight. They were at the mercy of powerful cartels and couldn't get fair prices for their grain or credit at a reasonable interest rate. In hopes of getting out from under the thumb of the out-of-state tycoons who were gouging them, they banded together to form a political organization called the Nonpartisan League (NPL). Some say the NPL was the idea of a former Socialist Party organizer named Albert Bowen. Others figure it was the brainchild of flax farmer-turned-political agitator A.C. Townley. One way or the other, Townley and Bowen teamed up, and Townley was soon driving across the state in a Model T Ford spreading the word about the NPL. Bowen and Townley enlisted tens of thousands of followers.

The NPL gained power by making use of a creation of the late-nineteenth-century progressives: the primary election. The primary system adopted in North Dakota and other states like Wisconsin not only gave voters the power to nominate major party candidates, it allowed voters to participate in a party's primary even if they did not belong to that party. By putting NPL-endorsed candidates up against those favored by the state's political machine, the NPL took over North Dakota's dominant Republican Party in 1916. A wheat farmer and NPL member named Lynn Frazier was elected governor with almost 80 percent of the vote, and NPL-backed candidates won every other statewide office except one as well as a majority in the state assembly. Upon gaining power, the NPL acted, giving farmers credit at significantly lower interest rates through the establishment of the state-run Bank of North Dakota, which opened in 1919. A state grain elevator was established in 1922, providing a fair market for grain and a source of feed and seed. Insurance was provided against fire, tornado, and hail damage.[18]

The NPL's enduring legacy in North Dakota stands as an inspiring example of what is possible when people declare themselves free of unresponsive major parties while simultaneously using elements of the two-party framework to force change. The NPL stands as proof that the dismal choice between lesser evil voting and wasted votes cast for spoiler candidates from minor parties is a false choice. There is another way. Almost a century later, anti-government feelings smoldered in poor, recession-ravaged communities and were fanned by rich right-wing ideologues, exploding into a prairie fire that swept the country. It was dubbed the Tea Party, but it was not a party at all. Its organizers took cues from those North Dakota socialists and embedded their insurgency within the Republican Party, and in a few short years, lightning struck again in the same place. The GOP was pretty much taken over.

Now go back to the nineteenth century. The progressives of the late 1800s tried for a time to establish a separate party but did not truly gain traction until their kind were embedded in both major parties. At one point, you had Teddy Roosevelt successfully running for president as a Progressive on the Republican ticket, and some years later, Woodrow Wilson was winning the presidency as a Progressive on the Democratic ticket. The major parties had no choice but to embrace the Progressive agenda and enact Progressive reforms. America was radically transformed. Consider what was done by Wisconsin's legislature in 1911 alone. Child labor laws and protections for women in the workplace were put in place. Workers' compensation was established to help injured laborers. There was also railroad regulation; insurance reform; the first state life insurance program anywhere in the country; the nation's first system of taxation based on ability to pay, namely the progressive income tax; and America's first vocational, technical, and adult education system. All done by a legislature made up almost entirely of Republicans and Democrats, with progressives embedded in those major parties.[19] All done by people who refused to accept the dismal choice we assume we are stuck with today.

Austerity is one of America's biggest enemies. Not the economic kind, although that's proven to inflict immense suffering, especially for the most financially vulnerable among us. I'm talking about political austerity. I'm talking about how those who are passed off as our nation's leaders are thinking so small at a time when the problems facing the country are so big. When we Americans are at our best, we are inventing and building and exploring new frontiers. We cannot be at our best with such austere politics. One party is busy tearing down what was built in the past, with no apparent intentions to build anything new. The other is just trying to stand in the way of the wrecking balls. Neither shows much interest in or excitement about what waits for us over the horizon. Neither is doing much imagining.

Everywhere I went in Wisconsin as a candidate for governor, I brought up the need to make education as affordable for future generations as it was for us. I made the point that past generations made it possible for their children and grandchildren to go all the way through high school for free, and then made college incredibly inexpensive. Today we are burying our kids and grandkids under a mountain of debt, forcing them to mortgage their American dreams. But when I said we have an obligation to do for future generations what past generations did for us, I was routinely asked by self-described progressives how we could afford to pay for that. I answered their question with a question. How did past generations afford to do what they did for us? They were, after all, substantially poorer than we are today. That never seemed to temper their skepticism.

"They'll call you a socialist if you talk that way."

Seriously? We can't even talk about doing what's right for our kids and grandkids because someone might call us a name? Is that what our politics has become? Middle school?

This is small politics.

Democrats puzzle over how farmers and other rural folks used to vote for them but generally no longer do. They puzzle until their puzzlers are sore. But they never seem to think about what Democrats thought before. Past generations of Democrats brought electricity to every barn and farmhouse. They built roads to get products more easily and quickly to market. They created market stability and economic security. Travel those roads and go to any rural community today, and you will find electricity. But the chances are great you won't be able to get a cell phone signal or a wireless internet connection.

Where are the calls from within the Democratic Party for the digital-age equivalent of rural electrification? Where is the commitment to bringing the power of what's popularly called the information superhighway to every doorstep in America? How could we possibly afford to pay for that? They'll call you a socialist if you talk that way.

We truly can't afford small politics. The challenges we face are way too big. There is no reason the future cannot be bright. Well, actually, there is one—political austerity.

If you look up the word *conservative*, Webster's says it means "tending or disposed to maintain existing views, conditions, or institutions." When you think about it, on today's American political landscape, the people who best fit that definition are actually those who describe themselves as progressives or liberals. For quite a few decades now, the ones wearing those largely interchangeable labels have been principally devoted to maintaining the status quo. They've focused on keeping the 80-some-year-old Social Security program and the half-century-old Medicare system safe and sound. They've tried, quite unsuccessfully, to protect the worker rights established by the more than 80-year-old National Labor Relations Act and the nearly as aged Fair Labor Standards Act. They resisted changes to the 1933 Glass-Steagall Act regulating banking only to see the law gutted in 1999, which contributed to the collapse of the U.S. economy in 2007 and the ensuing Great Recession.[20] Their calls to restore Glass-Steagall's protective wall between commercial and investment banking have been ignored ever since.

Contemporary progressive or liberal thinking is firmly rooted in the twentieth century. Over the past several decades, the list of new ideas or policy innovations for the twenty-first century coming from the left is a short one. Even the signature Democratic policy reform in recent memory—the Affordable Care Act—was borrowed from the right-wing Heritage Foundation and was known as Romneycare in Massachusetts before it became Obamacare nationally.

This is not to say that self-proclaimed conservatives and progressives have swapped places, with conservative forces becoming the engine of innovation for the twenty-first century. If today's progressives seem stuck in the twentieth century, conservatives of this day and age seem bound and determined to return us to the nineteenth century. They not only are intent on rolling back the New Deal reforms enacted on the heels of the Great Depression, but they also are working in places like Wisconsin to demolish century-old laws ranging from civil service protections against cronyism and political patronage to prohibitions against corporate political spending that were inspired by the trauma of the economic depression in the 1890s brought on by the excesses of the Gilded Age.

A big problem in American politics today is the absence of true progressive impulses. We have conservatives who call themselves progressives, and retrogressives who call themselves conservatives. The right is determined to turn the clock back to the 1800s, and the onslaught-weary left is willing to settle for keeping us in the 1900s. Missing is a forward-looking vision for what America can and should become in the twenty-first century and the drive to get us there.

If my travels over the last several years have taught me anything, it's that America—or at least one little corner of it here in Wisconsin—is in the midst of an identity crisis. I was given the opportunity to meet with every kind of group—urban and rural, young and old, haves and have nots and used to haves, white and black and brown, left and right. We met in churches, schools, bowling alleys, taverns, VFW and American Legion halls, public libraries, and bookstores. Everywhere I went, I was given a chance to share some thoughts. But I also got to ask questions and listen. I asked the same questions at nearly every stop: What are your core values? What do you believe in?

When I talked with conservative or Republican audiences, I was always struck by how quickly, confidently, and uniformly they answered those questions. Six themes surfaced time after time: less government, lower taxes, free market economics, individual liberty, old-fashioned family values, and patriotism. Sometimes the kind of freedom they profess to love seems to clash with their definition of family values. Sometimes their love of country takes the form of military might or homeland security. Other times it comes out sounding like fear or even hatred of foreigners.

When I met with Democrats or left-leaning groups and asked them my questions, I would typically hear crickets. I got puzzled looks. Pregnant pauses. Some would bring up issues or causes they care about. I stopped them and asked again. What are your *values*? What principles form the basis of your positions on issues? Sometimes answers never came, only shrugs. When answers were offered, they generally were neither confident nor uniform.

In the vacuum that forms, Republicans define Democrats by default. Since Republicans say they are for less government and lower taxes, that puts Democrats on the side of more government and higher taxes. This current understanding will probably persist until either Democrats reach a consensus on what values guide them, or a blossoming Republican identity crisis reaches full bloom. Now that the GOP is Donald Trump's party, the commitment to limited government is fading. Trump promised both guns and butter, both a massive military buildup[21] and a trillion-dollar domestic building program.[22] Free trade has given way to protectionism under Trump. Intrusive government authoritarianism is increasingly trespassing on personal freedoms. Both in his private life and his public behavior, Trump is at odds with what Reagan-style conservatives considered traditional virtues. Those on the right are having a harder time recognizing their party and agreeing on what it should stand for.

America can't be unscrewed until Americans have a shared sense of national purpose. That means a common set of core values. Time and again, I asked people of every political stripe: What are your values? The answers were not exactly confidence inspiring. Quite often, there were no answers. Instead, I was asked to list mine. I never hesitated, figuring that spelling out what I think America's values are might stimulate thought and discussion and rumination.

I start with **equality**. We are all created equal, with inalienable rights. Equality is a bedrock American value rooted in the rejection of royalty. It comes out of a sense of fairness and distaste for privilege. No one should get to start at third base. There are no lesser beings.

Next on my list is **democracy, both political and economic**. Democracy is more than a form of government; it is a way of life. Yes, the government needs to be of the people, by the people, and for the people. But so does the economy. And democracy cannot just be something we have; it has to be something we do. It's more verb than noun.

Then there's **freedom**. But I distinguish the kind of freedom I want and what America needs from mere individual liberty. To me, freedom means being able to be who you are and live the life you want. But it doesn't mean doing as you damn well please. True freedom is more than individual liberty. With freedom comes the responsibility not to hurt others with our actions. Each individual has a right to be free, but with that right also comes an obligation to make sure others are free as well. Contrast this with the warped, sociopathic mindset that, for example, leads the filthy rich to believe "freedom of speech" entitles them to spend as much money as they want to amplify their voices, even if it drowns out your voice and denies you representation. A commitment to true freedom plus equality plus democracy equals social and economic justice.

Caretaking is fourth on the list. That means looking out for one another and having each other's back. It also means taking care of the land, water, and air.

Last but certainly not least is **service**. To community. To country. To each other. Service is an extension of caretaking. It is neighbors helping neighbors. It is communities coming together. It is concern for the common good. It is civic duty. It is thinking less about what we are entitled to and more about debts we owe to society. It is caring for the planet we call home and all of its inhabitants.

No doubt about it, Americans are at each other's throats, politically speaking. Some consider themselves Democrats, and most of them are not terribly fond of their party but can't stand Republicans. Others call themselves Republicans, and most have no great love for their party either but are driven mad by Democrats. Most numerous of all are the self-proclaimed independents, who are turned off by both and refuse to wear either major party label. But even the officially unaffiliated tend to lean when it comes time to vote, reliably favoring one of the major parties.[23] The thing is, these days they lean not toward what they like most but rather in the opposite direction of what they fear and hate.[24]

Most people in this country currently think both major political parties suck, and not without good reason. The Republican Party started as a party of liberation under Lincoln and was a party of opportunity that worked for a broad expansion of the middle class under Eisenhower. Even a corrupted soul like Richard Nixon once proposed a guaranteed basic income for every American family, something he called a negative income tax. The GOP has since morphed into a party of privilege. Both its rhetoric and actions regularly show devotion to hierarchy—rich over poor, man over woman, white over brown or black, old over young, straight over gay, management over labor. The Democratic Party, on the other hand, has become synonymous with handouts. It is widely seen as the party of entitlement. This irks loyal Democratic partisans to no end, but the truth is the party's actions over the years have repeatedly reinforced this image.

Our nation was born out of rebellion against a king's power. The rejection of royalty is in our DNA, giving us a natural sense of fairness and distaste for privilege. But at the same time, there is a widespread belief that you should earn your keep. Taking without paying and getting without giving rubs your average American the wrong way too.

Reflecting on the famous line in John F. Kennedy's 1961 inaugural address, it's hard not to notice that we Americans have been mostly asking what our country can do for us since at least the 1980s. In their own ways, both major parties mirror the self-centeredness of the modern American psyche. Republican politics has been of the "me first" variety, focusing on how best to enable the most ambitious, enterprising, ruthless, and privileged among us to elbow their way to the front of the line. The result has been heretofore unimagined levels of prosperity for some, but also historic levels of income and wealth inequality. Democratic politics has been of the "me too" kind, concentrating on getting previously excluded or disadvantaged segments of the population more rights and opportunities. As a result, historic advances have been made in such areas as civil rights, women's rights, gay rights, and disability rights. The gains have not come without a cost to Democrats as they have lost much of their appeal to blue-collar Americans, especially working-class white men.

Two generations' worth of emphasis on individual advancement has been both good and bad. Americans have grown more equal in some ways and more unequal in others. Some have prospered, while others have been left behind. Many have finally secured a seat at the table, which is good. America is more politically polarized than it has been in a very long time, which is bad.

The major parties are a reflection of the preoccupation with self-fulfillment in American society. Both privilege and entitlement are products of me-focused politics. But conditions require a politics that is more we-centered, and visible signs indicate movement in that direction.[25] The trouble is the major parties are in step with where we've been but out of step with where we need to head. Entitlement needs to give way to a focus on service, to each other, and to society as a whole. A commitment to equality and democracy must replace privilege. The longer the parties fail to change their ways and remake themselves, the more likely it becomes that a new major party will eventually emerge. Voters are increasingly despising the old parties, and it's not a sustainable condition.

Against this backdrop of political dysfunction, it can be hard to see where to start the search for common ground in America. Part of the problem is that we've all been conditioned to think and talk about politics in ways that drive wedges between us and make us active participants in our own disempowerment. One secret to escaping the trap we're in is to consciously and creatively work to change our political vocabulary, discarding words like *left* and *right* and *liberal* or *conservative* in favor of terms that could knit us together instead of tear us apart. The old political labels have grown worthless, even toxic.

Another strategy worth trying is to steer conversations away from programs, policies, and politicians and toward discussions of what kind of society we want. We argue about things like food stamps and other forms of public assistance. One person sees a safety net; another sees a hammock. The argument accomplishes nothing except to further convince each that the other is evil. How about changing the conversation, focusing instead on how to create an economy where if you work, you won't be poor. Each side has little choice but to admit that we don't currently have such an economy. That's some common ground right there. Some more might be found once we start talking about how to build one.

We could talk about how there's a way to end old welfare programs that discourage gainful employment and replace them with a new policy that rewards work, without saying so long to compassion. Nixon noticed in his time that when we continue to spend so much money on welfare programs, there is a perverse incentive not to work. Recipients have to be poor to get help, and they have to stay poor to keep it. Because income eligibility thresholds inevitably get workers to the point where earning one more dollar causes them to lose far more, low-wage workers come out ahead by cutting back on their hours to stay eligible for public assistance. Nixon was thinking then what we could be thinking now: Shouldn't we have a system where the harder you work, the better off you are? Shouldn't you be able to climb the ladder and keep right on climbing? And isn't there a way to create a stable foundation allowing all workers to do that? One that in our day and age creates economic security and financial stability for vulnerable workers, relieves the anxiety that comes with watching their employment automated out of existence? One that frees people to be more attentive to family or leave dead-end jobs and take the risk of starting a business, empowering would-be entrepreneurs and stimulating the economy? Call it whatever you want—a negative income tax like Nixon did or a basic income program as many today do—but, say, $1,000 a month isn't enough to live on. There will be no choice but to work. But if low-wage employment is all you can find, the security of what amounts to a universal American prosperity dividend makes it possible to work for low wages and not be doomed to living in poverty.

Robots are here, and more are on the way. With each passing day, they replace more assembly line workers. Their impact won't just be felt in factories. With robots that now can perform gymnastics, does anyone really think the day's not coming when robots are laying bricks, hanging drywall, pouring cement, installing carpet, and doing a hundred other such tasks? Driverless vehicles are coming. When they arrive, what happens to all the truck drivers, the bus drivers, the taxi drivers, the millions of Americans who drive for a living? We can talk about how we are going through an economic revolution and think creatively about how to adapt to it, how to hold our society together when an increasingly jobless economy, where workers are considered disposable, is upon us. We can remember it's no coincidence that trade unions, child labor laws, unemployment compensation, workers' compensation for those injured in the workplace, and Social Security for the elderly all were outgrowths of and adjustments to industrialization a century or more ago. Americans at the time were anxious, frightened, and politically fractured but had the kinds of conversations we need to have today, and they were able to find common ground. We can take a stab at those conversations and search for common ground. What do we have to lose? We could lose welfare as we know it and the emotional distress and growing mental health crisis[26] that today's economic uncertainty breeds.

When pondering the pressing need to turn our politics from me to we, my brother Dan comes to mind again. Along with the many other names he was called, more than a few called him a gun nut, as he was a card-carrying lifetime member of the National Rifle Association. He had a way of pushing my buttons and bringing out the worst in me. But in the end, through witnessing the power of his example, I was able to recognize the best in me. He made me more caring and compassionate and concerned for the needs of others than I fear I would have been had I not grown up in his shadow. For that, I am forever grateful. Dan was an uncommonly brave and decent man who did more than anyone else to make me the person I have become. I needed him and he needed me. That gun nut is still very much with me, guiding me to this day.

Inspiration can come from the unlikeliest places. ✚

CHAPTER TWELVE
ON THIN ICE

O f the countless illustrations of America's schisms, one of the more amusing is the silly argument over whether the U.S. is a democracy or a republic. Not too many years ago, you never heard this argued. The terms were treated as interchangeable and commonly used by people of every political persuasion. Americans of every stripe proudly proclaimed our nation the world's greatest democracy. By that, they meant a representative democracy—a democratic republic.

Now quibbling partisans insist the two words are mutually exclusive. The argument rages, even as evidence mounts that America is neither. Most notable in the accumulating proof is the 2014 analysis by Princeton's Martin Gilens and Northwestern's Benjamin Page of the way Congress and the executive branch dealt with nearly 1,800 different policy issues over two decades. They concluded that economic elites and narrow interest groups succeeded in getting their favored policies adopted about half of the time, and they blocked legislation they opposed nearly all of the time. The wishes of ordinary citizens, on the other hand, had virtually no independent effect at all. "The preferences of the average American appear to have only a minuscule, near-zero, statistically non-significant impact upon public policy," the professors wrote.[1]

Maybe part of the problem is that we can't even agree on what to call our system of government, much less talk to each other and decide together what kind of society we want. Having that conversation is getting harder as political polarization intensifies and rhetoric coarsens. Republican democracy or democratic republicanism, whatever you want to call it, is not possible without active, engaged, and influential citizenship so the many, not the money, can decide the direction of our society. Meaningful civic engagement is endangered as large numbers of people are turned off and tuned out.

If our representative democracy or democratic republic, whatever you care to call it, is allowed to circle the drain, there is little hope for economic justice, environmental sanity, a stronger sense of community and greater concern for the common good, less hate, more compassion, and better physical and mental health. As emphasized in chapter 2, our political system is supposed to be built on a foundation of representation. For authentic representation to be possible, it has to be realistic for people who are truly reflective of the general public to run for office. Running for office the way it's typically done today costs a fortune. Few have access to the kind of money needed to compete in this environment.

In the 1990s, the late sociologist and senator Daniel Patrick Moynihan coined the phrase "defining deviancy down" to describe the tendency of societies to respond to destructive behaviors by lowering standards for what is permissible. Today it's clear the same thing has happened to political representation. Here in Wisconsin, we've unquestionably grown more tolerant of political corruption, and the same goes for the whole country. All across America, standards for what it means to be represented have been lowered. We still have the habit of calling elected officials our "representatives" even though we are convinced they don't care what we think, put their own interests ahead of the country's, and are slaves to wealthy donors.[2]

Even though we have elections for Congress and state legislatures where one party gets the most votes, but the other party wins the most seats, we are considered represented. Supermajorities of voters in cities and small rural towns, in Republican and Democratic strongholds alike, have made it abundantly clear they think there is too much money in politics.[3] Their "representatives" think there is not enough and have gone to work changing laws to allow vastly larger political donations with considerably less donor disclosure.[4] Wisconsin voters crossed party boundaries to show support for increasing the minimum wage.[5] Their "representatives" ignored their wishes. Voters cast ballots in favor of Wisconsin accepting federal funds to expand health care coverage.[6] Their "representatives" did the opposite, rejecting the federal money. They not only disregarded what voters wanted, but they actively worked to make it harder to vote.[7]

It's clear the representation that is a central feature of any true republic has been diminished, demeaned, and devalued in today's America. It's equally clear that supposed representatives are not undertaking the restoration of authentic representation. This work will have to be done by the supposedly represented. Standards for what it means to be represented will have to be raised. Intolerance of corruption and what currently passes for representation will have to grow. And we need to question everything about how the system works because it isn't working for most of us at the moment.

With the advanced information technology we now have, why isn't there automatic voter registration? Why do we have winner-take-all elections? Why do voters have to choose just one candidate for an office? Why can't we rank all the candidates in order of preference? Why do we still need primary and general elections? In this computer age, we could save a lot of money by having instant runoffs. For that matter, why do we have just one representative in each office? If one candidate gets 55 percent of the vote and another gets 45 percent, why pretend the top vote-getter represents everyone? Computer technology could easily be put to work in the halls of government to allow both to serve as representatives, with their representation of the voting jurisdiction instantly apportioned according to the percentage of the vote each received. That way, the wishes of all those voters would be reflected in decisions made by governing bodies, not just the wishes of just over half of them. Why do we still vote on Tuesdays? The practice dates to a law made in 1845. Back then people traveled a day or longer by horse and buggy to reach the county seat to vote and a day or longer to get back home. Traveling on a sabbath wasn't permitted, so Tuesdays it was.[8] There is absolutely no reason to continue this custom today.

While we are questioning the system, we also have to question our habits. Why do we call elected officials our representatives if we do not feel they represent us? Why do we call officeholders our nation's or state's or community's leaders when they do very little leading? Besides, aren't they supposed to be taking their cues from us? Why don't we recognize ourselves as the leaders and them as our servants?

What happens when we define political deviancy down and respond to destructive behaviors by lowering standards for what is permissible? We got a taste in 2016.

There were two competing storylines at the 2016 Democratic National Convention in Philadelphia. Democrats made history by becoming the first major party to nominate a woman for president. Then there were the tens of thousands of emails made public by Wikileaks showing how the Democratic establishment played favorites in the race for the nomination and went to great lengths to sabotage Bernie Sanders' campaign.[9]

In the euphoria of finally achieving the long-awaited and historic selection of a woman to be the party's candidate for the nation's highest office, Democrats looked past the fact that their nominee was not only a female but also someone who personified the political establishment at a time of intense anti-establishment feelings among voters and one who ran as a centrist at a time when there was no center in American politics. In 2016, there was rampant populism, taking the form of both an authoritarian populism embodied by Republican nominee Donald Trump and a democratic populism that Bernie Sanders was tapping into. Noticing the disappearance of the political middle, Barack Obama's labor secretary Robert Reich said at the time, "If Hillary Clinton and the Democratic Party don't recognize this realignment, they're in for a rude shock … because Donald Trump does recognize it."[10]

Successful politicians are like mirrors. When voters look at them, they see their hopes or fears or ways of seeing the world reflected back at them. If you accept my premise that one of the major parties has grown frightening and the other frightened, it would have been hard in 2016 to find two better mirrors of Democratic and Republican voters than Hillary and Trump. It's said that good politicians campaign in poetry and govern in prose. Hillary campaigned in uninspiring prose and most likely would have painted by numbers when it comes to governing. She'd have been cozy with Wall Street, there would have been no significant rearrangement of the economy, and she'd have been a hawk on foreign affairs. She'd have taken few risks.

The strongest impulse of the largest bloc of Democratic voters is to play it safe. They saw Hillary as the least risky choice. Her resumé, impeccable. Former First Lady. One-time U.S. senator. Cabinet secretary. Her name recognition, second to none. She had the money, and she had the endorsements. She is incredibly disciplined politically, scripted to a fault. It's no surprise then that she had the establishment's wholehearted backing. Because of those strengths, her supporters were more than willing to overlook all the baggage she carried. On the issues, Hillary is socially progressive and status quo economically, which makes her an accurate reflection of today's Democratic Party.

Trump, on the other hand, campaigns in vulgarity and governs by intentional chaos. Republican voters, at least those in the heartland states that usually decide national elections, are frustrated and angry, and that has them feeling downright reckless. Trump was a reckless candidate, the ultimate throw-caution-to-the-wind choice. He is the consummate anti-politician, cocksure of himself, full of bluster and boastful promises, an easy answer for every vexing question. Concerned about immigration? I'll build a wall spanning our entire southern border and make the Mexicans pay for it. Worried about your job? Don't fret. I wrote *The Art of the Deal*. I'll make the economy hum. How? Hey, I'm Donald Trump. Establishment Republicans were having night sweats over what Trump was doing to their party, with his unsubtle appeals to racism and xenophobia. In truth, the strength of his candidacy was the natural byproduct of what they had made their party into. Trump was the embodiment of the anti-establishment mood of voters they courted and invited into their party.

The Democratic establishment and mainstream Democratic voters couldn't seem to fathom how people could fall for a billionaire reality TV star whose message began with fear-mongering, race-baiting, and anti-immigrant nativism and ended with the conceit that he alone can keep us safe, maintain order, and make us prosper economically. Perhaps they couldn't wrap their heads around it because they were not sufficiently aware of the anger fueling the raging populism in both of its forms. When you or I lose our temper, I mean really blow our stacks, we aren't rational in the heat of the moment. Emotion overwhelms reason. We later regret things we say or do out of anger. Why should we expect that this all-too-familiar and all-too-human behavior will never come into play when it's time to vote in elections?

There is a significant segment of American society that can tell the politicians aren't listening to them and are not working on their behalf, and they are steamed. When they are told the economy is getting better, they aren't feeling it. When they are told the nation's crime rate is dropping, all they know is they do not feel safer or more secure. Is it so hard to understand how tens of millions of Americans who feel they've been left behind could be drawn to someone who tells them they are right to feel the way they are feeling and then assures them he will make their lives better?

Like most Americans, I had never seen anything quite like it before—the 2016 presidential race, that is. It was so dark, so ugly, so ridiculously comical at times. I thought it must signal something. The fall of an empire. The birth of a new American fascism. A major party coming apart at the seams. Something.

Whatever it signaled, the outcome of the 2016 election did not turn on whether enough Americans were ready to break the ultimate glass ceiling. It hinged on who best understood and responded to the causes of rising American populism. It's clear that national politics is reflecting nationwide angst. The causes of that anxiety did not suddenly appear in 2016; they had been mounting for several decades. America is being socially transformed. Civil rights. Women's rights. Gay rights. For many, this all feels right. It was about time. Some find the social upheaval discomforting, but they're adjusting. For others, such change is intolerable, and they are pushing back. Hard. The ferocity of the political backlash is itself a sure indication of how transformative recent social movements have been and continue to be.

We are in transition economically at the same time our country is experiencing dramatic social change. Economic dislocations are always painful and traumatic, and the fear and uncertainty and sense of loss that accompany them always find a political outlet. When large numbers of people left the land and went to factories and offices more than a century ago, there was political turbulence. With a global economy emerging, with factory jobs here at home disappearing, with great recessions and jobless recoveries, and rapidly expanding income and wealth inequality, there is political turbulence.

All of this has many Americans convinced that the country's best days are in the rearview mirror. They are wrong. A three-year journey across America didn't reveal a dying nation to journalist James Fallows. Instead, in place after place—Sioux Falls, South Dakota; Bend, Oregon; Columbus, Mississippi; Holland, Michigan; San Bernardino, California; Duluth, Minnesota; Bethlehem, Pennsylvania; Greenville, South Carolina—Fallows repeatedly found evidence of reinvention and renewal and revival.[11]

America is being remade, both socially and economically. This makeover didn't start in 2016, and it won't be completed any time soon. Fallows observed that Americans are adapting better and faster to the shifting ground beneath our feet than people in much of the rest of the world, but our national politics is lagging behind and dragging us down. That means the U.S. has a harder time taking the steps that would make adjusting to the challenges of our time less painful and more productive. For example, workers now have to change jobs more frequently than in the past. Guaranteeing access to medical care by making health insurance truly portable so it follows workers regardless of where they are employed makes all kinds of sense in this new economy. The political system has so far proven incapable of meeting the need. This is why there is so much anti-establishment fervor. This is why the race for the White House in 2016 was so ghastly. America is being remade, both socially and economically. It needs to be transformed politically too.

In case some out there still need persuading that the U.S. is on the verge of political system failure, look back at the 2016 presidential election, where American voters were doomed to a choice between the two most disliked major party nominees[12] in polling history.[13] The Democratic establishment was hellbent from the get-go to nominate one of the world's best-known political figures who also happened to be one of the least trusted[14] and most unlikable politicians around.[15] The silver lining to her unpopularity was that Republican insiders proved incapable of preventing an even more unpopular and distrusted character from capturing their party's nomination.[16] Elections are, by their nature, popularity contests to one degree or another. The 2016 presidential election was an unpopularity contest. But that's not what decided the outcome.

The greatest danger in continuously forcing voters to determine who they fear and hate the least is how nose-holding steers the public's thinking away from what America's future should look like and diverts our attention from what we all hope for and dream about. The badly corrupted and unresponsive government we have today is the product of decades of voters choosing the lesser of evils. The continuation of the American experiment has depended on some good luck along the way. The U.S. could have come apart at the seams on more than one occasion. In our darkest moments, gifted leaders like Lincoln and FDR emerged to light a path forward. We are again at a moment of truth. The major parties have grown calcified and estranged from the masses and incapable of replacing growing darkness with light.

What might come from such conditions is uncertain. The emergence of a new major party is highly unlikely because America has a two-party system that actively discriminates against this outcome, but it is no longer inconceivable that either or both of the major parties could splinter or even disintegrate. Parties deserve this fate when they no longer appeal to your hopes and dreams but rather can only play on your worst fears to gain power.

It is up to us to refuse to go where the ruling elites want to take us. It is up to us to look for chances to unite when they see endless opportunities to divide. If you are alarmed by Trump, you need to realize that obsessing over the horrors of a Trump presidency didn't prevent one—it helped him. Fear figured prominently in both parties' campaigns in 2016 and again in 2020. Now more than ever, the American people need to prove once again that this is the land of the brave. When we are told what we should hate, we need to say what we love. When we're told what is being destroyed, we need to say what we want created. In this oppressive darkness, it is up to us to shine light.

I'm not one of those who thinks you can't tell apart the two major political parties in America. I don't buy for a second that they are two wings of the same bird. I recently ran for statewide office as a Democrat. More than thirty years ago, I worked as an aide to three Republican state representatives. Two of the three clearly could not stand where they stood then and belong to today's Republican Party. The third might manage to still fit, but it would be iffy. Today's Republicans and Democrats have very real and substantial differences. But both parties have been corrupted, and each is failing the country in its own way.

On the surface, Republicans and Democrats talk and act differently. I confess, I don't understand Democrats. Today's Republicans I get. It's easy enough to see what kind of society they want. It's just not a fit place to live. Democrats, on the other hand, are hard to figure. I hear what they say they want to do. But when they are actually in power—like they were in Wisconsin and in the nation's capital in 2009 and 2010—they never seem to do those things. I'm not alone in losing count of the number of times Democratic lawmakers have been overheard saying they couldn't afford to act because it would jeopardize their ability to get re-elected and hold on to their majority. Then one of them after another was not re-elected anyway, and they lost their majority. I'm not alone in losing count of the number of times Democrats have been reluctant to deal with some issue or another because the polling didn't show strong enough public support. Right there is a major difference between Democrats and Republicans. Democrats are resigned to polls shaping their message and guiding their actions. Republicans believe their message and actions will shape the polling.

Then there is the Democrats' chronic habit of compromising with themselves. This tendency has been on prominent display all across the country, including in the 2016 presidential race. Democratic voters seemed to love the ideas Bernie Sanders put out there, so much so that he went from more than 50 percentage points down in the national polls to more or less even with Hillary Clinton.[17] Yet Clinton was considered the presumptive nominee. Curiously, you rarely heard Democratic voters say they preferred Clinton's ideas to Sanders'. They said they doubted his ideas could ever become law. They said ideas like debt-free college and health care for all and a higher minimum wage— ideas they claim to believe in—are impractical or even "pie in the sky" or "pipe dreams." Congress will never pass them, they said. Hillary's the safer choice, the more practical option.

How do you ever win by making unilateral concessions? It's Negotiation 101, people. Never compromise with yourself. Never move in the direction of the other side unless and until the other side also moves toward you. Ask for a little, and you get nothing. Ask for a lot, and you can't get less than nothing. More often than not, you eventually get at least some of what you want. As for Hillary being the safer choice, did it dawn on those thinking that way that there were unusually strong anti-establishment feelings among voters in 2016? Did it occur to them that for Donald Trump to have a path to the White House, he desperately needed to run against an establishment figure? There were good reasons why national polls showed Sanders running stronger against Trump than Clinton. Those polls showed significant risk for Democrats in a Clinton versus Trump matchup.

Never insult voters. That should be the first rule of politics. Hillary Clinton broke that rule when she said out loud that half of Trump's supporters were deplorables and irredeemable. She said what she and many of her supporters surely believed to be true, and she probably lost the election at that very moment. Mitt Romney made the same mistake in 2012 with his "47 percent" remark when he wrongly assumed he was speaking privately to supporters who undoubtedly shared his belief that close to half of Americans are deadbeats and slackers. Breaking the first rule did him in as well.

Elections are about representation. That should be the second rule of politics. Sifting through supposedly scientific exit polling data in hopes of explaining one of the biggest upsets in American political history, a mystified *Washington Post* reporter concluded that "people weren't voting on issues. Like, at all."[18]

They usually don't. Like, hardly ever. An occasional election becomes a referendum on some burning issue, but that's not the norm. Elections aren't generally about issues; they are about representation. Voters are shopping for a mirror, someone who is saying what they are feeling. A few among us might be single-issue voters, but most of us are just looking for someone who reflects our current thinking, generally speaking, and hoping those we elect will look out for our best interests. It's simply not possible to find candidates who agree with you on every issue. It is possible to find ones who seem to share your values and appear to be thinking what you are thinking.

Academics try to treat politics as a science, but like friendships and marriages, it's far more art than science. Issues don't typically decide elections. Connecting with voters decides elections. Hillary Clinton ran on her qualifications, her experience, and her readiness for the job. The problem for her was that voters weren't in the mood to buy what she was selling. If large numbers of voters had been more or less satisfied with the direction of the country and more or less satisfied with how our government was functioning, maybe they would have looked for a steady, seasoned hand. Maybe they would have put a premium on what Clinton offered. But tens of millions of voters were thinking America was on the wrong track, and their belief in government had been badly shaken. Donald Trump's talk of draining the swamp better reflected their thinking.

Most of those tens of millions were willing to overlook what they intensely dislike about Trump because he did more to reflect their frustrations than Clinton ever had. They overlooked what they find distasteful about Trump not only because he said what they were thinking, but also because of what he didn't say. He didn't tell working-class people in places like Wisconsin who supported Obama in the previous two elections that they are irredeemable. Democrats have been losing most elections for the past several decades, and after each beating, they react with a mixture of utter bewilderment and anger directed at tens of millions of voters who they believe are ignorantly voting against their own interests. Even if they don't say it out loud, they think it: These voters are deplorable and irredeemable.

Going forward, Democrats will have a hard time winning the presidency without winning battleground states like Wisconsin. And they will struggle to win over Wisconsin unless they think long and hard about the first two rules of politics.

The fact that so many were shocked about the turn our country took in 2016 is what's perhaps most shocking. Media pundits, the beltway operatives, and party insiders they count on as sources have a habit of overanalyzing elections and overthinking politics. Seen from flyover Wisconsin, what happened was not that complicated. Anti-establishment feelings were running sky-high. Hillary Clinton was seen as the stay the course, more of the same candidate. Clinton emphasized her experience and qualifications and readiness for the job, while Trump talked of draining the swamp. Compared to Clinton, Trump was the clear change candidate. If voters had been in a stay the course state of mind, Clinton would be president. A huge number were in no such mood. Tens of millions felt the urge to extend a middle finger to the powers-that-be. Trump was the biggest middle finger they could find. Democrats insisted on nominating a consummate insider at a moment when anti-establishment fervor was reaching a boiling point. Curiously, in talking to both party insiders and mainstream Democratic voters, they all seemed to think they were playing it safe. They couldn't see they were making one of the riskiest choices imaginable.

Democrats either don't understand or don't care how hated they are by voters who live in small towns or out on the farm. Judging from what I've experienced over the last year or two, the party's name has become a dirty word in most rural areas. By all appearances, Democratic leaders have written off large swaths of rural Wisconsin and rural America. What they don't seem to realize is this strategy makes it difficult, if not impossible, for them to construct governing majorities.

The Democratic Party is an amalgamation of a dizzying array of issues and causes and constituencies, the sum total of which does not add up to a governing majority in most parts of the country. Think of the group behavior of Democrats, and you are reminded more of cats or rabbits than bees or geese. There's even a metaphor commonly used to describe this trait that runs particularly strong in Democrats. They are said to each be in their own issue silo. Having grown up on a farm, I can say from personal experience that silos are no fit place to live. They are cramped, cold, and dirty. They work well for storing feed for cattle but not so well for storing the hopes and dreams of Democrats.

Over the years, Democrats earned a reputation as water carriers for organized labor. This reputation served Democrats well when you could find a union member in nearly every household in the country. But the vast majority of working people in the U.S. don't belong to unions anymore. Unions now represent only about one in ten American workers. In the private sector, it's more like one in fifteen. The masses of nonunion blue-collar laborers see the Democrats fighting for those few, but not for them.

For their part, Republicans keep emphasizing self-reliance. Successful people are self-made. Achievement comes from discipline and individual initiative. Failure is the fault of individual weakness or lack of effort, not a scarcity of opportunity or the absence of social justice. Government just gets in the way. The less government, the better. Of course, today's Republicans have an infidelity problem. There's the dirty little secret that the biggest expansion of the federal government in the last half-century was the doing of a Republican administration with near-universal support of Republicans in Congress.[19] That would be the creation of a vast new federal bureaucracy devoted to domestic surveillance and a radically enlarged police presence. Republicans used to be for local control but aren't anymore. They no longer act on the belief that the best government is the one closest to the people. In Wisconsin alone, close to 130 laws taking away community decision-making authority have been made since 2011.

For all the talk of limited government and individual liberty, today's Republican Party favors an activist and intrusive government with respect to our personal lives, morality, and sexuality. Republicans talk a good game about trusting in individuals to make their own life choices and placing faith in families to serve as the moral backbone of our society. But there is a big gap between word and deed. Modern-day Republicans have repeatedly supported interventions that effectively put government everywhere from the bedroom to the doctor's office. They have repeatedly sought to dictate who can love and marry whom and have not hesitated to meddle in doctor-patient relationships and medical decision making.

Your average Democrat, on the other hand, does not summon an overarching principle or core belief when explaining a stance or justifying an action. Democrats prefer facts and have large collections of them. The problem is when facts and values collide, most people will discard the facts and hold on tight to their values. While analysis often produces paralysis in Democrats, Republicans plunder. They are hellbent on destroying public education. They continuously feed the rich, not minding in the least the savage inequality that results. They enshrine privilege at every turn and pulverize the common good. They are not the least bit squeamish about making blunt appeals to racism, sexism, xenophobia, and other dark impulses to secure and hold on to power. All of this leaves them more unpopular with the American people than they've been in nearly a quarter of a century.[20] Yet they rule the country, thanks in part to the lengths they'll go to hold on to power and in part due to the Democrats' own identity crisis.

We live in dangerous times. Republicans have positioned themselves to rule most states and largely get their way on Capitol Hill by making the classic deal with the devil, swapping essential pieces of the party's soul for temporary supremacy. Democrats not only do not appear to have a plan to counter the GOP's power play, they seem reluctant to acknowledge they have a problem.

All of this leaves America's future far more in peril than need be. For different reasons and in different ways, both the Democrats and Republicans are missing something. Both are convinced their world view is superior, and both seem oblivious to the fact that most people embrace elements of both world views. Most people put great value on discipline and personal responsibility but also see the importance of lending a helping hand and making sure that everyone gets a fair shake. Few love paying taxes, but most see the sense of pooling our money to pay to do those things that need to be done together. The future belongs to the party that figures out that, philosophically speaking, we're mutts not purebreds and reconciles itself to the unpleasant fact that we see how both parties are slaves to special interests. They favor different constituencies, but they both cater religiously to those constituencies. The future belongs to the party willing to truly dedicate itself to making the government and the economy work for all of us, not just a few of us.

So much time and energy are wasted fruitlessly arguing over which party wants more government and which one wants less when the evidence shows that both are equally adept at enlarging government and extending its reach, albeit in different ways. If we spent half as much time zeroing in on government's purpose—what it does and for whom—as we spend assigning blame for its size, we could get somewhere. Both major parties have proven they are for big government. Both have shown a distressing tendency to put government to work for a few at the expense of the many. That needs to change. We need a repurposed government, one that is serving the whole of society both consistently and well.

No dictionary ever captured the essence of democracy's meaning better than Abe Lincoln did in his legendary Gettysburg Address. Lincoln defined it as government "of the people, by the people, and for the people." For a century and a half after the Civil War, the Republican Party was the party of Lincoln. Modern-day Republicans have rejected

Lincoln's commitment to equality as they flirted for decades before eventually jumping in bed with white supremacy. They also have renounced Lincoln's idea of democracy. For years now, the likes of Rush Limbaugh have been saying time and again that America is a republic, not a democracy, and dittoheads across the country dutifully repeat the mantra.[21]

It's pointless to argue over whether America is one or the other when we were so obviously intended to be both. The U.S. was set up to be a democratic republic. The republic the founders gave us can also accurately be described as a representative democracy or a constitutional democracy. The founders wisely and ingeniously struck a balance between majority rule by elected representatives of the people and protection of individual and minority rights by rule of constitutional law. To say we are a republic but not a democracy is to not only disregard the true meaning of these words but also to disrespect the founders' delicate balancing act. They understandably wanted no more to do with a monarchy and sought to replace a king's rule with democracy. But they also were rightly fearful of mob rule and felt the need to temper the democratic will with "inalienable" rights for individuals that could not be voted out of existence. They did a better job designing the system than we have done taking care of it.

At a time when the republic faced perhaps the greatest threat to its continued existence, Lincoln gave the country not only the perfect definition of democracy but also reason to believe a new birth of freedom in America was possible. In our time, all of us—whether Republican, Democrat, independent or something else—need to channel our inner Lincolns and dedicate ourselves to a new birth of democracy and equality. We need to figure out how to restore government of the people, by the people, and for the people. We also need to imagine an economy that is of the people, by the people, and for the people and strive to make it so.

We need Lincoln's spirit now more than ever. The party of Lincoln has waved goodbye to Abe. The rest of us need to summon him back. Too much is made of red voters and blue voters and red states and blue states, as if they make up two separate Americas (they do not), and their differences are forever irreconcilable (they are not). But for the moment, there is no denying that partisan divisions have intensified in recent years and that America is more politically polarized than at any time in at least two decades. It can be a challenge to find values and attitudes that unite Americans of every political persuasion. But people of every imaginable stripe stand on common ground when it comes to the broadly shared exasperation with money's dominion over democracy. Four out of five Republicans agree with four out of five Democrats and a supermajority of independents that the U.S. Supreme Court messed up bad when it ruled in 2010 that unlimited political spending is a constitutional right.[22]

It is helpful to remember that Supreme Court rulings come and go. Our nation's highest court once ruled that people could be property. It took not only a presidential proclamation but a bloody civil war and amendments to the Constitution to relegate that shameful decision to its rightful place in the trash bin of history. Today's Supreme Court blesses oligarchy with the similarly warped logic that property can be entitled to the constitutional rights of a person. In time, this legal malpractice will find its way to the dumpster too.

Undoing the harm this ruling has done already and continues to do need not involve warfare but could require a constitutional amendment if the Supreme Court in the fairly near future does not come to its senses and overturn that 2010 decision before a twenty-eighth amendment is ratified. How this all plays out and how promptly this inevitable outcome is brought about largely depends on legal creativity bordering on hubris. Lincoln's Emancipation Proclamation declaring three million slaves free was based on what's been called a "highly contentious, thin-ice reading of the presidential war powers."[23] Ample evidence suggests Lincoln knowingly and dramatically exceeded his legal and constitutional authority, and the nation is so very fortunate that he did.

American democracy needs a modern-day equivalent of the Emancipation Proclamation. Whether in the form of an executive order, an act of Congress, or measures enacted by states or local communities, the Supreme Court's ruling in the *Citizens United v. FEC* must be defied. The constitutional right of unlimited political spending invented by the court in this decision must be exposed for what it is—the legalization of bribery. Elected representatives of the people anywhere and everywhere should knowingly and dramatically exceed what the Supreme Court says is the limit of their legal authority and declare our government free from its current state of indentured servitude to billionaires and corporations. Whenever justices dictate injustice, legal ingenuity is required. Executive orders should be issued, and laws should be passed declaring that giving more than $200 to anyone holding or pursuing public office, or any group helping to elect a politician, is a bribe and therefore a felony.

In throwing down this gauntlet, the Supreme Court's warped logic is countered with this alternative reasoning: If you wish to demonstrate your support for politicians, their parties or surrogates, giving $200 is demonstration enough. Giving $200 or less does not distinguish you much from your many fellow citizens who are likewise giving small amounts or the much larger number who give nothing at all. But go past the $200 threshold, and you are among less than one percent of the population with that habit.[24] It makes you stand out, separates you from the crowd, and makes it start looking like you might want more than just the honor of participating in a democracy. Lincoln-style hubris is needed because we are beyond the point where campaign financing can be reformed. It can't be reformed because we no longer have campaign finance in America. We have legal bribery, and there's no reforming bribery. It has to be outlawed.

All laws and respect for the rule of law, in general, are demeaned and ultimately undermined when any law ceases to be rooted in reality. The reality is that most Americans—Republicans, Democrats, and independents alike—see big political donations for what they are, namely bribes. The law of this land needs to reflect that reality. Instead, the Supreme Court has imposed a fictitious alternate reality on us, ordering us to think of property as part of "we the people" and see massive sums of money spent on elections as "free speech." Just as a past court ordered all Americans, including President Lincoln, to accept that people could be regarded as property. Lincoln defied that court. He was said to be on thin ice legally when he did. The ground held beneath his feet.

In defense of democracy in our time, we need to be willing to stand on what we're told is thin ice. Two hundred dollars is plenty. Anything more is a bribe. ⬤

CHAPTER THIRTEEN
KEEPING IT

Mainstream media continually reinforce the twisted world of American elections. Read any run-of-the-mill news story about an upcoming election and you see why so many people find media coverage of politics unbearably exasperating. The story treats the election like a horse race. It handicaps the race. It tells readers who is *likely to win* the election but gives readers little useful information to help them decide for themselves who *should win*. The story quotes an "expert" or two—some campaign operative or political industry insider—repeating for the umpteenth time the conventional wisdom that elections are all about money. They go on to say which candidates have the most and are therefore worth paying attention to.

After following the pack for the duration of the 2016 presidential race, watching how the candidates campaigned and how the media covered the circus, *Rolling Stone* writer Matt Taibbi came away struck by how the whole process "was dysfunctional and that people were turned off by it. The people who did campaigning for a living, both politicians and the press, were wrapped up in their own little world."[1]

The warped perceptions of those wrapped up in that little world too often become self-fulfilling prophecy. Believing that money is the only thing that matters in elections helps make it so. Politicians with the most money win, and then your own elected representatives have little choice but to ignore your wishes to cater to the demands of their biggest donors. To hell with that. People are starving for more empowering elections that are about what kind of society we want to live in and how we could create such a place together. They are starving for more nourishing election coverage than what amounts to a Vegas betting line telling us that conventional politicians are all we've got to choose from because the odds are stacked against any alternative, no matter how inspiring that alternative might be.

Satisfying these cravings will require new journalism and new politics. Without it, the ideal of representation is debased because nearly all Americans can't realistically run for office. The way things are done dooms us to "representation" that is far older, richer, whiter, and more likely to be male than the average American. Our country is poorer for it.

Despite the impoverishing effects of the way things are done, it's amazing how many still go with the flow and campaign conventionally. Long before candidates for public office give their first stump speech, they go to school—candidate school, that is. Consulting operations run these training programs. A few have some unique wrinkles, but for the most part, they are assembly lines that churn out cookie-cutter candidates. And they all emphasize the development of one skill over all others: fundraising prowess. These schools teach from the same curriculum. Central to the course material is getting would-be candidates over the perfectly natural discomfort with asking people for money. Candidates are coached on how to see this grubby chore as a blessing … how they are really giving people a glorious gift by inviting them to invest in such a noble cause. They are taught not only to be shameless about fundraising but to take pride in their newfound shamelessness. In a nutshell, they are trained to see their fellow citizens as little more than ATMs.

They are taught to think this way because of the vast industry that has grown up around modern politics. The beast needs constant feeding by candidates who take the advice of multi-millionaire investment banker, one-time White House chief of staff, and former congressman and Chicago mayor Rahm Emanuel: "The first third of your campaign is money, money, money. The second third is money, money, and press. The final third is votes, press, and money." For those keeping score at home, that's money 6, votes 1.[2]

The pollsters, media consultants, telemarketers, list brokers, direct mail firms, and advertising agencies who profit from devising ways to spend all that money sell the idea that there is a formula for election campaigning, and if you follow the formula, you win. The formula isn't shared in the form of an equation, but if it were, it would look something like this for a small-scale state legislative campaign in a rural part of Wisconsin:

$$V = E + \cfrac{70K}{22314 \to 7DM + \cfrac{pm}{r+pa} + \cfrac{gotv}{rc+dh}}$$

One local candidate's experience explains the formula. He was told to avoid taking positions on issues as much as possible and steer clear of controversy. He was told victory (V) depended on gathering endorsements (E) and raising $70,000 with most of it sent to an Alexandria, Virginia, (zip code 22314) marketing firm to pay for seven mass-produced direct mailings (DM), and the rest going for a little paid media (pm) including some radio (r) and print advertising (pa) and get-out-the-vote (gotv) expenses like robocalls (rc) and printed door hangers (dh). He followed the script and lost by a large margin. The formula failed him. Yet hundreds of candidates have continued following the script in legislative contests throughout Wisconsin, which is why close to $36 million was spent on 2018 campaigns.[3] Adjust the formula for an election for a statewide office like governor, with a lot of paid media including an abundance of pricey TV ads, and the spending tally reaches the stratospheric $93 million seen in the 2018 election for Wisconsin's highest office.

Spending heavily on paid media—television, radio, print, online—is political gospel. The conventional wisdom is looking less wise when you consider that public trust in advertising has been falling.[4] This trend is sure to continue in the future because young millennials are especially distrustful of advertising.[5] TV ads, in particular, are losing effectiveness, partly because viewers are increasingly wary of them and partly because it is getting easier to avoid them, using digital recording and online video streaming to watch programs but skip the accompanying ads.[6] Yet the vast majority of election campaign spending still is devoted to TV and other traditional forms of advertising. It makes the political professionals and media corporations billions. It turns voters' stomachs and starves democracy.

So what works better? Word of mouth. The information we trust most comes from people we know, especially friends and family,[7] which makes it all the more curious that neighbor-to-neighbor outreach programs like street teams and other kinds of direct voter contact are so hard to find in the conventional campaign playbook. With face-to-face campaigning downplayed and a premium placed on paid media, the playbook says attack your opponent at every turn. It is an article of faith among political professionals that negative advertising "works." It certainly does, if the goal is to shrink and polarize the electorate.[8] If the goal is to persuade or motivate voters, or make our society governable, then a growing body of evidence challenges the devotion to scorched earth campaigning.[9]

Outside Philadelphia's Independence Hall at the close of the Constitutional Convention of 1787, a woman approached one of the departing delegates, Benjamin Franklin, and asked, "What have we got—a republic or a monarchy?" Franklin famously replied, "A republic, if you can keep it."

Keeping it is now iffier than at any time in living memory. When it comes to having a truly representative democracy and a government responsive to all of the people, let's face it, the odds are stacked against us. Money has been crowned king of American politics by the highest court in the land. That means as the rich get richer, they also get more politically powerful. As they gain more and more power, they are increasingly able to rig the system in their favor.

Keeping the republic means finding ways to beat the odds and elect representatives who break the mold and dare to be different. When running for office, especially for the first time, the natural impulse is to look at how others have done it and copy them. Going with the flow and campaigning conventionally means embracing the vast industry that has commandeered modern politics and locking arms with the industry professionals—pollsters, media consultants, campaign operatives, political strategists, telemarketers, list brokers, fundraising experts, and advertising agents—who make a living selling the idea that there is a formula for election campaigning and that if you follow it, you win.

In the end, the formula fails our entire society and does violence to our republic. It destroys faith in democracy and trust in government. Money can buy a lot of things, but it can't buy faith or trust. Keeping the republic we inherited comes down to refusing to play by rules that favor the rich and powerful. It comes down to building relationships and earning trust and restoring faith. More than anything, it comes down to enough of us being undaunted by the unfairness of the fight and the steepness of the odds.

More than ever, America needs subversives who consciously choose to resist the impulse to look, sound, and act like your typical politician and who instead break the mold and dare to be different. Our society needs subversives who run for office as if they intend to leave our political system in better shape than they found it and who seek to overcome money power with people power ... discovering and putting to use other political currencies to combat the oppressive influence of big money in politics. This is the only way to upend the emerging oligarchy that threatens U.S. democracy—or has already replaced it if researchers like Gilens and Page are to be believed. Corruption must be subverted to keep the republic.

Those subversives also will have to embrace a fuller, more meaningful definition of victory that allows our whole society, and not just the candidate, to win. Imagine a campaign that 1) changes the dynamics of the race by bringing previously ignored problems to the forefront; 2) reframes the debate by changing what is discussed, how it's talked about, and how voters are engaged on these topics; 3) measurably moves public opinion on key issues; and 4) creates a highly competitive contest that heightens interest in the race and increases voter turnout.

Say a campaign does all these things, but the candidate does not get the most votes but does shape the campaign platform and policy agenda of the eventual officeholder. Was it a losing campaign? Did the candidate fail? If the purpose of running for office is to make change, to make our society better, the answer to those questions is clearly no. Candidates dwelling only on getting the most votes routinely say whatever they think people want to hear rather than saying what needs to be said. Many take the low road—cutting ethical corners, accepting tainted money, and engaging in character assassination of opponents—and drag our elections into the gutter. Those candidates might win but our democracy loses, and trust in government is lost. A candidate running subversively might lose an election but win something far more valuable for our society. In the end, what matters in elections is which values are promoted and what actions our government is prompted to take and what problems end up getting solved.

Money is powerful in politics, no question about it. The U.S. Supreme Court's 2010 decision in *Citizens United v. FEC* allowing wealthy individuals and corporations to spend as much as they want to influence elections and the court's 1976 ruling in *Buckley v. Valeo* equating money with speech created a new political reality for anyone thinking of running for office. Unless you are independently wealthy or have very rich friends, you are going to be up against opponents with vastly more money. But again, money is not the only political currency. There are other currencies that, when combined, can make a concoction potent enough to overcome conventional political power. India was freed from British colonial rule using what Mahatma Gandhi called *satyagraha* or "truth force." A disciple of Gandhi's, Martin Luther King Jr. put what he called "soul force" to equally effective use in the fight for racial justice and civil rights in America. Many different ingredients can be substituted for large sums of money in a recipe for a successful campaign. Here are four:

1. People power, creatively employed. While opponents spend like drunken sailors, subversive candidates run on a shoestring by saying no to the herd of political professionals who descend on campaigns offering their assistance. They rely on volunteers instead of paid professionals.

Rather than paying a telemarketing firm for automated phone calls, volunteers make the calls and send texts from their own phones. Instead of paying an outdoor advertising company for billboard space, volunteers make large banners and display them in heavy traffic areas. They plant inexpensive yard signs on lawns and erect hand-painted road signs and billboards on supporters' property. Old-fashioned shoe leather is combined with new-age cyberstumping. The power of social media and other web-based tools complement volunteer effort.

2. Big ideas, fearlessly shared. Money is a form of political capital, and it's pretty much the only one recognized by conventional politicians. Just as organized people are an alternative political currency, so are provocative ideas. Professional political operatives teach conventional candidates to play it safe and avoid saying or doing anything controversial. Defeating convention necessarily involves risk. Subversive campaigns make friends with controversy.

3. Revolutionary spirit, properly understood. America is the product of revolt against a king's power. Distrust of government is in our nation's DNA. Most Americans hate politics and politicians with a burning passion. Most dislike both major parties. Subversive candidates swim with these currents. They don't defend the system. Conventional politicians fawn over VIPs. Subversives aim their affections in the opposite direction, putting the "little guy" on a pedestal. They make privilege the enemy. Large numbers of people see both the political system and economy rigged against them. They see both politics and economics working well for a few at everyone else's expense. Subversives embrace what they see.

4. Love, publicly displayed. Hate is an undeniably powerful emotion. It incites people to action, even to violence. Fear and the hatred that grows out of it are regularly put to use for political gain. Love is a powerful emotion, too, and can inspire social action just as readily as hate does. With hate on the rise in our society, never has there been a greater need for love, empathy, compassion, and concern for the common good in politics. We can't be afraid to say it's important to look out for each other and that we are our brother and sister's keeper. Our society has become self-centered and driven by greed. Now more than ever, "me" politics needs to be assertively challenged by "we" politics, with love put on public display.

The odds are still stacked against candidates running this way. A few will capture public offices, as Alexandria Ocasio-Cortez did in New York. Many more will fall short of that goal, as I did in Wisconsin. But all can run impactful campaigns that help unscrew America if they are run with a clear understanding that when facing opponents with brute strength—namely an abundance of their own money or rich friends—following a formula that heavily relies on money is a huge strategic mistake if you don't have that kind of strength. You need another kind—the willingness and ability to truly lead.

Those intent on subverting the American oligarchy have to be willing to go where no one else is going, alone if necessary. Most politicians won't move a muscle without polls and consultants telling them to. Genuine leaders let their conscience be their guide. Conventional politicians have a sixth sense about where to find a parade, and then quickly run to the front and grab a drum. True leaders don't follow the crowd. They have the courage of conviction that makes others want to follow them.

The secret sauce of a subversive campaign is an extensive network of volunteers. It takes a movement to beat the machine. For a strong grassroots campaign, an ambitious but feasible rule of thumb is one volunteer for every 2,500 to 3,000 people living in the area where you are running. There are ninety-nine state assembly districts in Wisconsin, and each has roughly 57,000 residents. Somewhere in the neighborhood of twenty volunteers are needed in a grassroots assembly campaign. State senate districts are three times the size of assembly districts, requiring about sixty volunteers in those races. For congressional elections in my state, the size of the volunteer corps rises to at least 250. For a statewide race, the number runs up to 2,000 or more.

Building such a network is hard work, but there's also some magic involved. Conventional campaign managers are control freaks. In subversive campaigns, magic happens when some control is surrendered, and volunteers are given freedom to make decisions and put their stamp on the campaign. Some will do cringe-inducing things. But occasional overzealousness or clumsiness is a price worth paying to build grassroots power. Challenging people to be full-fledged citizens, empowering them to take action and giving them the freedom to exercise creativity fuels volunteer commitment. Cut the fuel supply, and the engine will stall.

When volunteers are trusted and empowered, there are so many things they can do: organize house parties and meet-the-candidate gatherings at popular locations in the community; gather signatures on nomination papers; make phone calls; monitor and post to social media; write letters to the editor to local newspapers; call into talk radio programs; record and share videos; canvas door to door; distribute yard signs and do literature drops; stuff envelopes; plan and carry out fundraisers; data entry; clerical assistance and help with bookkeeping or required campaign filings; drive the candidate to events and other campaign appearances; staff information tables at fairs, neighborhood festivals, and other community events; and get-out-the-vote activities like texting, phoning, and handwriting postcards to friends and neighbors.

Volunteer-driven campaigning is far more cost-effective than the money-fueled, consultant-guided electioneering that has become the norm, and this frees the candidate from the corrupting money chase. The goal of any campaign advertising is to get the candidate's name and message out there. Reaching that goal doesn't have to cost a fortune. Volunteers can become walking advertisements, working in shifts of one to two hours holding banners in parades and at busy intersections or highway overpasses to create an ongoing, visible presence for the campaign. It can be done weekly or even daily, depending on the number of volunteers. Creative citizens like Veronica Wolski of Chicago have pioneered this kind of subversive volunteerism, turning expressway overpasses into "Bernie Bridges" for Senator Sanders' presidential campaign and then passing along her methods to others, including the political greenhorns who formed the "people powered billboard" crew that became a signature element of my quixotic, low-budget campaign for governor.

Banners printed on durable, waterproof vinyl with metal grommets are relatively inexpensive and can be displayed by volunteers or hung on highly visible buildings. Or the signs can be homemade at next to no cost. Experienced volunteer leaders like Veronica freely offer guidance to anyone wishing to take this route: Make the signs big, preferably about four feet by six feet, even larger if possible. They need to be visible from a distance while moving. Make the lettering large, ideally twelve to fourteen inches high in bold, block capital letters. If the background is light, use dark lettering. If the background is dark, use white or very light lettering. Again, it needs to be easily visible from a distance. Use heavy-duty cloth. Canvas tarps work great. Bedsheets with a high thread count can be used but are not ideal. Use permanent markers or paint that doesn't smudge or wash off when it gets wet. Tape can be used to make letters on vinyl or plastic tarps. Keep the message simple—the candidate's name and the office being sought and little else—three to four words, tops.

As mentioned earlier, for machine politicians like Rahm Emanuel, the first third of a campaign is money, money, money. The second third is money, money, and press. The final third is votes, press, and money. Running subversively doesn't mean running with no money, but relying on small donations from regular folks does mean running on a shoestring. So it's more like this: The first third of the campaign focuses on building organizational infrastructure, assembling and growing your campaign team, media outreach, and grassroots fundraising. The second third is community events, candidate appearances, more media outreach, on-the-ground volunteer deployment, and some continued fundraising. The final third is street-level campaign visibility, voter engagement, media attention (including supporter-generated letters to the editor and the like), targeted advertising and get-out-the-vote operations, along with enough fundraising to get to the finish line.

Running subversively means swimming against powerful currents. It means standing out from the crowd. When you think of running for office, the natural impulse is to look at how others have done it and copy them. Following this instinct leads you to mimic how they dress, how they carry themselves, how they talk, and how they campaign.

Think about where succumbing to this impulse inevitably leads. Ask just about anyone what they think of politicians, and what do you hear? Liars. Crooks. Cheats. Sellouts. A profession that confers upon its practitioners the title "The Honorable" is seen as the least honorable of all lines of work.[10] Or, as one pollster found, somewhere between cockroaches and traffic jams in the public's estimation.[11]

Running subversively is based on the belief that good politics is not formulaic. Politics is an art, not a science. Politics is about relationships. Running subversively involves identifying and utilizing other political currencies that, when used creatively, can be more powerful than money. It depends on resisting the impulse to play by rules that favor your opponents. But it also hinges on using their strengths against them.

Think of it as political jiu-jitsu. Jiu-jitsu is the martial art based on the concept that a smaller, weaker person can successfully defend themselves against a bigger, stronger assailant by using proper technique and leverage. The principles of jiu-jitsu can be applied to election campaigning.

Political money and all that it buys is like fire. If the fire is big enough, fighting it is fruitless. You'll never have enough water to put it out. You're going to get burned. You've got to make the fire fight itself. The trick is to turn your opponents' greatest strengths into liabilities and transfer your weaknesses to your opponents. This maneuver depends on two things:

1. An honest accounting of your own and your opponents' strengths and weaknesses. You need to see yourself with honest eyes, as others see you. Just as important is the ability to recognize your opponents' best traits, or better yet, admire them. Those who campaign subversively can't be haters. Overcoming powerful opponents depends on understanding their strengths well enough to use those strengths against them. Hate blinds us to the characteristics of our opponents that we most need to understand. It also ends up obscuring what is best in us.

2. Willingness to focus on and openly deal with both your own greatest weaknesses as a candidate and your opponents' greatest strengths. This is completely counterintuitive. The natural impulse is to gloss over your shortcomings and draw no attention to your opponents' strong suits. Political jiu-jitsu hinges on resisting this impulse and acting counterintuitively.

Remember, when questions arose about whether Ronald Reagan was too old to bear the burdens of the presidency, he did not dodge the subject or try to fake youthful vigor. He famously quipped that he was "not going to exploit, for political purposes, my opponent's youth and inexperience." If your opponents have more money, make money an issue. Hammer away at what all that money buys, especially that stable of political professionals at their service. Hammer away at how you don't have anyone telling you what to think, what to say, or what to do, which in turn draws attention to your opponents' puppet strings. If you are seen as inexperienced, and your opponents' resumes look more impressive, make their experience an issue. The mess that's been made is their doing, not yours. Make them own it. Similarly, if they've got more endorsements and establishment support, make the establishment an issue.

There's another dimension to practicing political jiu-jitsu. It's best described using a practical illustration. Let's say you are seen as a tax-and-spend big-government liberal. You've got a problem. Most people don't think much of government and aren't thrilled about paying taxes. Trying to convince people that government is good is futile. Trying to get people to like paying taxes is just as fruitless. Both maneuvers also are violations of the basic principles of political jiu-jitsu. You can push against these forces with all your might, but they will still overwhelm you. Here's the thing. You don't need to convince people that government is good for them to support putting government to constructive use. And you don't need to get people to like paying taxes for them to pay for massive government undertakings willingly. There has always been strong anti-government and anti-tax sentiment in America. Yet people paid for vast public works programs to lift the country out of the Great Depression, paid to fight the Nazis, paid to build the railroads and the interstate highway system and Hoover Dam, and paid to boost seniors out of poverty with Social Security and Medicare. If you are seen as a big-government liberal, don't shy away from talking about taxes and government spending. Just don't waste time defending government and taxation. Focus instead on identifying areas of agreement on how to put government and our tax dollars to the best possible use.

Every day on the campaign trail, you encounter people who don't see eye to eye with you on everything. There are sharp divisions in our society, and the citizenry is highly polarized politically. Keeping conversations civil is challenging. Finding common ground can seem next to impossible sometimes. But through trial and error, I found there are ways to make it possible to reach an understanding, if not agreement, even in the most contentious encounters. Here are four I found to be most effective:

1. Keep it personal, if at all possible. If you are talking to a single individual, keep the conversation focused on the two of you. Your life stories. Your experiences. Your politics. Your religions. Your successes and failures. Your pet peeves. Your favorite things. The two of you will almost certainly find you have some things in common, even if the other person's politics are vastly different than your own. A human connection is made, allowing you to stop seeing each other as mere caricatures of the enemy and even opening the door to understanding one another. Same goes if you are talking to several people at once or even a fairly sizeable group. Keep the conversation focused on those involved in the exchange and what's going on in their lives. The more the topics of conversation expand outward—to Donald Trump and Hillary Clinton or Democrats and Republicans, for example—the more tribal instincts kick in, and you'll be at each other's throats in no time. Minds close and walls go up. Any hope for a meeting of the minds is lost.

2. Speak the other side's language. Meet people on their turf. Describe your values using their vocabulary. For example, if you're talking to people favoring less government and lower taxes, there's a big difference between saying, "We need to raise taxes on the rich," and saying, "No new taxes are needed, but we ought to make sure everyone pays the ones we've got." The two statements make the same basic point about tax policies favoring the ultra-wealthy. One probably ends the conversation because all they hear is "raise taxes." The other leaves room for further discussion because they hear "no new taxes." Leaders like Martin Luther King Jr. melted stiff resistance to civil rights with appeals that not only drew heavily from scripture but also the nation's founding documents written by slaveholders. Public opinion about homosexuality shifted dramatically when gay rights advocates shrewdly and very consciously recalibrated their message from one that emphasized differences but demanded equal treatment to one focusing on love and marriage and commitment to family. The stubborn stereotype of gay people as recklessly promiscuous gave way to far more widespread acceptance of same-sex families. In 1988, barely one-tenth of Americans believed gay couples should have the right to marry, and over three-fourths said gay sex is "always wrong." Just three decades later, more than two-thirds of Americans supported gay marriage.[12]

3. Avoid old labels. Labels are shorthand. They allow people and policies to be categorized for easy reference. They are used to make sense of political debates, elections, and acts of governing by describing where all the participants fit on an ideological spectrum running horizontally from right to left. But with the highly polarized political landscape we have today, the traditional labels—progressive, liberal, moderate, conservative—only serve to promote division. They become baggage that weighs us down. Never carry baggage you don't pack yourself. Try to start each conversation with an empty suitcase. That means resisting old labels and establishing your own identity.

4. Think and talk vertically, not horizontally. As the old labels indicate, we've all been conditioned to think about politics horizontally, from right to left. This way of thinking needlessly divides us by magnifying our differences and glossing over our commonalities. Turn the political spectrum on its head and think top to bottom instead of left to right, and a magical thing can happen. Picture a man and a woman. He's white. She's black. He's a farmworker, she's a child care provider. Both are struggling to make ends meet. He votes Republican, she votes for Democrats. On the old horizontal political spectrum, they are far apart, her on the left and him on the right. We see them as enemies. They see each other the same way. They are divided and conquered. Now think vertically. Who's on top and who's at the bottom? Who has the most money, and who has the least? Who has power and who doesn't? Whose voices are heard and whose aren't? These two people are in the same spot on a vertical political spectrum and have more in common than either they or we have been trained to see. Talking vertically involves talking about royals and commoners or have-lots and have-littles, not liberals and conservatives or left-wingers and right-wingers. Thinking vertically not only has the potential to unite those who are currently divided but also empower those who are presently conquered.

To unscrew America, we have to be real with each other. In this post-truth, alternative-fact world we now live in, *messaging* is a popular buzzword in political circles. Those who win are convinced superior messaging is the secret of their success. Those who lose are convinced that faulty messaging was their downfall, and all they need to do to win is get better at it. There are messaging gurus on both sides. They get a lot of attention and make a lot of money doling out advice. Messaging has become something of an obsession, especially on the Democratic side. To hear Democratic insiders tell it, their party has lost power across the country because of bad messaging, and improved messaging will bring about a Democratic resurgence. It won't—at least not on its own.

Don't get me wrong. Effective communication is important in politics. But if you stand for nothing, it doesn't matter how clever and polished your messaging is. Your message is still about nothing. If your ideas have gone bad, or your steps take you in the wrong direction, sweet words can't rescue sour thinking or rotten actions. If the messenger isn't trusted, the message will be rejected no matter how artfully it is expressed.

Success as a candidate depends heavily on describing why you are running and why you are the best one for the job and doing so simply, briefly, clearly, and memorably and saying it over and over again. Your success depends on telling your story, and your story is much more than a message. Like a compelling message, a good story is well told and memorable and bears repeating. But good stories also bare the soul. They are windows into the storyteller. That creates a bond between the storyteller and the audience, and that's what builds trust. It's not just *what you believe*. It's about *who you are*. Voters want and deserve to know.

As recently as a generation ago, public service was widely seen as noble. Many, if not most, Americans no longer think of public service that way because they have a hard time seeing today's elected officials as public servants. The best imaginable messaging can't change that. Saying over and over again that public service is noble won't make people think it is. They've seen too many public offices used as stepping stones to more lucrative gigs. They see the revolving door. They see career politicians holding some office and then later trading on the connections they've made to pull in $250 or $300 an hour or more as lobbyists or campaign consultants.

It does no good to tell people about the value of public service. They have to be shown. Leadership is required. Messaging is a lot of things, but it is not leadership. Real leading is done by example. When people see public service treated as preparation for cushy jobs on K Street or elsewhere in the political, industrial complex paying six- and seven-figure salaries, that example trumps any messaging to the contrary. The only way to restore faith in public service is to replace countless self-serving acts of me politics with public-spirited acts of we politics. No matter how much the messaging gurus are paid to persuade us to think otherwise, what generations of parents have been teaching their children still rings true. Actions speak louder than words.

Some years ago, the Stand by Your Ad law was made requiring candidates for federal office to identify themselves by name in their campaign advertisements and declare, "I approve this message." This law is not the only reason most of today's politicians are so tolerant of the vast array of front groups and dark money operations that dot the American political landscape, but it is a significant reason. Considering the content of the average political ad, it's no wonder politicians are reluctant to stand by their ads and prefer that surrogates spew the bile.

Most of these politicians and their surrogates profess to be church-going, God-fearing people. Nearly all claim to have accepted Jesus Christ as their Lord and savior. So what kind of message would Jesus approve in this day and age?

Would it not be something along these lines? "If you want to know my opponents' failings, you will have to discover them for yourselves. You will not hear of it from me. I will not tear them down to build myself up. If you wonder whether their attacks on me are true or false, you will have to determine that for yourselves. Believe them if you wish. I have nothing to offer in my defense. I have neither the time nor any justification to condemn those who speak against me. The well-being of the weakest and most vulnerable among us will be my first concern and top priority. The last will be put first. Blessed are those you call slackers and moochers and deadbeats. I will be their servant. I will stake their claim to a rightful share of our nation's bounty. I am not worthy to represent you, but only say the word, and I will do my best to lead our society toward the way of love, forgiveness, and charity. I am Jesus of Nazareth, and I approve this message."

In this land that so many insist is a Christian nation, would this message win the approval of a majority of voters? Not a chance. That says a lot about our politics, our morals, our practice of religion, and the condition of America's soul.

To hear professional political operatives tell it, winning elections is about nothing more or nothing less than mathematical calculations. It's all about data, and it's algorithmic. You gather all kinds of data about voters, use that data to target those most likely to vote for your candidate, write a formula for reaching your "win target," plug all the data into your formula, and out pops a victory. Sounds great, all scientific and everything, until what pops out is a loss.

One of the most glaring examples of data gone wrong was the 2016 presidential election. Clinton headquarters had the math all figured out. They shunned persuasion campaigning, meaning they didn't want to waste time trying to win over voters their computers told them were not likely to support the Democratic nominee. They saw it purely as a "base turnout" election. In other words, their data told them that if those identified as core Democratic supporters went to the polls and voted as expected, Hillary Clinton is elected president. In places like Wisconsin, Pennsylvania, and Michigan, where the election was decided, that didn't happen.[13]

They didn't factor into their equation Clinton's unpopularity and her inability to persuasively communicate reasons to support her. That left her base unenthusiastic and her opponents energized. This was hardly the first time voters have confounded the political mathematicians armed with all their data and their computers, nor will it be the last. In 2014, Democratic operatives in Wisconsin insisted that if turnout was high in the election for governor, their nominee Mary Burke would win. If turnout was low, Scott Walker would be re-elected. Voter turnout ended up being a record high for a regular election for governor in Wisconsin,[14] and yet Walker won. Like Team Clinton in 2016, Wisconsin Democrats concentrated on turning out their base for Burke in 2014. If their computers said you were a likely Burke voter for one reason or another, you were hounded. You got phone calls, emails, texts, and junk mail. People knocked on your door. You got so many reminders to vote that you were ready to scream. If the Democratic algorithm didn't have you down as a target, you were left alone. You were given no reason to think about voting for Burke. It turns out their algorithm was wrong.

There's a good reason why political algorithms are unreliable. Elections aren't algorithmic. Politics is more art than science. How voters make decisions can't be reduced to mathematical equations or scientific formulas. There is a human dimension that computers can't account for. Elections are about representation. Voters are looking for someone who gets them, someone who is saying what they are feeling and who reflects their thinking and will be somewhat likely to act accordingly. They look at candidates differently than computers do. They look at who a candidate is, where they're from, and what they stand for.

They look for someone they feel a connection with, someone they can relate to.

No algorithm can be written to produce that. And no algorithm can keep the republic. ✪

CHAPTER FOURTEEN
ENDING THE AGE OF BULLSHIT

In an election year with more than its share of too-strange-for-fiction storylines and salacious sideshows, one of the more meaningful stories of the 2016 presidential race was little told. Donald Trump spent about half as much as Hillary Clinton on his way to the White House.[1]

That fact didn't square with conventional wisdom. Most journalists have bought into the idea that money is the single most newsworthy factor in elections and confer viability on the candidates with the biggest war chests. Neither the reporters nor their go-to sources seem to have noticed, much less learned anything from what happened in the 2016 election for the nation's highest office. In the 2018 election for governor in Wisconsin, news media in the state had tiered coverage of the candidates based on their fundraising prowess. The state's second-largest newspaper, the *Wisconsin State Journal*, was most overt about it, expressly choosing to focus on the candidates who had raised enough money to hire campaign staff. I was fortunate to reach that qualifying threshold and was among those who were paid some attention. Close to a dozen other announced candidates who were actively campaigning did not and were ignored.

The reporters' stock in trade is conventional wisdom, and they are sticking to it. Who has the most money, and who's ahead in the polls is what passes for election news most days. Perhaps this helps explain why fewer people read what the reporters write and why so many of the companies employing them are slowly but surely going out of business. This is no gratuitous cheap shot. This is harsh reality. According to *Editor & Publisher*'s Newspaper DataBook, there were 126 fewer daily newspapers in 2014 than in 2004.[2] More than one out of every five local newspapers in America have closed since 2004, creating news deserts in communities across the country.[3]

Maybe those in the media are right about money being the thing that matters most in elections. Maybe they're wrong. I happen to believe they are wrong. But this I know for sure: If they're right and elections are mostly about money, then the people can't win. Some politician with the most money will win, but you won't. Your own elected representatives will have no choice but to ignore your wishes because they will be busy catering to the wishes of their biggest donors.

Elections should be about what kind of society we want to live in and how we could create such a place together. Instead, we're told by manipulative politicians that somebody living somewhere else is to blame for all our problems. We're told somebody somewhere is getting something we're not. And we're told by jaded journalists that those politicians are all we've got to choose from because they have enough money to be taken seriously, and those without enough money—however they define enough—aren't worth considering no matter how refreshing or inspiring they may be.

Once the votes are counted, and those elected are sworn in, their actions are reported in pretty much the same way the elections are covered. We're told which officials are most likely to get their way and which party stands the best chance of gaining the upper hand when all is said and done. Not much attention is given to how these actions will affect people's lives and whether their solutions to our problems will work.

In a front-page story in early 2019 about the proposed state budget put forward by Wisconsin's new governor Tony Evers, the *State Journal* told readers that the Republican-controlled state legislature "wholesale rejected his proposal."[4] Neither house had voted on it. They hadn't even held hearings on it yet. The article went on to quote former GOP assembly speaker Scott Jensen, saying, "The governor is trying to make happy all the Democratic constituency groups that helped him win this election narrowly. Unfortunately, that means he's built a budget that's a fantasy." The story neglected to mention that a clear majority of people in Wisconsin—Republicans, Democrats, and independents alike—favor much of what Jensen dismissed as fantasy.[5] The two reporters who wrote the story failed to grasp that Evers wasn't the one being "wholesale rejected" by lawmakers. They were telling the people of our state, most of whom support the governor's budget priorities, to get lost. Most want Wisconsin to capture federal funds to expand Medicaid and want the state to withdraw from the lawsuit aiming to repeal the federal health care law. Most want more funding for public schools and support increasing the minimum wage. Most want a nonpartisan approach to drawing the state's political boundaries. Most want marijuana use legalized.

The story also provided no useful context about the reporters' trusted source Scott Jensen, who was charged in 2002 with three felonies and a misdemeanor for criminal misconduct in office and was convicted on all charges in 2006 and sentenced to fifteen months in prison. He filed multiple appeals and delayed proceedings against him for years, finally convincing a state appeals court to grant him a new trial on a technicality and move the second trial to his home turf of Waukesha County, a Republican stronghold. In 2010, an old friend and political ally, then-Waukesha County district attorney and eventual state Attorney General Brad Schimel, offered him a plea deal, dismissing the felonies and letting Jensen plead no contest to an ethics code violation and pay a fine. Jensen went on to cash in on his connections with and service to billionaire school privatization advocates like the Walton and DeVos families to land a $200,000-a-year lobbying gig.[6]

At the same time, the online political news service WisPolitics.com was featuring Jensen and fellow disgraced politician Chuck Chvala—both barred from ever holding office in Wisconsin again—in an ongoing video series called *The Insiders* showcasing their views on Wisconsin politics and government. As chronicled in chapter 2, Chvala's career ended when he was charged with nineteen felonies for misconduct in office and making and extorting illegal campaign contributions. He pleaded guilty to two felonies and served a nine-month jail sentence.

Wisconsin's state capitol has become a house of ill repute and the legislature a parliament of whores. We are in the midst of total political system failure,[7] with the will of the people utterly disregarded, and journalists reporting for the *Wisconsin State Journal* and those who run WisPolitics.com feed their audiences the insights of career crooks. Regular working people are being screwed over, their wishes ignored by elected officials too busy fellating wealthy donors, and what's left of the capitol press corps—our eyes and ears in the halls of power—does its best Sergeant Schultz impersonation.

Good journalism is never neutral. Good journalists come down squarely on the side of truth and justice. They comfort the afflicted and afflict the comfortable. Bad ones are accomplices. With so many official lies and too many accessories to the crime, our current times will go down in history as the age of bullshit. Unless, of course, the manure spreaders somehow figure out a way to prevent the truth from ever being recorded for posterity. The powerful and privileged have always found honesty inconvenient. It has this pesky way of interfering with their plans. Their problem got way bigger in the twentieth century with the advent of radio and then television. Never before in human history could more sources of information reach mass audiences so quickly. The powerful and privileged knew they had to do something.

Step one was to do away with the Fairness Doctrine[8] and weaken other public interest obligations enshrined in the Radio Act of 1927 and the Communications Act of 1934 that for decades ensured everything from coverage of local issues to children's educational programming. Step two was to methodically demonize legitimate news reporting and convince a significant segment of the population to no longer trust what is reported. Not only were lies told, but a highly organized effort was made to persuade the public that no one was telling the truth. Journalism was being de-legitimized. Step three was the construction of their own alternative "news" operations. Free of the old requirements to serve the public interest, they could build their own propaganda machine. And they did.

The completion of these three steps brought about this era of fake news and alternative facts we now live in—the age of bullshit. The powerful and privileged succeeded. They may have been too successful for their own good. At first, they had to be delighted by how efficiently their machine worked. All across the nation, public offices were occupied by people who benefited from the falsehoods the machine spread but at least appeared to understand the truth. But now, a large and growing segment of society clearly embraces the lies and either won't or can't distinguish fiction from fact. More public offices are being occupied by such people, which has brought us to the point where those who've been empowered to govern aren't governing. Perhaps they've been entertaining fantasies and scapegoating and demonizing for so long that they've forgotten how to govern. Or maybe they never learned how. In any case, they can't possibly deliver what their propagandized constituents expect them to accomplish. They can't simultaneously cut taxes, drastically increase military spending, protect Social Security, balance the budget, and bring down the national debt. They can't create a private health insurance system with no government involvement that will cover everyone and cost less. They have no way of bringing back all the lost U.S. factory jobs in heavy manufacturing.

One of the minions of the powerful and privileged who helped spread the manure—longtime Milwaukee right-wing radio gabber Charlie Sykes—deserves credit for at least admitting he helped "create a monster" as he reflected on a president who "gives every indication that he is as much the gullible tool of liars as he is the liar in chief."[9] In 1795, Thomas Jefferson wrote that "light and liberty go together." By 1816, Jefferson's thinking on the matter sharpened: "If a nation expects to be ignorant and free in a state of civilization, it expects what never was and never will be." It sharpened more by 1821, almost as if he could see what was coming: "No nation is permitted to live in ignorance with impunity." One can only imagine what Jefferson would have to say in our day and age, with the U.S. ranking as one of the five most ignorant countries globally, according to the research firm Ipsos MORI's 2016 Index of Ignorance.[10]

If you take the long view of history, it's not only journalism that has strayed far from its mission. So has our educational system. What today are called public schools in America formerly were known as common schools. Central to the mission of common schools was civic literacy, which was seen as necessary to make democracy possible. The idea of schools as first and foremost laboratories of democracy and builders of social capital took root in the late 1700s and early 1800s, then started to fully blossom as the twentieth century dawned. In 1911, Wisconsin identified schools as "social centers" where not just students but anyone in the community could gather to discuss the issues of the day and develop solutions to the challenges facing society.[11]

Somewhere along the line, this mission has been lost. Today's schools focus on preparing the populace to participate in the economy but not our democracy. They concern themselves more with producing skilled workers than good citizens. Neither the school day nor the school year has been lengthened to speak of, but more hours of math and science have been ordered, and technology classes and vocational training have been added, meaning civic instruction is pushed aside.

How strange that in a country that boasts of being the world's greatest democracy, we really don't teach democracy. The workings of government are taught, sparingly and half-heartedly, but citizen engagement is not. It is exceedingly rare to find courses on the dynamics of social movements, or how to organize, or even how to responsibly consume media and distinguish between news and propaganda. Today's students spend less time exercising in gym class than I did when I was a boy, but even less time is devoted to learning how to exercise the five freedoms enshrined in the First Amendment to the Constitution.

In just forty-five words, our nation's founders gave us freedom of religion, freedom of speech, freedom of the press, the right to assemble peaceably, and the right to petition our government. Precious little time is spent in school examining those forty-five words much less exploring how to put them to use. Not surprisingly then, these five freedoms have never been more threatened than they are today. Press freedom is under assault as the president branded the news media an "enemy of the American people."[12] Free speech has become anything but free as the U.S. Supreme Court has ruled that money is speech, and corporations are citizens with speech rights, thereby blessing unlimited corporate election spending. Lawmakers in states all across the country have sought to criminalize freedom of assembly and peaceful protest.[13] Both of the First Amendment's religious freedom clauses are being ignored as non-Christians are subjected to increasing discrimination and even targeted for deportation.[14] The first of the two, namely the establishment clause, is disregarded as more and more American taxpayers are being forced to fund religious schools.

Here again, Wisconsin was America's weather vane. Nearly three decades ago, Wisconsin lawmakers blazed a new trail by creating the nation's first scholastic welfare program. It started in Milwaukee, expanded to Racine, and then was taken statewide. It started small, with just over 300 students. Now there are more than 30,000 in the program. It's officially called the Parental Choice Program. But if there were truth in labeling, it would be called what it is: taxpayer-subsidized private schooling. The small number of families getting the subsidies already had a choice. In fact, most of them were exercising their option to have their children privately schooled before state handouts were ever offered.[15] People who have the means to send their children to private schools can continue to send them to private schools but have the rest of us taxpayers pay their tuition for them.

The real kick in the teeth for taxpayers is that the value of the public-funded vouchers for private schooling is considerably higher than the amount of state aid for each student attending a public school in Wisconsin. By 2017, the state was spending more than $250 million on the Milwaukee, Racine, and statewide "parental choice" programs while cutting state aid to public schools by over $80 million to help pay for it. Taxpayers were picking up the tab to the tune of more than $7,300 for each elementary and middle school student and more than $7,900 for

MIKE McCABE

each high school student. Meanwhile, when you look at all the different forms of state aid to public schools, the amount being spent on each of the more than 870,000 students attending public schools is less than $6,000.[16] Let that sink in for a moment. The private schools serving scholastic welfare recipients are getting roughly 20 percent more state aid per student than the public schools educating everyone else's children are getting.

The lobbyists who sold Wisconsin lawmakers on this scheme more than a quarter of a century ago insisted at the time that the program would create competition and ultimately boost student achievement. It hasn't. After all these years, students getting taxpayer-subsidized private schooling are doing no better than their counterparts in public schools. If anything, they actually are doing somewhat worse.[17] And that holds true in other states that followed Wisconsin's lead.[18]

Scholastic welfare is a raw deal for taxpayers and a decades-long failure as an educational policy, but it has been very good for the campaign coffers of politicians.[19] And why is so much money thrown at politicians to keep expanding a program that has never delivered on its promises? To prop up private and parochial schools whose enrollments have been plummeting nationwide.[20] While private school enrollments in Wisconsin were falling statewide, they were increasing in the counties where the scholastic welfare program was started.[21] Keeping failing private schools alive is the one thing this program has succeeded in doing. That's why Wisconsin's program was expanded statewide in 2013.

"School choice" is one of the latest in a series of fads that have blown over American education. It was promoted as a miracle cure for what ailed American education. As it became increasingly clear that taxpayer-subsidized private schooling had no magical powers, the "school accountability" movement took hold, and students started being tested to death. It enriched the standardized testing industry but has done little else. Then came the "school to work" craze and "STEM education"—shorthand for a school curriculum focused on science, technology, engineering, and mathematics. These fixations haven't prevented the American education system from continuing to slide toward mediocrity internationally[22] but have driven teaching of the arts and civics to the brink of extinction.

Education is important, and good schools are preferable to mediocre or poor ones, so we must rearrange our priorities because America is no longer even close to providing the best education in the world. The road to an improved U.S. education system is long and winding, but spend some time talking to the front-line soldiers in the education wars—classroom teachers—and they'll clue you in on some good places to start the journey.

First, keep state and national politicians as far away from schools as possible. It's a crying shame it has come to this, but the less education is pondered on Capitol Hill and in state capitols, the better off schools will be. Restoring local community control of schools needs to be job one.

Second, stop testing kids to tears. All the incessant testing done nowadays hurts students by cutting deeply into the time devoted to actual teaching and learning. The politicians' testing fetish grew out of a desperate desire to do an end run around a reality they find intolerably uncomfortable: Even the very best educators will almost always fail when they work in inadequately equipped schools and are tasked with teaching profoundly disadvantaged students. Rather than try to eliminate, or at least diminish, the disadvantages, the politicians look for an easier route. Nonstop testing gives them someone to point fingers at. It produces a plentiful supply of scapegoats but does little or nothing to help struggling students learn better or all students learn more.

Third, align expectations with investments. Excellence doesn't come cheap. It is no coincidence that the best performing schools are consistently found where education spending is highest.[23] But this is another reality that politicians find uncomfortable, which is why they are forever in search of the scholastic equivalent of fairy dust and why American education is so prone to fads.

The national group Parents Across America points to one strategy in particular that has proven effective over the years: class size reduction.[24] But having smaller classes means hiring more teachers, and that costs money. Replacing the industrial-age factory model of schools and the mass-production, assembly-line approach to instruction with a more personalized, flexible, and interactive approach can reverse the decline of U.S. educational performance. Still, it requires smaller classes and smaller schools, and that gives politicians the willies. As a society, we have decisions to make and priorities to set. If we expect excellence, we need to act like that's what we want. If we can live with diminished international competitiveness that comes with increasing educational mediocrity here at home, then fads and fairy dust will do just fine.

From the time of our nation's founding through the first 180 years of the American experiment, our country's motto was *E Pluribus Unum*. In 1956, it was officially changed to *In God We Trust*. But with legions of Americans pessimistic about the future[25]—even more pessimistic than people in economically underdeveloped countries[26]—it's almost as if the unofficial slogan of the U.S. has become *No We Can't*.

When it is suggested that we should stop sentencing the nation's youth to debt and make education as affordable for our children and grandchildren as past generations made it for us, this aspiration is widely dismissed as a pipe dream. Some bitterly grumble about "free stuff," while many others wonder aloud how we could possibly pay to extend the promise of free public education through college. Seemingly forgotten is that past generations of Americans created and paid for a system of free public education through high school, and they were far poorer than we are now when they did it. Many who paid had no high school diploma of their own at the time but knew that industrialization meant that many of their kids and grandkids would be leaving the land and heading to factories and offices and would need more education and job training if they were to have a shot at experiencing the American Dream. So they dug deep and provided future generations that shot.

Is a high school diploma alone a sure pathway to the American Dream today? The answer is obvious. No. Then where is the resolve in us that our grandparents and great-grandparents had in such abundance? Where in us is their willingness to pay it forward?

When it is suggested that every American should be able to get medical care, this ambition is roundly condemned as pie in the sky. Calls for universal health insurance produce more griping about free stuff and many a baseless claim that guaranteeing medical care for everyone would be the mother of all job killers. Forgotten is how past generations of Americans who had far less than we have today made rampant poverty among the nation's elderly a thing of the past by creating and paying for such things as Social Security and Medicare, and these inventions didn't ruin the economy. They didn't even slow it down. The U.S. economic engine roared as never before.

When it is suggested that high-speed internet and mobile phone service be brought to every doorstep in America, this digital-age necessity is shouted down as an unaffordable extravagance. More complaining about free stuff ensues. Forgotten is how past generations of Americans found it within their limited means to pay to bring electricity not only to every city neighborhood but every farmhouse and barn in the country. Electric companies would never have taken on the expense of stringing electrical wires down every backroad just to pick up a handful of additional customers. Rural electrification took a decades-long national effort. We all benefit today from that massive undertaking past generations of Americans were willing to support. Today's telecoms aren't going to lay fiber-optic or erect cell towers or mount transmitters in every nook and cranny of the country just to get a few extra customers. The realization of universal access to high-speed internet and wireless voice services will again require a sustained national effort.

In so many ways, we have more going for us today than past generations did. We have more money than they had, we are more highly educated than they were, we have far more material possessions, more free time on our hands, not to mention more and better ways to communicate with each other. The one and perhaps only thing they had, and we seem to lack, is their optimism and boundless faith in America's potential.

We won't rediscover that faith with ongoing and escalating attacks on the separation of church and state that threaten religious freedom. State-endorsed religion is a small step from state-sponsored religion, which is another small step away from state-imposed religion. Faith in America's future won't be restored by passively accepting the equating of money and speech that is transforming a central First Amendment right into a commodity that must be purchased at great expense. When calls to limit the capacity of the rich and powerful to buy politicians and own our government are savaged as assaults on free speech, we are essentially being told we can try to deal with corruption in government, or we can have free speech, but not both. This is a false choice and must be seen as such. We can have freedom *and* democracy. We can guarantee all people the right to speak freely without, at the same time, granting them a license to buy off our elected representatives and corrupt our government.

Seeing through patently false choices and genuinely fake news is integral to bringing the age of bullshit to a close and unscrewing America. To ultimately succeed, we have to recommit ourselves to teaching democracy. And we the people are going to have to prove that the land of the free is still the home of the brave. We're going to have to demonstrate courage in defending dissent and condemning attacks on peaceful protest. We're going to have to stand up for a free press and make it clear we do not see journalists as our enemies but rather as indispensable defenders of democracy. If we don't, those forty-five words describing five precious freedoms won't be worth the parchment they were written on. ✪

CHAPTER FIFTEEN
THE ART OF THE ORDEAL

It seems almost everyone is down on America. Talk to foreigners and you get the sense that the consensus around the world is that Americans must be taking leave of their senses. There is a lot of head scratching about the political choices we are making and a lot of head shaking about the general direction of the country. Talk to Americans pretty much anywhere and you get the sense that the belief here is that the country's future has never been cloudier and that national decline is more or less inevitable.

Shrewd investors buy when almost everyone's selling and sell when others are buying. Apply that logic to the fate of nations, and now must be a good time to be bullish on our country.

Yes, politics here is ugly at the moment—a national embarrassment. But it's worth remembering that gutter politics is as old as the republic. George Washington was called a "thin-skinned tyrant" by his opponents. John Adams' supporters slammed Thomas Jefferson as an "apostle of anarchy and a trickster." Teddy Roosevelt once said President William McKinley had the "backbone of a chocolate eclair." Abraham Lincoln was maligned as a "third-rate backwoods lawyer." That was the tamest of insults aimed in his direction. *Harper's Weekly* said he was a "filthy story-teller, ignoramus, despot, old scoundrel, big secessionist, perjurer, liar, robber, thief, swindler, braggart, tyrant, buffoon, fiend, usurper, butcher, monster, land-pirate, and a long, lean, lank, lantern-jawed, high-cheeked-boned, spavined, rail-splitting stallion."[1] Makes "Crooked Hillary" seem like child's play.

Yes, Americans currently are politically polarized, and partisan divisions are sharp. But we've been at each other's throats many times before. The union survived civil war. Not only did the highest court in the land once declare that people could be property, it also once blessed forcibly sterilizing people deemed unfit to procreate.[2] As many as 70,000 people became victims of state-ordered sterilization, some because they were considered "feebleminded" or "mentally deficient," others because they were deaf, blind, or diseased. Minorities and the poor often were targeted. The mood of the country in 1927 was such that it wasn't a close vote. Legal giant Oliver Wendell Holmes wrote for the eight-to-one majority, favoring selective breeding to purify the national gene pool, with liberal lion Louis Brandeis among those who joined him.

Yes, the challenges facing us today are enormous and vexing, from the ecological threat of an overheating planet to the economic trauma associated with deindustrialization and globalization. But America is in the process of being transformed in spite of our backward politics. The collective thinking of Americans about sexual orientation, gender, and race has been evolving and will continue to. This evolution has triggered a powerful backlash, but the arc of American beliefs and values bends toward greater tolerance and social justice. The road to economic renewal is a bumpy one, but Americans are slowly but surely adapting to both the savagery and opportunities found in the new global economy.

Yes, this is an uncomfortable time. Living in interesting times is said to be the Chinese curse. We're living in uncomfortable times. That's the American blessing. Life in America is changing rapidly, and change is discomforting. Discomfort brings about renewal. Comfortable people don't move. They stay where they are because they are comfortable there. To make them move, they have to be made uncomfortable. It's like the basic law of physics: An object at rest will remain at rest, unless some force makes it move. A corrupted society will stay corrupt, unless some force makes the powers-that-be change their ways. That force is discomfort.

Anxiety and fear about the country's future are running high among tens of millions of Americans. The only thing that seems certain for the time being is uncertainty. Official reassurances that unemployment is falling and the economy is booming mean nothing to someone who once earned twenty-five dollars an hour working in a factory before that work was exported overseas, and the best available replacement job pays maybe twelve or thirteen dollars an hour. For someone whose standard of living has been cut in half, claims of economic prosperity are an abstraction. For them, the American Dream appears to be in the process of downsizing. And worse yet, their gut tells them their children will probably have it harder than they've had it.

The discomfort this reality produces fueled a reactionary, authoritarian populism that gave rise to the Tea Party movement and paved a route to the White House for Donald Trump. America now stands at a crossroads. We can take a divisive, backward-looking, destructive path, or we can choose a uniting, forward-looking, constructive route. For the moment, a large segment of the population appears to favor the former for lack of a well-defined and compelling alternative. A better road won't be paved until people who are disturbed by the direction we're currently heading get uncomfortable enough to blaze a different trail. Those alarmed by the actions of the radical right are going to have to warm up to agitation and provocation. They are going to have to make friends with discomfort.

America needs a revolution. Nothing less than the overthrow of the creatures who have commandeered our public institutions will do. I use the word *creatures* deliberately because not all of those doing the commandeering take a human form. The majority of judges on the highest court in our land stretched the definition of "we the people" to include things created and operated by actual people, namely corporations. Defining things as people and bestowing on those things what amounts to full rights of citizenship does horrific violence to democracy. It leaves us with a rigged political system, one where the

MIKE McCABE

supposed representatives of we the people shamelessly and shamefully cater to a wealthy few and ignore the wishes and needs of the masses.

America's dormant revolutionary spirit needs reawakening. Say the word *revolution* today and people squirm, seemingly forgetting that the U.S. is the product of revolt against a king's power. For too many of us, revolution sounds uncomfortably subversive. We overlook for comfort's sake that our nation's founders were nothing if not subversive. Thomas Jefferson believed each generation should have its own revolution and went so far as to suggest that every generation should tear up the Constitution and start over. Jefferson famously said that expecting each new generation to forever live by the customs and laws of past generations is like expecting adults to wear the same clothes that fit them as children. Jefferson had to have known he was speaking not only to his living fellow countrymen but to future generations as well. His unquestionably subversive, revolutionary thinking is still there for us to ponder.

The clothes no longer fit. Yes, America needs a revolution—a revolution of spirit.

Yes, we have to rescue democracy. The likes of Gilens and Page say we don't have a democracy in America anymore. It's not just academic researchers who are saying it. I hear it or see it almost every day. Somebody says it at a meeting or posts it as a comment on an internet message board or social media site. It's embedded in a question asked at some public forum. It's on a sign at a demonstration. Democracy in America has been killed. It's dead. I disagree for many reasons, not the least of which is that democracy is more verb than noun, and verbs can't be killed. Democracy is something we will have so long as it continues to be something enough of us do. There's no overlooking the fact that democracy is gravely ill in many respects. There is a crisis of faith in the American political system and almost total lack of confidence in elected officials and the major political parties. Most Americans do not believe their votes count for much, do not believe their voices are heard, and do not believe their interests are being served. They have good reasons for those beliefs. Democracy is dependent on many things, but none more important than the consent of the governed. What passes for consent of the governed nowadays is frightening when you consider what most Americans think of those doing the governing and further consider how elected officials demonstrate that they don't care what the general public thinks. To unscrew America, democracy has to be resuscitated. But that's not enough.

Yes, we have to rediscover our sense of national purpose and rekindle faith in the American Dream. There is not only a crisis of faith in the political system, but also a crisis of faith in the form of a widespread fear that future generations will be worse off than those who came before them. This anxiety leaves too many among us resigned to the inevitability of national decline. Broad public acceptance of the notion that the American Dreams of future generations must necessarily be downsized is as poisonous to our country as the subversion and perversion of democracy. Today's lack of trust in government is as understandable as it is correctable. But given the upbringing of so many of us, the erosion of faith in the future of our country is curious. So many of us were taught to believe in the Resurrection, to believe in one who conquered death, and to believe that He will come again. Yet despite this fidelity to gospel, the idea that America's best days are behind her has spread among us like a virus. Nagging doubt about our nation's ability to bounce back has become contagious. This loss of spirit can be overcome only through the sheer force of will. To unscrew America, we have to start thinking big again, the way we did when we shot for the moon. But that's not enough.

Yes, we need to democratize our economy. America is growing apart economically. We need to grow together. We need three bottom lines in business. We need financially profitable companies that treat workers and customers justly and are careful stewards of natural resources. We need to come to terms with how immigrants and racial minorities get scapegoated when jobs paying a living wage are hard to come by and when family-supporting employment is being outsourced, offshored, or automated out of existence. To unscrew America, we need an economy that is of the people, by the people, and for the people. But that's not enough.

MIKE McCABE

Yes, we need a moral reckoning and a new social contract, a covenant between us describing what we all are called to do for our country and each other. We need to remember the forgotten people living in forgotten places. We need to figure out how to have civil conversations and build solid relationships with those we currently count as enemies. And we need to face down our greatest national demon—race. No nation filled with hate can be great. To unscrew America, we need to overpower hate. But that's still not enough.

Yes, we need to rethink our relationship with our planet. This is a matter of our species' survival. We cannot hurt the planet without harming ourselves. We cannot destroy Earth and somehow sidestep our own destruction. Try as we might to ignore it or deny it, our fate is tied to the place we inhabit. The climate crisis is real, and of all our planet's inhabitants, we are by far the most responsible for it. To unscrew America, we need to stop viewing environmental protection as the enemy of economic development and start seeing how kicking our fossil fuel addiction and becoming the first nation to be fully powered by renewable energy is not only essential to the well-being of the planet but also can usher in the next industrial revolution. But that's not enough.

Yes, we need to get serious about civic education and commit ourselves to teach democracy again. And we need to re-legitimize journalism. The old model of news gathering and information dissemination is breaking down. We need to make a new one. No nation can be ignorant and free. We need to aspire to intelligence, not belittle it. Becoming well educated and informed and thinking critically has to be valued and expected, not feared or obstructed. It is our best hope for building a better and more prosperous future and our best weapon against economic and social decline. To unscrew America, we need to harness the power of knowledge and favor uncomfortable truths over convenient lies. But that's not enough.

As Gandhi said: "As human beings, our greatness lies not so much in being able to remake the world as in being able to remake ourselves."

I've been blessed to travel to every part of America's weather vane to meet with people living in very different places and living very different lives. Everywhere I've gone, I've heard about people's challenges, hopes, fears, dreams, and nightmares. What I've heard sometimes sounds defeatist. Other times powerless. Occasionally hopeless. Or even helpless. I get where these feelings come from. So much inequality. So much injustice. So much economic insecurity. So many barriers to real political representation. So many looming threats on the horizon. So many reasons to believe America is screwed. People want to curl up in a ball.

Acting on this impulse, many abandon civic duty and withdraw from public life. They say they don't want to talk about politics much less take part in it. They say it does no good. The major parties are useless, and the system is rigged. Voting only encourages them, they say. Many choose not to think about the climate crisis. In all my travels—more than four times around the world without once leaving Wisconsin—I lost count of the number of people I encountered who you could probably classify as climate change deniers. Yet only a few deny the weather is changing. Only a handful dispute that human behavior is driving the change. They just don't think we can act quickly enough to do anything about it, so they choose not to worry. They don't want to talk about it or think about it.

This is the biggest reason why America is screwed. It's not the economy. It's not the government. It's not the schools. Or the news media. It's not even apathy. It's powerlessness.

There is a world of difference between apathy and powerlessness. Apathy is not caring. From what I can tell based on thousands of conversations in hundreds of places, the powerless seem to care a great deal about what's happening in our country. They just don't think there is a damn thing they can do about it.

I'll grant you, the odds are stacked against us. The odds have never favored common folk. But the abolitionists did end slavery. The suffragists got women the vote. The progressives who were up against the robber barons in the Gilded Age beat them. The exploited West

Virginia coal miners formed unions. Textile mills were forced to respect child labor laws. Civil rights activists ended Jim Crow. Marriage equality, regardless of sexual orientation, is now the law of the land.

All of these advances were made against seemingly insurmountable odds. Many who were instrumental in bringing about the change never were able to enjoy the fruits of their labor. Think for a moment about those suffragists. So many women who fought for the right to vote did not live long enough to ever cast a ballot. Giants in the women's suffrage movement like Susan B. Anthony, Elizabeth Cady Stanton, and Lucy Stone all passed away more than a decade before the Nineteenth Amendment, giving women the right to vote was ratified in 1920. Stone's death came more than twenty-five years before the Constitution was amended. Suffragists not only marched for the right, but some were beaten and imprisoned and tortured in jail.[3] Countless lesser-known crusaders for the vote devoted their lives to the cause but did not live to see the Nineteenth Amendment ratified. Rowena Granice Steele died in 1901, but not before her novel *The Victims of Fate* became the first written by a woman to be published in California. Esther Hobart Morris, who became the first woman justice of the peace in the U.S., died in 1902. Helen Pitts, perhaps best known as the second wife of Frederick Douglass, died in 1903. Sarah E. Wall, who led a successful anti-tax protest in Massachusetts defending a woman's right not to be subjected to taxation without representation, died in 1907. Julia Ward Howe, best known for writing "The Battle Hymn of the Republic," died in 1910.[4]

At the time of their deaths, it could have been said that all of these women lost. After all, they died without winning the right they devoted their lives to securing. But knowing now how they paved the way for generations of women after them to have the vote and gain political clout, knowing now what they never knew during their lifetimes, it is clear they did not fail. The losses they endured served a grand purpose.

Just as apathy and powerlessness are two entirely different things, so too are optimism and hope. As the Czech dissident and author turned statesman Václav Havel wrote: "Hope ... is not the same as joy that things are going well, or willingness to invest in enterprises that are obviously headed for early success, but rather an ability to work for something because it is good, not just because it stands a chance to succeed. The more unpromising the situation in which we demonstrate hope, the deeper that hope is. Hope is not the same thing as optimism. It is not the conviction that something will turn out well, but the certainty that something makes sense, regardless of how it turns out."[5]

More than half a century before Havel wrote that, the suffragists understood and acted on it. They had hope, and they gave it to those who followed in their footsteps.

There is a lesson there for all of us who are anguishing over the condition of our country today. Americans are obsessed with winning. Few things bother most Americans more than losing. A great football coach once summed up the American psyche: "Winning isn't everything, it's the only thing." That line is often attributed to legendary Green Bay Packers coach Vince Lombardi.[6] Lombardi wasn't the first to say it. Maybe he heard it first from college football coach Red Sanders, who said it close to a decade before Lombardi made the aphorism famous. Maybe he lifted his signature saying from the 1953 John Wayne movie *Trouble Along the Way*. But eventually, even Lombardi came to realize winning isn't the be-all and end-all. Roughly three years after he made the "only thing" remark, he offered an amended version: "Winning isn't everything, but wanting to win is."[7]

Good coaches are good teachers, and they realize that more can be learned from a loss than a win. They tend to see long winning streaks as fool's gold because they know from experience that bad habits have a way of forming while their teams are stringing together wins, and those habits are only exposed as damaging after they lead to a defeat. So it is in politics and life. You win some and you lose some. But when you lose, you need to lose with a purpose. Something has to be gained from every defeat. Seeds planted during today's loss grow into the fruits of tomorrow's victory. How you lose is what defines you.

In recent times, Republicans have lost much more purposefully than Democrats. Democratic Party dominance in the 1960s, and especially

Barry Goldwater's landslide loss in 1964, inspired the 1971 Powell Memo that was a blueprint for a merger of corporation and state and an accompanying Republican renaissance.[8] The Democratic establishment's response to what the Powell Memo has wrought has been curious. Back in 2014, I wrote about a young woman from farm country who ran for a seat in the state assembly a couple of years earlier and how she was coached by Democratic operatives to avoid being pinned down on issues and to steer clear of controversial stands. The Democrats' nominee for governor at the time similarly advised her to be as vague as possible on the issues and said her job as a candidate was to be "present and pleasant." She took their advice. She lost.[9]

Since then, I've lost count of the number of former candidates for state and federal offices who have told me they received the same coaching. They followed the same advice and also lost. In fact, Democrats lost twice in these instances. They lost those elections, but by saying or doing little or nothing to challenge the other side's orthodoxy and to get voters to start thinking differently, conditions favorable to winning future elections are not created. Democrats across the country have made a habit of running scared for the sake of "electability" and then gone on to lose anyway.[10] You lose sometimes. I ran and I lost. But every loss has to have a purpose. There was a purpose to the early suffragists' losses. In 1964, Barry Goldwater ran defiantly as an unabashed defender of conservative values. He lost, but it sparked a movement that transformed the Republican Party. There was a purpose to Goldwater's defeat. It paved the road Ronald Reagan took to the White House a decade and a half later. Present and pleasant serves no purpose.

There is nothing more integral to unscrewing America than ditching the "winning is the only thing" mindset and gaining an appreciation for the importance of losing purposefully. While sport is less important than politics, it is a far better teacher. Politicians didn't teach me the value of patience, stamina, and faith. Sports did. More specifically, baseball did. Great teams lose seventy games in a season. Good major league hitters fail more than seven out of every ten times they go to bat. Perhaps more so than in any other sport, baseball players have to make peace with failure.

Then there's my favorite team. I am a lifelong, diehard Chicago Cubs fan. I inherited the affliction from my dad, who inherited it from his. One hundred and eight years. That's how long Cubs fans had to wait. My dad didn't live to see it. I did.

If David Ross's story had been peddled in Hollywood as a movie script, it surely would have been rejected as stranger than fiction—too corny and implausible. Ross was an aging backup catcher, playing out the final year of an unspectacular career for a team that had become synonymous with futility. He had never been an All-Star. He had never led his team in any offensive category. His career batting average was a paltry .229. Then he hits a home run in game seven of the World Series and gets carried off the field on the shoulders of his teammates, a hero and champion.[11]

The 2016 World Series was epic. Truly one for the ages. And from my admittedly biased vantage point, what the Cubs did ranks among the single greatest accomplishment in the history of any sport. It's right up there with the Miracle on Ice and Secretariat's still-unparalleled record-smashing run to the Triple Crown and Jesse Owens winning four gold medals in the 1936 Berlin Olympics with Hitler watching. The Cubs not only broke a 108-year championship drought, but they won it all with a target the size of Donald Trump's ego on their backs. Before the first stretching exercise or the first warm-up pitch in spring training, the nation's sportswriters, TV commentators, and baseball analysts made the Cubs the odds-on favorite to win the World Series. These Cubs had to deal with the added pressure that comes with having nearly everyone saying that anything short of a title would be an underachievement. And that's not the only burden they were carrying. They had a monkey the size of King Kong on their backs. Winning a World Series is hard under any circumstances. But proving you can run and throw and catch and hit better than any other team in Major League Baseball is impossibly difficult while carrying a billy goat, a black cat, Steve Bartman, and the torment of millions of fans on your shoulders.[12]

The Cubs did the impossible. And to do it, they had to dig out of a three-games-to-one hole, twice winning elimination games with their backs to the wall to force a deciding game seven. And then they had to overcome the trauma of blowing a commanding 5–1 lead in that do-or-die situation. David Ross entered the game in the fifth inning as a defensive replacement with his team holding that four-run lead over the relentless Cleveland Indians. With a runner on first base and needing just one out to end the inning, Cleveland's Jason Kipnis hit a dribbler in front of the plate. The player teammates and fans alike called Grandpa Rossy fielded the ball and threw it wildly, well out of the reach of Cubs first baseman Anthony Rizzo. The runners advanced to second and third. Then Cubs pitcher Jon Lester spiked a curveball in the dirt in front of home plate that bounced up and hit Ross in the mask, ricocheting toward the Cubs dugout on the first base side. Two runs scored, slicing the Cubs' lead to 5–3.

Ross redeemed himself in the top of the sixth, hitting the unlikeliest of home runs with two strikes against him off Cleveland ace reliever Andrew Miller to get the lead back up to 6–3. In the bottom of the eighth, the first two Cleveland hitters were retired. Jose Ramirez kept the Indians' hopes alive with a single up the middle. Brandon Guyer worked the next at-bat to a 3–2 count against Cubs flame-throwing closer Aroldis Chapman before ripping a double to deep center field, scoring Ramirez and cutting the Cubs' lead to 6–4. With Guyer on second, with a 2–2 count on Indians outfielder Rajai Davis, Ross thought Chapman could get a blazing fastball past Davis to end the inning, and he signaled the Cubs' pitcher to throw his heater. Davis somehow caught up with the pitch and hit a line drive down the left-field line for a two-run home run tying the game at 6–6.

With the Cubs' lead surrendered and the momentum swung decisively in favor of Cleveland, what happened next seemed to me to be nothing short of heavenly intervention. It rained. It was as if Harry Caray, Ernie Banks, and multitudes of departed Cubs fans like my dad and mom and sister Linda and brother Dan decided these Cubs were carrying too heavy a burden and needed a moment to gather themselves. The rains came down. The game was stopped for something like seventeen minutes. It was as if Cubs fans from the great beyond were telling all these Cubs what the grizzled Ross told his teammate Rizzo in the dugout earlier in the game when the young first baseman said within range of television microphones that he was an "emotional wreck." With the tarp briefly covering the field, the whole team was given a chance to "just continue to breathe."

The Cubs immediately struck in the top of the tenth, scoring twice to take a two-run lead. Of course, it wasn't going to end like that. Of course, the Indians would fight back to draw to within a run in the bottom of the tenth. Of course, the tying run was going to be on base and the winning run at the plate when the last out was finally made. This was not going to be easy. And then did you see what I saw? A smile crossed third baseman Kris Bryant's face before he fielded the grounder and made the throw across the diamond to Rizzo at first base to end it. The kind of smile that comes when a great burden is lifted. They did it. They won it all.

In times of need, inspiration comes to us from unexpected sources. It's hard to imagine a more unexpected source than those lovable losers on Chicago's north side. But inspire they did. They showed us faith is rewarded, even if it takes 108 years for the reward to come.

With so many Americans feeling screwed over and believing their country is screwed up, it's worth reminding ourselves that the challenges we face today are not new. They are as old as the hills. It's useful to remember that it's darkest before the dawn. The intensity of the efforts by America's current rulers to plunge the country into total darkness must be a sure sign that dawn approaches. In his first inaugural address, Franklin Delano Roosevelt famously told a nation facing one of America's darkest hours that the only thing we have to fear is fear itself. The resolve and emotional toughness Roosevelt called upon as the country descended into a Great Depression is conspicuously missing today. America is full of fear, largely because the nation's very un-Roosevelt-like leaders and the mass media keep feeding us reasons to be afraid. We are told to fear for our safety. We are told to fear foreigners. We are told to fear people we think look like foreigners. We are constantly warned of predators in our midst who aim to scam us or rob us or do us physical harm. Republicans tell us to fear Democrats. Democrats tell us to fear Republicans.

We are better than this. Or at least we could be. In a speech to Congress delivered on January 6, 1941, Roosevelt spoke of "basic things expected by our people of their political and economic systems," including "equality of opportunity for youth and for others, jobs for those who can work, security for those who need it, the ending of special privilege for the few, the preservation of civil liberties for all, and the enjoyment of the fruits of scientific progress in a wider and constantly rising standard of living." He then spelled out four essential freedoms. The first was freedom of speech and expression, not just in America but everywhere in the world. Second, FDR spoke of freedom of worship. He emphasized the importance of allowing every person to worship God "in his own way" and again emphasized such freedom needs to be guaranteed everywhere in the world. To FDR's way of thinking, religious freedom and religious tolerance went hand in hand. They were, in fact, inseparable. And for anyone to be free, everyone must be free. Roosevelt's third freedom was freedom from want. Roosevelt said that meant "economic understandings which will secure to every nation a healthy peacetime life for its inhabitants everywhere in the world." Last, but certainly not least, was freedom from fear. He dreamed out loud of curtailing war-making capacity so that no nation would be in a position to commit an act of physical aggression against any neighbor anywhere in the world.

His words are a timely reminder about the importance of dealing with the countless fears and insecurities that have Americans so spooked today. What he described is not too much to expect in our own time. This is not too much to aspire to. This is nothing to be afraid of.

I am like that aging backup catcher reaching the end of an unspectacular career. I've become well acquainted with losing. I am better for the losses. They haven't made me love my country less or shaken my faith in her potential. Still, there are nagging questions.

How come we need so many gates and locks and walls? How'd so many scaredy-cats take up residence in the home of the brave? Growing up on the farm, we didn't have locks on our doors. Now there are gated communities with home security systems and video surveillance.

Why have we become so suspicious and fearful of strangers? Mom *always* had a fresh-baked cake or pie on hand in case someone came calling. Extending hospitality to strangers was a duty. I get why little children are told not to talk to strangers. I don't get why so many adults think they shouldn't either.

When and why did we become so quick to judge and eager to condemn others? We're all human. We all make mistakes. But we grow less willing to cut anyone some slack. In his book *One Summer: America, 1927* author Bill Bryson wrote there "may never have been another time in the nation's history when more people disliked more other people from more directions and for less reason." It feels like the 1920s again in that regard.

How'd we let ourselves get so addicted to entertainment? As our collective hunger to be entertained continues to grow, our thirst for news and knowledge and human interaction diminishes. For evidence, look no further than the evolution of television programming in America. TV feeds us what we are hungry for. Today's menu is nothing if not an alarm bell.

What happened to saving for a rainy day, picking up after ourselves, and putting things back where we found them? Somewhere along the line, a whole lot of us decided to reject those teachings from our childhood. We want it all, and we want it now. Buy today, pay tomorrow. At the same time, we are growing increasingly disconnected from the land. We don't see ourselves as guests on this planet, we see ourselves as owners. That arrogance not only threatens Earth, it imperils the human species.

Why and how have so many of us come to feel so helpless in the face of political corruption and economic inequality, and somehow

unworthy to be agents of change? Our country has faced impossibly difficult-to-solve problems and mammoth crises many times before, and past generations of Americans consistently rose to the occasion and came up with solutions and brought about a better day. They were less educated than we are, had less money than we do, and had far fewer means of communication. Yet they proved smart enough, showed themselves to be plenty enterprising, and found ways to make their voices heard. Time after time, through the sheer force of will, they made America a better country. Why not us, why not here, and why not now?

Yes, America has some king-sized challenges. Economic insecurity. Stagnant wages. Growing inequality. Nagging fear that the nation's children will end up worse off than their parents. Strained social relations. Political parties that offer empty promises and false choices when they are not pointing fingers of blame at the other side. Collapsing public confidence in those parties and the democratic process. Those fond of domestic tranquility are in for a bumpy ride and a bitterly disappointing next few years. America is on a collision course with social, economic, and political upheaval.

In their provocative book *The Fourth Turning*, authors William Strauss and Neil Howe suggest there is a predictable rhythm to social conditions and change, with alternating periods of progress, decay, and renewal. According to Strauss and Howe, each generation has distinct characteristics that contribute to the perpetual change and occasional upheaval societies experience. Over the course of what they describe as a "natural century," or roughly the length of a normal human life, there are four identifiable phases or "turnings."

A first turning is marked by a **high**, that euphoric buzz that accompanies a recent overhaul of the social order. Faith in institutions is high, and society is confident of where it is headed collectively. These heady times are followed by an **awakening** when institutions begin to be questioned and attacked in the name of personal autonomy. Just when society is reaching a high tide of public progress, people tire of communal discipline and long for more individual satisfaction and enjoyment.

Awakenings invariably produce an **unraveling**. Public institutions become weak and distrusted. Individualism flourishes. More than one observer has noticed that the early part of the twenty-first century has amounted to a "great unraveling."[1314] After unraveling comes **crisis**. Fourth turnings are phoenix moments when societies are reborn—as if arising from the ashes—and national identity is redefined. Institutions are torn down and rebuilt from the ground up in response to a perceived threat to the nation's very survival. Civic life revives, and a sense of community purpose reemerges.

America's last fourth turning began with the stock market crash of 1929 and climaxed with World War II, followed by a prolonged post-war high, closely tracing the telltale pattern Strauss and Howe identified. Highs follow crises when society senses it must coalesce and rebuild. Unravelings come on the heels of awakenings when the social impulse is to fragment and enjoy. As the title of their book implies, the U.S. is now entering a fourth turning. Our country has gone through this three times before. The first was at the time of the nation's founding and culminated with the American Revolution. The second was the nation's reckoning with the scourge of slavery and the resulting Civil War. The third was the Great Depression and World War II.

The impending crisis in our day and age grows out of the chaos of economic globalization, the concentration of wealth and power in fewer and fewer hands, and global environmental emergency. Public institutions are in tatters, having fallen victim to the loss of civic consciousness that came with the great unraveling. The major political parties are failing. The Republican Party was established by radicals who sought to overthrow morally bankrupt institutions and remake the social order. It now works to ward off social change and protect the privileges of the high and mighty. The Democratic Party has spent an enormous amount of energy trying to make amends for being on the wrong side of history with respect to slavery and even emerged as a force for considerable good under the leadership of FDR at a time of national and global crisis. But since then, the Democrats have experienced their own great unraveling, to the point where it is known to most Americans simply as the party of more government and higher

MIKE McCABE

taxes. At a time when society has grown wary, if not resentful, of public authority and once-stout public institutions are being torn to pieces, being the party of government is not solid ground to stand on. Today's Democrats are easy prey for opponents wishing to caricature them as a party that takes from people who work and gives to people who don't.

Meanwhile, economic and environmental challenges and demand for social change are reaching a boiling point. Another phoenix moment fast approaches. With the enormity of today's challenges, this is no time for pussyfooting.

America is never finished. It is always a work in progress. Instead of throwing up our hands, we can get to work making our country what we want it to be. We don't need hate to fuel us. We can follow the Golden Rule. We can love thy neighbor. We can lean on each other and look out for one another. We don't need to tear someone down to build ourselves up. That's what bullies do. We can be better than bullies. We don't need to worry about greatness. We do need to concentrate on goodness, now more than ever. We don't need to repeal any unjust laws for us to make change. When we make change, then those unjust laws will be repealed. We don't need what all that money buys the politicians. We don't need pollsters to tell us what to think. We can think for ourselves. We don't need speechwriters and teleprompters to put words in our mouths. We can speak for ourselves. We don't need public relations firms and ad agencies to mold our images. We can just be who we are. We don't need political professionals to do the work for us. We can do the work of citizenship. We can flood the democratic process rather than flee it. We can throw our hats in the ring, worrying less about running victoriously and more about doing so impactfully. Not many of us have the time, but we can make the time. We need not fear failure. Failure can be a great teacher and is one of the most important secrets of success. We don't need to be afraid of the dark. Darkness is no match for millions of people shining light.

America is never finished. It is always in the making. ✪

ABOUT THE AUTHOR

Mike McCabe got his start in life on the farm milking cows and working the land with his family. He brings that farming background and a lifetime of experience in politics, journalism and nonprofit leadership to his writing. He is now executive director of Our Wisconsin Revolution and ran a spirited underdog campaign for governor of Wisconsin in 2018. Before that he started the grassroots group Blue Jean Nation. For 15 years Mike led the independent watchdog group Wisconsin Democracy Campaign. In that role, Mike blew the whistle on wrongdoing by elected officials and earned a reputation as one of the nation's best political money trackers. Under his leadership, the Democracy Campaign was named the Citizen Openness Advocate of the Year in 2012 by the Society of Professional Journalists and Wisconsin Freedom of Information Council. In 2015 the University of Wisconsin-Madison School of Journalism honored him with its Distinguished Service Award. While leading Blue Jean Nation, Mike produced a radio commentary series that was among the Wisconsin Broadcasters Association's 2016 Awards for Excellence winners for best editorial commentary in large market radio programming. He appeared in the documentary films *Citizen Koch* (2013) and *Pay 2 Play: Democracy's High Stakes* (2014), and previously authored *Blue Jeans in High Places: The Coming Makeover of American Politics*, which is in its fourth printing. *The Progressive* magazine named it one of the best books of 2014. ✪

ENDNOTES

INTRODUCTION

1 Amy B. Wang, "Did the 2011 White House correspondents' dinner spur Trump to run for president?" *Washington Post*, February 26, 2017, https://www.chicagotribune.com/nation-world/ct-white-house-correspondents-dinner-trump-20170226-story.html.

2 Liam Stack, "Glenn Beck Says Opposing Trump Is 'Moral, Ethical' Even If It Means Clinton Wins," *The New York Times* October 11, 2016.

3 Katherine Krueger, "Conservative Pundit Owns up to Role in Trump's Rise: 'We Created This Monster,'" *Talking Points Memo*, August 15, 2016, https://talkingpointsmemo.com/livewire/charlie-sykes-conservative-media-created-trump-monster.

4 Hadas Gold, "Charlie Sykes to end his radio show," *Politico*, October 4, 2016, https://www.politico.com/blogs/on-media/2016/10/charlie-sykes-to-end-his-radio-show-229102.

5 Jonah Goldberg, "Republicans are wishing upon a 'star,'" *Wisconsin State Journal*, October 12, 2016.

6 David Brooks, "Donald Trump's Sad, Lonely Life," *The New York Times*, October 11, 2016.

7 George Will, "Trump's vile candidacy is chemotherapy for the GOP," *Anchorage Daily News*, October 10, 2016, https://www.chicagotribune.com/opinion/commentary/ct-donald-trump-gop-chemotherapy-george-will-20161010-story.html.

8 "At least 110 Republican leaders won't vote for Donald Trump: Here's when they reached their breaking point," *The New York Times*, August 29, 2016.

9 Ibid.

10 Eliza Collins, "Poll: Clinton, Trump most unfavorable candidates ever," *USA Today*, August 31, 2016.

11 Robert Schlesinger, "Ka-Ching: Donald Trump is raking in big bucks from emoluments foreign and domestic," *U.S. News & World Report*, March 5, 2018, https://www.usnews.com/opinion/articles/2018-03-05/how-is-donald-trump-profiting-from-the-presidency-let-us-count-the-ways.

12 "Taxpayers footed a $1,000 bar tab at Trump's Mar-a-Lago. That's just for starters," *Los Angeles Times*, March 4, 2019.

13 Cenk Uygur, "Why Millennials Love Bernie Sanders," *Huffington Post*, May 4, 2016, https://www.commondreams.org/views/2016/05/04/why-millennials-love-bernie-sanders.

CHAPTER ONE

1 Tina Nguyen, "You Could Fit All the Voters Who Cost Clinton the Election in a Mid-Size Football Stadium," *Vanity Fair*, December 1, 2016.

2 Sabrina Tavernise and Robert Gebeloff, "They Voted for Obama, Then Went for Trump. Can Democrats Win Them Back?" *The New York Times*, May 4, 2018.

3 Joseph Ranney, "Law and the Progressive Era, Part 3: Reforming the Workplace," *Wisconsin Lawyer*, November 2005.

4 Daniel Nelson, "The Origins of Unemployment Insurance in Wisconsin," *Wisconsin Magazine of History*, Winter 1967–68.

5 John O. Stark, "The Establishment of Wisconsin's Income Tax," *Wisconsin Magazine of History*, Autumn 1987.

6 Larry DeWitt, Social Security Administration Historian's Office, "Research Note #8: The Special Role of the University of Wisconsin in the History of Social Security," July 2000, https://www.ssa.gov/history/wiscrole.html.

7 Tom Kertscher, "Under Scott Walker, Wisconsin lags U.S. in wage, job growth, *Meet the Press* host Chuck Todd says," PolitiFact Wisconsin, November 28, 2014, https://www. politifact.com/wisconsin/statements/2014/nov/28/chuck-todd/ under-scott-walker-wisconsin-lags-us-wage-job-grow/.

8 Scott Gordon, "Wisconsin's 'Comparatively Unimpressive' Jobs Recovery," WisContext, September 12, 2016, https://www. wiscontext.org/wisconsins-comparatively-unimpressive-jobs-recovery.

9 Shawn Johnson, "Wisconsin Lost Manufacturing Jobs in 2016," *Wisconsin Public Radio*, May 26, 2017, https://www.wpr.org/ wisconsin-lost-manufacturing-jobs-2016.

10 Kathleen Gallagher, "Wisconsin Ranks Last Again for Start-Ups," *Milwaukee Journal Sentinel*, August 25, 2016, https://www.jsonline.com/story/money/business/ onramp/2016/08/25/wisconsin-innovation-last-again/89313028/.

11 Scottie Lee Meyers, "Wisconsin Has Seen Largest Middle-Class Decline of Any State, Study Finds," *Wisconsin Public Radio*, April 2, 2015, https://www.wpr.org/wisconsin-has-seen-largest-middle-class-decline-any-state-study-finds.

12 Katelyn Ferral, "National Report: Half of Wisconsin's roads are in poor or mediocre condition," *The Capital Times*, September 18, 2018, https://madison.com/ct/news/local/govt-and-politics/national-report-half-of-wisconsin-s-major-roads-are-in/article_01841742-0cf0-55ea-85d6-3e4d7c3dbe65.html.

13 Rick Barrett, "Wisconsin broadband speeds lagging," *Milwaukee Journal Sentinel*, August 8, 2016, https://www.jsonline.com/ story/money/2016/08/08/wisconsin-broadband-speeds-lagging/88416370/.

14 Bill Lueders, "Wisconsin lags on renewable energy," The Wisconsin Center for Investigative Journalism, October 8, 2014, https://www.wisconsinwatch.org/2014/10/wisconsin-lags-on-renewable-energy/.

15 "Wisconsin Earns a C-Plus on State Report Card, Ranks 11th in Nation," Education Week, January 2, 2015, https://www.edweek.org/ew/qc/2015/state-highlights/2015/01/08/wisconsin-education-ranking.html.

16 Ron Seely, "Bacteria in Wisconsin's Drinking Water is a 'Public Health Crisis,'" Wisconsin Center for Investigative Journalism, May 1, 2016, https://www.wuwm.com/post/bacteria-wisconsins-drinking-water-public-health-crisis#stream/0.

17 Hope Kirwan, "Western Wisconsin Led Nation in Farm Bankruptcies in 2017," *Wisconsin Public Radio*, January 24, 2018, https://www.wpr.org/western-wisconsin-led-nation-farm-bankruptcies-2017.

18 David Wahlberg, "As Wisconsin farmers struggle, new effort aims to prevent suicide," *Wisconsin State Journal*, January 27, 2019.

19 George Joseph, "How Wisconsin Became the Home of Black Incarceration," CityLab, August 17, 2016, https://www.citylab.com/equity/2016/08/how-wisconsin-became-the-home-of-black-incarceration/496130/.

20 "Wealth Inequality in the United States," Inequality.org, https://inequality.org/facts/wealth-inequality/.

21 Rakesh Kochhar, "The American middle class is stable in size, but losing ground financially to upper-income families," Pew Research Center, September 6, 2018, https://www.pewresearch.org/fact-tank/2018/09/06/the-american-middle-class-is-stable-in-size-but-losing-ground-financially-to-upper-income-families/.

22 Sarah Kendzior, "Geography is making America's uneven economic recovery worse," Quartz, https://qz.com/672589/geography-is-making-americas-uneven-economic-recovery-worse/, April 29, 2016.

23 Jeffrey Brown, "How schools are forced to close as rural populations dwindle," PBS NewsHour, https://www.pbs.org/newshour/show/how-schools-are-forced-to-close-as-rural-populations-dwindle, November 27, 2018.

24 An excellent assessment of this phenomenon is Katherine Cramer's book *The Politics of Resentment*, https://www.press.uchicago.edu/ucp/books/book/chicago/P/bo22879533.html.

25 Brian Alexander, "What America Is Losing as Its Small Towns Struggle," *The Atlantic*, October 18, 2017, https://www.theatlantic.com/business/archive/2017/10/small-town-economies-culture/543138/.

26 Jeff Cox, "The U.S. labor shortage is reaching a critical point," CNBC, July 5, 2018.

27 Kelly Meyerhofer, "Wisconsin had 4th biggest drop in per-student spending for higher education," *Wisconsin State Journal* (April 25, 2019).

28 Katie Reilly, "Read Hillary Clinton's 'Basket of Deplorables' Remarks About Donald Trump Supporters," *Time*, September 10, 2016, http://time.com/4486502/hillary-clinton-basket-of-deplorables-transcript/.

29 U.S. Department of Agriculture statistics, http://www.nass.usda.gov/Statistics_by_State/Wisconsin/Publications/County_Estimates/milk_cows.pdf.

30 U.S. Census population figures, https://census.gov/quickfacts/fact/table/US/PST045218.

31 "Wisconsin Is Definitely Not Close to Full," *Wisconsin State Journal*, April 24, 2019.

32 Dale Knapp, Director of Research and Analytics, "Falling Behind: Migration Changes and State Workforce," Forward Analytics, April 2019, https://www.wicounties.org/blog/forward-analytics-issues-falling-behind-migration-changes-and-state-workforce/.

33 Adam Ozimek, Kenan Fikri, and John Lettieri, "From Managing Decline to Building the Future: Could a Heartland Visa Help Struggling Regions?" Economic Innovation Group, April 2019, https://eig.org/wp-content/uploads/2019/04/Heartland-Visas-Report.pdf.

CHAPTER TWO

1 Matt DeFour, "Mike McCabe: We are all in this together, and we've got to look out for each other," *Wisconsin State Journal*, July 21, 2018.

2 Special Reports, Wisconsin Democracy Campaign, https://www.wisdc.org/news/special-reports.

3 Major Accomplishments, Wisconsin Democracy Campaign, https://www.wisdc.org/about-us/major-accomplishments.

4 "WDC Files 43 Complaints Against Fat Cat Donors, Ex-Governor," Wisconsin Democracy Campaign, May 13, 2003, https://www.wisdc.org/interest-group-spending/3224-wdc-files-43-complaints-against-fat-cat-donors-ex-governor.

5 "Two Violate $10,000 Contribution Limit in 2007," Wisconsin Democracy Campaign, April 16, 2008, https://www.wisdc.org/events/1460-two-violate-10-000-contribution-limit-in-2007.

6 "WDC Requests Ethics Probe of Supreme Court Candidate," Wisconsin Democracy Campaign, March 19, 2007, https://www.wisdc.org/about-us/major-accomplishments/26-rss/3019-wdc-requests-ethics-probe-of-supreme-court-candidate.

7 Caucus Scandal Archive, Wisconsin Democracy Campaign, https://www.wisdc.org/about-us/major-accomplishments?id=3314: caucus-scandal-archive&catid=6.

8 "Reform Groups File Complaint Over Caucus Scandal," Wisconsin Democracy Campaign, June 6, 2001, https://www.wisdc.org/follow-the-money/32-campaign-finance-profiles-2009/3128-reform-groups-file-complaint-over-caucus-scandal.

9 Driessen memo, Wisconsin Democracy Campaign, https://www.wisdc.org/news/press-releases/69-press-release-2001/3116-driessen-memo.

10 Phil Brinkman, "Chvala doesn't want GOP to get more, donors warned," *Wisconsin State Journal*, May 26, 2001.

11 "Lobbyist's Pay-to-Play Memo Turns Out to Be Prophetic, Analysis Shows," Wisconsin Democracy Campaign, October 15, 2001, https://www.wisdc.org/news/press-releases/69-press-release-2001/3115-lobbyist-s-pay-to-play-memo-turns-out-to-be-prophetic-analysis-shows.

12 Joe Tarr, "Mike McCabe for Governor?" *Isthmus*, May 4, 2017, https://isthmus.com/news/news/mike-mccabe-for-governor/.

13 "We Support Mike McCabe for Governor of Wisconsin in 2018," change.org petition, https://www.change.org/p/sign-the-petition-mike-mccabe-for-governor-of-wisconsin-in-2018.

14 "Wisconsin Governor's Race Cost Nearly $82 Million," Wisconsin Democracy Campaign, March 9, 2015, https://www.wisdc.org/news/press-releases/76-press-release-2015/4875-wisconsin-governor-s-race-cost-nearly-82-million.

15 "May 2018 State Occupational Employment and Wage Estimates – Wisconsin," U.S. Bureau of Labor Statistics https://www.bls.gov/oes/current/oes_wi.htm.

CHAPTER THREE

1 For two examples of this, check out my earlier book, *Blue Jeans in High Places*, pages 84–86.

2 Jessie Opoien, "Wedge Issues: Mike McCabe says governors should be 'servants, not masters,'" *The Capital Times*, August 3, 2018, https://madison.com/ct/news/local/govt-and-politics/election-matters/wedge-issues-mike-mccabe-says-governors-should-be-servants-not/article_9155a262-d2f4-58ca-9782-af7b36209618.html.

3 Bill Kraus, "Early handicapping on the governor's race: Walker assumed favorite, but … " WisPolitics.com, August 10, 2017, https://www.wispolitics.com/2017/14780/.

4 "Timeline: The life and career of Madison's 'Mayor for Life' Paul Soglin," *Wisconsin State Journal*, July 17, 2018.

5 John Nichols, "Best ideas of campaign: basic income, pardons to achieve justice, state bank," *The Capital Times*, August 7, 2018, https://madison.com/ct/opinion/column/john_nichols/john-nichols-best-ideas-of-campaign-basic-income-pardons-to/article_7784bebb-3010-5202-b8ac-11dc7e225129.html.

6 Samantha West, "Mike McCabe says Minnesota is imprisoning half as many people as Wisconsin, with same crime rates," PolitiFact Wisconsin & *Milwaukee Journal Sentinel*, September 5, 2018, https://www.politifact.com/wisconsin/statements/2018/sep/05/mike-mccabe/mike-mccabe-says-minnesota-imprisoning-half-many-p/.

7 Report 15–3, "Wisconsin Economic Development Corporation," State of Wisconsin Legislative Audit Bureau, May 2015, https://legis.wisconsin.gov/lab/reports/15-3full.pdf.

8 Report 17–9, "Wisconsin Economic Development Corporation," State of Wisconsin Legislative Audit Bureau, May 2017, https://legis.wisconsin.gov/lab/media/2627/17-9full.pdf.

9 Scott Bauer, "Audit finds ongoing problems with WEDC, tax credits for jobs created in other states," Associated Press and *Wisconsin State Journal*, May 11, 2019.

10 Rick Romell, "Wisconsin is last among states in startup activity," *Milwaukee Journal Sentinel*, May 18, 2017, https://www.jsonline.com/story/money/2017/05/18/third-straight-year-wisconsin-ranks-last-business-startup-activity/328803001/.

11 Molly Beck, "DPI: 73 percent of statewide voucher students already enrolled in private schools," *Wisconsin State Journal*, October 30, 2013.

12 John Nichols, "Mike McCabe's right: Wisconsin must renew local democracy," *The Capital Times*, May 29, 2018, https://madison.com/ct/opinion/column/john_nichols/john-nichols-mike-mccabe-s-right-wisconsin-must-renew-local/article_e4afdd37-11be-5408-84a5-8076928ead11.html.

13 Dave Zweifel, "Kudos to Mike McCabe for pitching return to local control," *The Capital Times*, May 25, 2018, https://madison.com/ct/opinion/column/dave_zweifel/plain-talk-kudos-to-mike-mccabe-for-pitching-return-to/article_f1a2a76c-71b6-529c-bb20-00f4776db21b.html.

14 "Dare to Dream," Wisconsin Democratic Convention speech, June 2, 2018, https://www.youtube.com/watch?v=dQDFFeizYDc.

15 A listing of capitol staffers who received taxpayer-financed legal representation authorized by the legislature as of October 2002, signaling that they were being questioned about or were implicated in the caucus scandal is published on the Wisconsin Democracy Campaign website at https://www.wisdc.org/2-uncategorised/3315-wdc-calls-on-doyle-to-challenge-caucus-legal-fees-5a8c4a0615b1a#assmdem.

16 Jake Ekdahl Twitter post, June 20, 2018, https://twitter.com/ JakeaEkdahl/status/1009492315868749824.

17 Matt DeFour, "Scott Walker has nearly four times more cash than Democratic field," *Wisconsin State Journal*, January 17, 2018.

18 "Wisconsin Governor's Race Cost Nearly $82 Million," Wisconsin Democracy Campaign, February 17, 2015, https:// www.wisdc.org/news/press-releases/76-press-release-2015/4875-wisconsin-governor-s-race-cost-nearly-82-million.

19 "Recall Race for Governor Cost $81 Million," Wisconsin Democracy Campaign, July 25, 2012, https://www.wisdc.org/ news/press-releases/73-press-release-2012/4112-recall-race-for-governor-cost-81-million.

20 "Record $37.4 Million Spent In Governor's Race," Wisconsin Democracy Campaign, February 8, 2011, https://www.wisdc. org/news/press-releases/72-press-release-2011/3662-record-37-4-million-spent-in-governor-s-race.

21 One good profile of the career of Senator William Proxmire was published by the Wisconsin Historical Society and is available online at http://www.wisconsinhistory.org/topics/ proxmire/biography.asp. An obituary written by The Associated Press after Proxmire's death also captures the essence of his political career. http://www.legacy.com/NS/Obituary. aspx?pid=15984365.

22 John Nichols, "Mike McCabe's right: Wisconsin must renew local democracy," *The Capital Times*, May 29, 2018, https:// madison.com/ct/opinion/column/john_nichols/john-nichols-mike-mccabe-s-right-wisconsin-must-renew-local/article_ e4afdd37-11be-5408-84a5-8076928ead11.html.

CHAPTER FOUR

1 "2018 Governor's Race Cost Record $93M+," Wisconsin Democracy Campaign, January 24, 2019, https://www.wisdc. org/news/press-releases/126-press-release-2019/6288-2018-governor-s-race-cost-record-93m.

2 Elisa Shearer, "Social media outpaces print newspapers in the U.S. as a news source," Pew Research Center, December 10, 2018, https://www.pewresearch.org/fact-tank/2018/12/10/social-media-outpaces-print-newspapers-in-the-u-s-as-a-news-source/.

3 Charlotte Alter, "'Change Is Closer Than We Think.' Inside Alexandria Ocasio-Cortez's Unlikely Rise," *Time*, March 21, 2019.

4 "Wealth Inequality in the United States," https://inequality.org/facts/wealth-inequality/.

5 Eleanor Krause and Isabel V. Sawhill, "Seven reasons to worry about the American middle class," Center for Children and Families and the Brookings Institution, June 5, 2018, https://www.brookings.edu/blog/social-mobility-memos/2018/06/05/seven-reasons-to-worry-about-the-american-middle-class/.

6 "75% in U.S. See Widespread Government Corruption," Gallup, September 19, 2015, https://news.gallup.com/poll/185759/widespread-government-corruption.aspx.

7 "America's Top Fears 2018," Chapman University Survey of American Fears, October 16, 2018, https://blogs.chapman.edu/wilkinson/2018/10/16/americas-top-fears-2018/.

8 Martin Gilens and Benjamin Page, "Testing Theories of American Politics: Elites, Interest Groups, and Average Citizens," Cambridge University Press, September 2014.

9 Bradley Jones, "Most Americans want to limit campaign spending, say big donors have greater political influence," Pew Research Center, May 8, 2018.

10 Jonathan Berr, "Media Companies Profit Handsomely From the Political Ads Voters Despise," *Forbes*, November 2, 2018.

11 "How Money Corrupts American Politics," Scholars Strategy Network, June 19, 2013, https://scholars.org/how-money-corrupts-american-politics.

12 Jacob S. Hacker and Nathan Loewentheil, "How Big Money Corrupts the Economy," Democracy, Winter 2013, https://democracyjournal.org/magazine/27/how-big-money-corrupts-the-economy/.

13 Shawn Johnson, "In Small Wisconsin Towns, Paved Roads Return To Gravel," *Wisconsin Public Radio*, March 2, 2017, https://www.wpr.org/small-wisconsin-towns-paved-roads-return-gravel.

14 "More bad news on the state of our roads," *Wisconsin State Journal* editorial, March 5, 2017.

15 "Wisconsin: Presidential County Results," *The New York Times*, December 9, 2008, https://www.nytimes.com/elections/2008/results/states/president/wisconsin.html.

16 https://www.nytimes.com/elections/2012/results/states/wisconsin.html.

17 Craig Gilbert, "The reddest and bluest places in Wisconsin," *Milwaukee Journal Sentinel*, December 3, 2014.

18 2018 WISDOM Gubernatorial Candidate Forum, June 11, 2018, https://www.youtube.com/watch?v=lMstEts94gc.

19 Ibid.

20 Jud Lounsbury, "Wisconsin: The Perfect Place to Address America's Apartheid," *The Progressive*, May 9, 2019.

21 "Political Expert Predicts Primary Election Surprise," *Here and Now*, Wisconsin Public Television, August 10, 2018, https://wpt4.org/wpt-video/here-and-now/political-expert-mordecai-lee-predicts-primary-election-surprise/.

CHAPTER FIVE

1 Christopher Rugaber, "Unemployment Hits 49-Year Low as Employers Add 263,000 Jobs," Associated Press, May 3, 2019, https://apnews.com/8a603c0717d44e9a9edca5f342129685.

2 Yun Li, "Dow jumps 190 points after unemployment falls to lowest in half century," CNBC, May 3, 2019, https://www.cnbc.com/2019/05/03/us-stocks-nonfarm-payrolls-in-focus.html.

3 Uri Friedman, "Trust Is Collapsing in America," *The Atlantic*, January 21, 2018, https://www.theatlantic.com/international/archive/2018/01/trust-trump-america-world/550964/.

4 Abe Voelker, "On the death of my family's dairy farm," March 6, 2019, https://blog.abevoelker.com/2019-03-06/on-the-death-of-my-familys-dairy-farm/.

5 Ibid.

6 Ibid.

7 Ibid.

8 Ibid.

9 Ibid.

10 Carrie Hribar, "Understanding Concentrated Animal Feeding Operations and Their Impact on Communities," National Association of Local Boards of Health, 2010, https://www.cdc.gov/nceh/ehs/docs/understanding_cafos_nalboh.pdf.

11 Abe Voelker, "On the death of my family's dairy farm," March 6, 2019, https://blog.abevoelker.com/2019-03-06/on-the-death-of-my-familys-dairy-farm/.

12 "Manure shower," YouTube video, November 27, 2017, https://youtu.be/ug31xUsCHcw.

13 Ron Seely, "Bacteria in state's drinking water is 'public health crisis,'" Wisconsin Center for Investigative Journalism, May 1, 2016, https://www.wisconsinwatch.org/2016/05/bacteria-in-states-drinking-water-is-public-health-crisis/.

14 "Study: Private Wells in Rural SW Wisconsin Are 91% Polluted," Associated Press, August 4, 2019, https://www.usnews.com/news/best-states/wisconsin/articles/2019-08-04/study-private-wells-in-rural-sw-wisconsin-are-91-polluted.

15 Abe Voelker, "On the death of my family's dairy farm," March 6, 2019, https://blog.abevoelker.com/2019-03-06/on-the-death-of-my-familys-dairy-farm/.

16 Alison Moodie, "Fowl Play: The Chicken Farmers Being Bullied by Big Poultry," *The Guardian*, April 22, 2017, https://www.theguardian.com/sustainable-business/2017/apr/22/chicken-farmers-big-poultry-rules.

17 Betsy Freese, "Pork Powerhouses: The 40 Largest Pork Producers in the U.S. Keep Growing Despite Trade Wars, Lawsuits, Disease Threats, and Falling Markets," *Successful Farming*, September 30, 2018, https://www.agriculture.com/livestock/pork-powerhouses/pork-powerhouses-2018-ramping-up.

18 Betsy Freese, "What the Swine Nuisance Verdicts in NC Could Mean for Midwestern Producers," *Successful Farming*, September 7, 2018, https://www.agriculture.com/news/livestock/what-the-50-million-swine-nuisance-verdict-could-mean-for-midwestern-producers.

19 Abe Voelker, "On the death of my family's dairy farm," March 6, 2019, https://blog.abevoelker.com/2019-03-06/on-the-death-of-my-familys-dairy-farm/.

20 George Packer, "The Broken Contract: Inequality and American Decline," *Foreign Affairs*, November/December 2011 Issue, https://files.foreignaffairs.com/legacy/attachments/PC1_Packer.pdf.

21 Alexander Eichler, "Young People More Likely to Favor Socialism Than Capitalism: Pew," *Huffington Post* report on Pew Research Center findings, December 29, 2011, https://www. huffpost.com/entry/young-people-socialism_n_1175218.

22 Mike P. Sinn, "Government Spends More on Corporate Welfare Subsidies than Social Welfare Programs," Think By Numbers, https://thinkbynumbers.org/government-spending/corporate-welfare/corporate-vs-social-welfare/.

23 Parth Shah, "Wisconsin Poverty Rate Reaches Highest Level In 30 Years," *Wisconsin Public Radio*, February 25, 2016, https://www.wpr.org/wisconsin-poverty-rate-reaches-highest-level-30-years.

24 Mike Ivey, "Wisconsin income gap widening faster than nation as a whole," *The Capital Times*, March 1, 2014, https://madison.com/ct/news/local/writers/mike_ivey/wisconsin-income-gap-widening-faster-than-nation-as-a-whole/article_acc8a776-a0be-11e3-a5f1-001a4bcf887a.html.

25 Heather Long, "56% of Americans think their kids will be worse off," CNN Business, January 28, 2016, https://money.cnn.com/2016/01/28/news/economy/donald-trump-bernie-sanders-us-economy/.

26 Union Members Summary, U.S. Bureau of Labor Statistics, January 18, 2019, https://www.bls.gov/news.release/union2.nr0.htm.

27 Steven Verburg, "State audit finds DNR ignoring own rules on water pollution," *Wisconsin State Journal*, June 4, 2016.

28 Todd Richmond, "DNR: Large farms will write own permits," Associated Press, November 30, 2016.

29 Steven Verburg, "After Scott Walker's office alerts farm lobby, clean water regulations scaled back," *Wisconsin State Journal*, August 1, 2016.

30 Henry Grabar, "The Shackling of the American City," Slate.com, September 9, 2016, https://grassrootschange.net/2016/09/shackling-american-city/.

31 "Media conglomerates: The Big 6," WebFX, https://www.webfx.com/data/the-6-companies-that-own-almost-all-media/.

32 "Global Wealth Inequality: Trends and Projections," World Inequality Lab, https://wir2018.wid.world/part-4.html.

33 Erik Sherman, "America Is The Richest, and Most Unequal, Country," *Fortune*, September 30, 2015, https://fortune.com/2015/09/30/america-wealth-inequality/.

34 Terence Burlij and Jennifer Agiesta, "CNN Poll: Opinion of the Republican Party falls to all-time low," CNN, September 25, 2017, https://www.cnn.com/2017/09/24/politics/cnn-poll-republican-party-approval/index.html.

35 Ryan Struyk, "Poll: Views of Democratic Party hit lowest mark in 25 years," CNN, November 7, 2017, https://www.cnn.com/2017/11/07/politics/cnn-poll-republicans-democrats-taxes/index.html.

36 Roberto Foa and Yascha Mounk, "Are Americans losing faith in democracy?" Vox, December 18, 2015, https://www.vox.com/polyarchy/2015/12/18/9360663/is-democracy-in-trouble.

CHAPTER SIX

1 "How the Koch Brothers Helped Scott Walker," Wisconsin Democracy Campaign, May 4, 2015, https://www.wisdc.org/press-releases/76-press-release-2015/4946-how-the-koch-brothers-helped-scott-walker.

2 "2018 Governor's Race Cost Record $93M+," Wisconsin Democracy Campaign, January 24, 2019, https://www.wisdc.org/news/press-releases/126-press-release-2019/6288-2018-governor-s-race-cost-record-93m.

3 Derek Willis, "To Understand Scott Walker's Strength, Look at His Donors," *The New York Times*, February 11, 2015, https://www.nytimes.com/2015/02/12/upshot/to-understand-scott-walkers-strength-look-at-his-donors.html.

4 "Walker's NRA Bankroll Topped $3.5 Million," Wisconsin Democracy Campaign, June 22, 2016, https://www.wisdc.org/news/press-releases/77-press-release-2016/5417-walker-s-nra-bankroll-topped-3-5-million.

5 Andy Kroll, "Inside Labor's Epic Battle in Wisconsin," *Mother Jones*, March 4, 2011, https://www.motherjones.com/politics/2011/03/wisconsin-protest-scott-walker-labor/.

6 Clay Barbour and Mary Spicuzza, "Organizers file more than 1 million signatures to recall Walker," *Wisconsin State Journal*, January 18, 2012.

7 "Recall Race for Governor Cost $81 Million," Wisconsin Democracy Campaign, July 25, 2012. https://www.wisdc.org/news/press-releases/73-press-release-2012/4112-recall-race-for-governor-cost-81-million.

8 Steven Walters, "Evers Too Slow on Prison Reform?" *Urban Milwaukee*, April 8, 2019.

9 Eric Litke, "Wisconsin Gov. Tony Evers flips position on dissolving WEDC," PolitiFact Wisconsin and *Milwaukee Journal Sentinel*, January 17, 2019, https://www.politifact.com/wisconsin/statements/2019/jan/17/tony-evers/wisconsin-gov-evers-flips-position-dissolving-wedc/.

10 Trisha Marczsk,"4 Examples of Corporate Welfare in Action," Taxpayers for Common Sense, August 21, 2013, https://www.taxpayer.net/budget-appropriations-tax/4-examples-of-corporate-welfare-in-action/.

11 John White, "How Corporate Welfare Is Killing Small Businesses," *Inc.* magazine, August 21, 2017, https://www. inc.com/john-white/how-corporate-welfare-is-killing-small-businesses.html.

12 Brent Gardner, "The Corporate Welfare Fable," *Forbes,* October 26, 2016, https://www.forbes.com/sites/realspin/2016/10/26/the-corporate-welfare-fable/#39fc02d23df0.

13 Joseph Holt, "Here's what's worrisome about Foxconn's plan to build a plant in the U.S.," CNBC, July 27, 2017, https://www.cnbc.com/2017/07/27/heres-whats-worrisome-about-foxconns-plan-to-build-a-plant-in-the-us-commentary.html.

14 Tim Culpan, "New York dodged an Amazon bullet. Wisconsin still faces a bazooka," *La Crosse Tribune,* February 19, 2019, https://lacrossetribune.com/opinion/columnists/tim-culpan-new-york-dodged-an-amazon-bullet-wisconsin-still/article_cd135ecb-3180-5be4-a6f6-d5539f5d6e45.html.

15 Lauly Li, Cheng Ting-Fang, and Gen Nakamura, "Foxconn opts to make smaller displays at Wisconsin plant," *Nikkei Asian Review,* May 23, 2018, https://asia.nikkei.com/Business/Companies/Foxconn-opts-to-make-smaller-displays-at-Wisconsin-plant.

16 Rick Romell, "Foxconn's first Wisconsin factory likely will be smaller than planned," *Milwaukee Journal Sentinel,* June 28, 2018, https://www.jsonline.com/story/money/business/2018/06/28/foxconns-first-wisconsin-factory-smaller-than-originally-planned/740627002/.

17 Yang Jie, Shayndi Raice, and Eric Morath, "Foxconn mulls importing Chinese skilled workers for Wisconsin plant," *Wall Street Journal* MarketWatch, November 6, 2018, https://www.marketwatch.com/story/foxconn-mulls-tapping-chinese-skilled-workers-for-wisconsin-plant-as-us-job-market-tightens-2018-11-06.

18 Jess Macy Yu and Karl Plume, "Foxconn reconsidering plans to make LCD panels at Wisconsin plant," Reuters, January 30, 2019, https://www.reuters.com/article/us-foxconn-wisconsin-exclusive/exclusive-foxconn-reconsidering-plans-to-make-lcd-panels-at-wisconsin-plant-idUSKCN1PO0FV.

19 Riley Vetterkind and Mark Sommerhauser, "After Trump intervenes, Foxconn says it will move forward with Wisconsin plant," *Wisconsin State Journal*, February 2, 2019.

20 "WisEye Morning Minute: Newsmakers – DOA Sec. Joel Brennan Discusses Foxconn," WisconsinEye, February 14, 2019, https://www.youtube.com/watch?v=qDACPt3j36M.

21 Sissi Cao, "Amazon Paid $0 in Federal Taxes Despite Making $11 Billion in 2018–And No One Knows Why," *Observer*, February 20, 2019, https://observer.com/2019/02/amazon-pays-zero-federal-tax-2018-accountant-explains-tcja-impact/.

22 Alanna Petroff, "U.S. health care admin costs are double the average," CNN Business, January 11, 2017, https://money.cnn.com/2017/01/11/news/economy/healthcare-administrative-costs-us-obamacare/index.html.

23 Ryan Gamlin, "Administrative costs are killing U.S. health care," *Medical Economics*, May 21, 2016, https://www.medicaleconomics.com/medical-economics-blog/administrative-costs-are-killing-us-healthcare.

24 Dan Mangan, "Medicare, Medicaid popularity high: Kaiser, CNBC, July 17, 2015, https://www.cnbc.com/2015/07/16/medicare-medicaid-popularity-high-ahead-of-birthday.html.

25 Diane Archer, "Medicare Is More Efficient Than Private Insurance," Health Affairs, September 20, 2011, https://www.healthaffairs.org/do/10.1377/hblog20110920.013390/full/.

26 Melissa Hellman, "U.S. Health Care Ranked Worst in the Developed World," *Time*, June 17, 2014, https://time.com/2888403/u-s-health-care-ranked-worst-in-the-developed-world/.

27 Lisa Du and Wei Lu, "U.S. Health-Care System Ranks as One of the Least-Efficient," Bloomberg, September 28, 2016.

28 Charles Blahous, "The Costs of a National Single-Payer Healthcare System," Mercatus Center at George Mason University, July 30, 2018, https://www.mercatus.org/publications/government-spending/costs-national-single-payer-healthcare-system.

29 Jake Johnson, "'Easy to Pay for Something That Costs Less': New Study Shows Medicare for All Would Save U.S. $5.1 Trillion Over Ten Years," *Truthout*, December 1, 2018, https://www.commondreams.org/news/2018/11/30/easy-pay-something-costs-less-new-study-shows-medicare-all-would-save-us-51-trillion.

30 "Income Inequality in the United States," Inequality.org, https://inequality.org/facts/income-inequality/.

31 Colin Gordon, "Growing Apart: A Political History of American Inequality," Inequality.org, March 14, 2018, https://inequality.org/research/growing-apart-political-history-american-inequality/.

32 "Minimum Wage Mythbusters," ICNA Council for Social Justice, September 18, 2016, http://icnacsj.org/2016/09/minimum-wage-mythbusters/.

33 Scott Neuman, "States That Raised Minimum Wage See Faster Job Growth, Report Says," *NPR*, July 19, 2014, https://www.npr.org/sections/thetwo-way/2014/07/19/332879409/states-that-raised-minimum-wage-see-faster-job-growth-report-says.

34 "Who Pays? A Distributional Analysis of the Tax Systems in All 50 States," Institute on Taxation and Economic Policy, October 2018, https://itep.org/whopays/.

35 "The Panama Papers: Exposing the Rogue Offshore Finance Industry," International Consortium of Investigative Journalists, https://www.icij.org/investigations/panama-papers/.

36 Jason Stein and Patrick Marley, "Wisconsin jobs agency failed in tracking taxpayer money, audit finds," *Milwaukee Journal Sentinel*, May 1, 2013, http://archive.jsonline.com/news/statepolitics/wisconsin-jobs-agency-failed-in-tracking-taxpayer-money-audit-finds-9a9pl8g-205595881.html/.

37 Catherine Clifford, "Why Amazon and other companies are trying 30-hour workweeks," CNBC, September 16, 2016, https://www.cnbc.com/2016/09/16/why-amazon-and-other-companies-are-trying-30-hour-workweeks.html.

38 Richard D. Kahlenberg and Moshe Z. Marvit, "A Civil Right to Unionize," *The New York Times*, February 29, 2012, https://www.nytimes.com/2012/03/01/opinion/a-civil-right-to-unionize.html.

CHAPTER SEVEN

1 John Nichols, "Scott Walker Promised $500K Donor He Would 'Divide and Conquer' Unions," *The Nation*, May 11, 2012.

2 Theodore Allen, *The Invention of the White Race* (New York: Verso, 1994), 185–186.

3 "Declaration in the Name of the People – 30 July 1676," University of Groningen, November 12, 2016.

4 Howard Zinn, *A People's History of the United States* (New York: The New York Press, 1997).

5 Mary K. Geiter and William Arthur Speck, *Colonial America: From Jamestown to Yorktown* (Macmillan: 2002), 63.

6 Theodore Allen, *The Invention of the White Race* (New York: Verso, 1994), 48–249.

7 Mary Giovagnoli, "Removal of 'Nation of Immigrants' from USCIS Mission Ignores Agency's Mandate and American History," American Immigration Council, February 26, 2018, http://immigrationimpact.com/2018/02/26/removal-nation-immigrants-uscis-mission/#.XeWIU-hKhPY.

8 "US authorities fire tear gas across border to repel Central Americans," Associated Press and *The Guardian*, January 2, 2019, https://www.theguardian.com/us-news/2019/jan/01/us-mexico-border-migrant-caravan-tijuana-tear-gas.

9 "Class War Chests," Wisconsin Democracy Campaign, January 26, 2004, https://www.wisdc.org/news/13-special-reports/1197-class-war-chests.

10 Melody Joy Kramer, "'Citizens United' Ruling Opened Floodgates on Groups' Ad Spending," *NPR*, October 7, 2010, https://www.npr.org/sections/itsallpolitics/2010/10/07/130399554/fresh-air.

11 "Race and the Drug War," Drug Policy Alliance, http://www.drugpolicy.org/issues/race-and-drug-war.

12 "New Voting Restrictions in America," Brennan Center for Justice, New York University School of Law, October 1, 2019, https://www.brennancenter.org/new-voting-restrictions-america.

13 "Myth of Voter Fraud," Brennan Center for Justice, https://www.brennancenter.org/issues/voter-fraud.

14 Christina A. Cassidy and Ivan Moreno, "In Wisconsin, ID law proved insurmountable for many voters," Associated Press and PBS NewsHour, May 14, 2017, https://apnews.com/624a00e48a444f2c8fbd2faa07d44ad5.

15 Zoltan Hajnal, "The results in voter ID laws are in – and it's bad news for racial and ethnic minorities," *Los Angeles Times*, September 8, 2016.

16 Ashley May, "#AllLivesMatter hashtag is racist, critics say," *USA Today*, July 13, 2016, https://www.usatoday.com/story/news/nation-now/2016/07/13/why-saying-all-lives-matter-opposite-black-lives-matter/87025190/.

17 Naomi Lim, "Rudy Giuliani: Black Lives Matter 'inherently racist,'" CNN, July 11, 2016, https://www.cnn.com/2016/07/11/politics/rudy-giuliani-black-lives-matter-inherently-racist/index.html.

18 Matthew Daly and Jill Colvin, "Trump: 'A Lot of People' Feel That Black Lives Matter Is Inherently Racist," Talking Points Memo and Associated Press, July 12, 2016, https://talkingpointsmemo.com/news/trump-black-lives-matter-divisive.

19 Jessie Opoien, "Wisconsin GOP legislator to introduce 'Blue Lives Matter' bill," *The Capital Times*, July 8, 2016, https://madison.com/ct/news/local/govt-and-politics/election-matters/wisconsin-gop-legislator-to-introduce-blue-lives-matter-bill/article_1e61b27c-3adb-5924-9e17-909bbb920ad2.html.

20 Rachel Charlene Lewis, "It's Time You Realize #AllLivesMatter Is Racist," *Advocate*, July 7, 2016, https://www.advocate.com/commentary/2016/7/07/its-time-you-realize-alllivesmatter-racist.

21 Kevin Roose, "The next time someone says 'all lives matter,' show them these 5 paragraphs," Splinter News, July 21, 2015, https://splinternews.com/the-next-time-someone-says-all-lives-matter-show-them-1793849332.

CHAPTER EIGHT

1 Naomi Oreskes, "The Scientific Consensus on Climate Change," *Science*, December 3, 2004, https://science.sciencemag.org/content/306/5702/1686.

2 Coral Davenport, "Major Climate Report Describes a Strong Risk of Crisis as Early as 2040," *The New York Times*, October 7, 2018, https://www.nytimes.com/2018/10/07/climate/ipcc-climate-report-2040.html.

3 "Global Warming of 1.5 °C," Intergovernmental Panel on Climate Change, October 2018.

4 Lee Bergquist, "DNR purges climate change from website," *Milwaukee Journal Sentinel*, December 28, 2016, https://www.jsonline.com/story/news/politics/2016/12/28/dnr-purges-climate-change-on-web-page/95929564/.

5 Lee Bergquist, "State OKs permit to triple Enbridge oil pipeline capacity," *Milwaukee Journal Sentinel*, June 12, 2014, http://archive.jsonline.com/news/wisconsin/state-oks-permit-for-enbridge-oil-pipeline-capacity-hike-b99290055z1-262917491.html.

6 "Brave Wisconsin meeting on Enbridge pipeline well attended," *Watertown Daily Times*, July 15, 2016, http://www.wdtimes.com/news/article_a0347a8e-4aa9-11e6-9918-5bbd160097a6.html.

7 Matt Gardner, "Enbridge Pipeline Forum Highlights Many Concerns," *Lake Mills Leader*, July 27, 2016, http://www.hngnews.com/lake_mills_leader/news/local/article_f57f4542-5354-11e6-ab42-b3ba1a14f74d.html.

8 Ibid.

9 Ibid.

10 Roger Bybee, "Masters of Our Domain: Foxconn and State Minions Seize Land," *The Progressive*, January 16, 2019, https://progressive.org/dispatches/eminent-domain-foxconn-seize-land-190116/.

11 Lawrence Tabak, "In Racine County, neatly maintained homes and dream houses are being designated 'blighted' to make way for Foxconn," *Belt Magazine*, April 11, 2018, https://beltmag.com/blighted-by-foxconn/.

12 Jeremy Van Loon, "Oil Sands and the Environment," *Bloomberg*, March 24, 2017.

13 "Frack Sand Industry Support Spikes With Mines," Wisconsin Democracy Campaign, May 21, 2013, https://www.wisdc.org/news/press-releases/74-press-release-2013/4271-frack-sand-industry-support-spikes-with-mines.

14 "Woman Describes Life 'Trapped' in Frac Sand Mining District," WIVoices TV, November 20, 2012, https://wivoices.org/2012/11/20/family-trapped-in-frac-sand-mining-district-called-collateral-damage/.

15 Arthur Thomas, "Wisconsin ranks last in Midwest clean energy jobs," *BizTimes*, March 22, 2016, https://biztimes.com/wisconsin-ranks-last-in-midwest-clean-energy-jobs/.

16 Kate Samuelson, "Renewable Energy Is Creating Jobs 12 Times Faster Than the Rest of the Economy," *Fortune*, January 27, 2017, https://fortune.com/2017/01/27/solar-wind-renewable-jobs/.

17 Seth Borenstein, "UN report: Humans accelerating extinction of other species," Associated Press, May 6, 2019, https://apnews.com/aaf1091c5aae40b0a110daaf04950672.

18 Ibid.

19 Lynette Kalsnes, "Great Lakes face increasing pressure for water from world, own backyard," WBEZ News, June 21, 2011, https://www.wbez.org/shows/front-and-center/great-lakes-face-increasing-pressure-for-water-from-world-own-backyard/8bdea30e-51cf-4d9e-80b9-67fc4ddc2e3d.

20 Sarah Zielinski, "The Colorado River Runs Dry," *Smithsonian Magazine*, October 2010, https://www.smithsonianmag.com/science-nature/the-colorado-river-runs-dry-61427169/.

21 Eliott C. McLaughlin, "5 things to know about Flint's water crisis," CNN, January 21, 2016, https://www.cnn.com/2016/01/18/us/flint-michigan-water-crisis-five-things/index.html.

22 Eric Litke, "Unsafe lead in 81 Wisconsin water systems," *Green Bay Press-Gazette* and *USA Today* Network-Wisconsin, March 18, 2016, https://www.greenbaypressgazette.com/story/news/investigations/2016/03/18/unsafe-lead-81-wisconsin-water-systems/81971958/.

23 Avory Brookins, "Report: Lead Poisoning Rate Among Wisconsin Children Nearly Equal to Flint," *Wisconsin Public Radio*, October 27, 2016, https://www.wpr.org/report-lead-poisoning-rate-among-wisconsin-children-nearly-equal-flint.

24 "Project: Groundwater supply," The Wisconsin Center for Investigative Journalism, https://www.wisconsinwatch.org/projects/groundwater-concerns/.

25 "Central Wisconsin's Disappearing Lakes & Rivers," Central Sands Water Action Coalition, September 2015, http://centralsandswater.org/wp-content/uploads/2015/09/Central-Wisconsin%E2%80%99s-Disappearing-Lakes-Rivers.pdf.

26 Ryan Schuessler, "Politicized environmental agency threatens Wisconsin's water, critics say," Al Jazeera America, November 11, 2015, http://america.aljazeera.com/articles/2015/11/11/wisconsins-water-woes-politicized-natural-resources-agency-threatens.html.

27 Ryan Schuessler, "Something's in the water in Kewaunee County, Wisconsin," Al Jazeera America, November 13, 2015, http://america.aljazeera.com/articles/2015/11/13/somethings-in-the-water-in-kewaunee-county-wisconsin.html.

28 Steven Verburg, "GOP leader's bill would loosen high-capacity well regulations," *Wisconsin State Journal*, February 22, 2017, https://madison.com/wsj/news/local/environment/gop-leader-s-bill-would-loosen-high-capacity-well-regulations/article_e268dd79-c781-54d5-9fd3-8728caa50572.html.

29 "Walker Donors Got DNR Well Permits," Wisconsin Democracy Campaign, November 4, 2016, https://www.wisdc.org/news/press-releases/77-press-release-2016/5540-walker-donors-got-dnr-well-permits.

30 "WMC, Big Ag Pressure Senate on High-Capacity Wells," Wisconsin Democracy Campaign, March 11, 2016, https://www.wisdc.org/news/press-releases/77-press-release-2016/5337-wmc-big-ag-pressure-senate-on-high-capacity-wells.

CHAPTER NINE

1 "Dane Co. grew jobs at 4x the rate of Wisconsin," WIBA Radio and WKOW-TV, June 1, 2017, https://wiba.iheart.com/content/2017-06-01-dane-co-grew-jobs-at-4x-the-rate-of-wisconsin/.

2 Ibid.

3 Judy Newman, "Epic Systems growth expected to continue," *Wisconsin State Journal*, January 4, 2016.

4 Barry Adams and David Wahlberg, "Verona approves one of the largest school referendums in Wisconsin history," *Wisconsin State Journal*, April 5, 2017.

5 Matt DeFour and Dee J. Hall, "Top Scott Walker aides pushed for questionable $500,000 WEDC loan," *Wisconsin State Journal*, May 18, 2015.

6 Valerie Strauss, "What the heck is going on with Wisconsin public education?" *Washington Post*, May 28, 2015.

7 Mary Spicuzza and Jason Stein, "Walker's welfare plan: Expand work requirements to parents," *Milwaukee Journal Sentinel*, January 23, 2017, https://www.jsonline.com/story/news/politics/2017/01/23/scott-walker-set-announce-welfare-overhaul/96942732/

8 Mike P. Sinn, "Government Spends More on Corporate Welfare Subsidies than Social Welfare Programs," Think by Numbers, https://thinkbynumbers.org/government-spending/corporate-welfare/corporate-vs-social-welfare/.

9 John Eligon, "Hate Crimes Increase for the Third Consecutive Year, F.B.I. Reports," *The New York Times*, November 13, 2018.

10 Uri Friedman, "Trust Is Collapsing in America," *The Atlantic*, January 21, 2018, https://www.theatlantic.com/international/archive/2018/01/trust-trump-america-world/550964/.

11 "Government tops 5th annual Chapman University survey of American fears," Chapman University, October 18, 2018.

CHAPTER TEN

1 "Politics really is ruining Thanksgiving, according to data from 10 million cellphones," *Washington Post*, November 15, 2017.

2 Nigel Barber Ph.D., "Does Trump Suffer From Narcissistic Personality Disorder?" *Psychology Today*, August 10, 2016 https://www.psychologytoday.com/us/blog/the-human-beast/201608/does-trump-suffer-narcissistic-personality-disorder

3 Ray Downs, "Poll: Major parties less popular as more Americans identify as independent," United Press International, January 8, 2018.

4 John Haltiwanger, "Most Americans Desperate for Third Major Political Party in Trump Era," *Newsweek*, September 27, 2017, https://www.newsweek.com/most-americans-desperate-third-major-political-party-trump-era-672540.

5 "Public Trust in Government: 1958 to 2019," Pew Research Center, April 11, 2019, https://www.people-press.org/2019/04/11/public-trust-in-government-1958-2019/.

6 "Government corruption tops 5th annual Chapman University survey of American fears," Chapman University Survey of American Fears, October 18, 2018.

7 Alec MacGillis, "Who Turned My Blue State Red?" *The New York Times*, November 20, 2015, https://www.nytimes.com/2015/11/22/opinion/sunday/who-turned-my-blue-state-red.html.

8 Barry Adams, "In rural school districts, declining enrollments— and hard choices," *Wisconsin State Journal*, March 14, 2010.

9 Corinne Jurney, "Maps Show Which Americans Have Broadband Access and Which Don't," *Forbes*, June 9, 2015, https://www.forbes.com/sites/corinnejurney/2015/06/09/maps-show-which-americans-have-broadband-access-and-which-dont/#446126b36a06.

10 Lisa Mullins, "162 Million Americans Lack Regular Access To Broadband Internet, Study Says," WBUR Radio, Boston, December 7, 2018.

11 Steve Lohr, "Digital Divide Is Wider Than We Think, Study Says," *The New York Times*, December 4, 2018.

12 Heidi Shierholz, Lawrence Mishel, and Jared Bernstein, *The State of Working America*, 12th Edition, Economic Policy Institute (Cornell University Press, 2012).

13 David Dayen, "This man made millions suffer: Tim Geithner's sorry legacy on housing," *Salon*, May 14, 2014, https://www.salon.com/2014/05/14/this_man_made_millions_suffer_tim_geithners_sorry_legacy_on_housing/.

14 "What the Democrats don't want you to know: Party lost more than 1,030 seats in state legislatures, governor's mansions and Congress during Barack Obama's presidency," Associated Press and DailyMail.com, December 24, 2016, https://www.dailymail.co.uk/news/article-4063898/As-Obama-accomplished-policy-goals-party-floundered.html.

15 Jonathan Martin, "Eric Cantor Defeated by David Brat, Tea Party Challenger, in G.O.P. Primary Upset," *The New York Times*, June 10, 2014.

16 Jochen Bittner, "Is This the West's Weimar Moment?" *The New York Times*, May 31, 2016.

17 Matt DeFour, "At least 25 companies have outsourced and received state funding award since 2005," *Wisconsin State Journal*, August 3, 2014.

18 Marc Hetherington and Jonathan Weiler, *Prius or Pickup?: How the Answers to Four Simple Questions Explain America's Great Divide* (Boston: Houghton Mifflin Harcourt, 2018).

19 John Nichols, "Sen. Tom Reynolds Gives New Meaning to 'Quirky'," *The Capital Times*, August 27, 2006, https://madison.com/news/opinion/sen-tom-reynolds-gives-new-meaning-to-quirky/article_87bf0da3-2c89-5d56-bf20-28a4aa300cb6.html.

20 Daniel Bice," Former Sen. Tom Reynolds jailed for contempt of court," *Milwaukee Journal Sentinel*, August 30, 2013, http://archive.jsonline.com/newswatch/221783381.html.

21 Michael Harriot, "How the Republican Party Became the Party of Racism," *The Root*, July 23, 2018, https://www.theroot.com/how-the-republican-party-became-the-party-of-racism-1827779221.

22 Frank James, "Political Scientist: Republicans Most Conservative They've Been in 100 Years," *NPR*, April 13, 2012, https://www.npr.org/sections/itsallpolitics/2012/04/10/150349438/gops-rightward-shift-higher-polarization-fills-political-scientist-with-dread.

23 Daniel J. McGraw, "The GOP Is Dying Off. Literally." *Politico Magazine*, May 17, 2015, https://www.politico.com/magazine/story/2015/05/the-gop-is-dying-off-literally-118035.

24 Lee Drutman, "Yes, the Republican Party has become pathological. But why?" *Vox*, September 22, 2017.

25 Elaine Kamarck, Alexander R. Podkul and Nicholas W. Zeppos, "Trump owns as shrinking Republican Party," Brookings Institution, June 14, 2018, https://www.brookings.edu/blog/fixgov/2018/06/14/trump-owns-a-shrinking-republican-party/.

26 John Kruzel, "Yes, the Democratic Party is at nearly its weakest point in a century," PolitiFact, June 15, 2018, https://www.politifact.com/punditfact/statements/2018/jun/15/fareed-zakaria/yes-democratic-party-nearly-its-weakest-point-cent/

27 John Feehery, "The Blue Dog: An Endangered Species," *The Hill*, August 1, 2007, https://thehill.com/blogs/pundits-blog/economy-a-budget/33840-the-blue-dog-an-endangered-species.

28 Bill Bishop, "'D' is for Disadvantage: Democrats have an Identity Problem in Rural America," 100 Days in Appalachia and West Virginia University's Reed College of Media, November 23, 2018, https://www.100daysinappalachia.com/2018/11/d-is-for-disadvantage-democrats-have-an-identity-problem-in-rural-america/.

29 Jay Cost, Losing the Suburbs," *National Review*, November 15, 2018, https://www.nationalreview.com/magazine/2018/12/03/losing-the-suburbs/.

30 Amber Phillips, "These 3 maps show just how dominant Republicans are in America after Tuesday," *Washington Post*, November 12, 2016.

31 The Sentencing Project is a valuable source of statistics on mass incarceration, http://www.sentencingproject.org/issues/incarceration/.

32 Scott Horsley, "Guns in America, By the Numbers," *NPR*, January 5, 2016, https://www.npr.org/2016/01/05/462017461/guns-in-america-by-the-numbers.

33 "U.S. Military Spending vs. the World," National Priorities Project, https://www.nationalpriorities.org/campaigns/us-military-spending-vs-world/.

34 Larry Schwartz, "35 soul-crushing facts about American income inequality," *Salon*, July 15, 2015, https://www.salon.com/2015/07/15/35_soul_crushing_facts_about_american_income_inequality_partner/.

35 Mike McCabe, *Blue Jeans in High Places: The Coming Makeover of American Politics*, (Little Creek Press, chapter 7).

36 Shankar Vedantam, "Nature, Nurture and Your Politics," Hidden Brain, *NPR*, October 8, 2018, https://www.npr.org/2018/10/03/654127241/nature-nurture-and-your-politics.

CHAPTER ELEVEN

1 David Zucchino, "Gen. Eisenhower had a second, secret D-day message," *Los Angeles Times*, June 5, 2019, https://www.latimes.com/nation/nationnow/la-na-eisenhower-d-day-message-story.html.

2 Abby Vesoulis and Abigail Simon, "Here's Who Found That Russia Meddled in the 2016 Election," *Time*, July 16, 2018, https://time.com/5340060/donald-trump-vladimir-putin-summit-russia-meddling/.

3 Noah Bierman and Tracy Wilkinson, "Donald Trump invites Russia to hack Hillary Clinton's emails," *Los Angeles Times*, July 27, 2016, https://www.latimes.com/politics/la-na-pol-trump-russia-emails-20160727-snap-story.html.

4 Jo Becker, Adam Goldman, and Matt Apuzzo, "Russian Dirt on Clinton? 'I Love It,' Donald Trump Jr. Said," *The New York Times*, July 11, 2017.

5 Louis Nelson, "Giuliani: Mueller probe 'most corrupt investigation I have ever seen,'" *Politico*, July 8, 2018, https://www.politico.com/story/2018/07/08/giuliani-trump-mueller-russia-investigation-702136.

6 "Rudy Giuliani calls for Trump accusers to apologize after Mueller report finds no Russia collusion," Fox News, March 25, 2019.

7 "The Mueller Investigation," *Frontline*, Season 37 Episode 18, PBS, March 25, 2019.

8 Sam Glick, "It's time to end our 'separate but unequal' approach to mental health," *World Economic Forum*, October 9, 2018, https://www.weforum.org/agenda/2018/10/it-s-time-to-end-our-separate-but-unequal-approach-to-mental-health/.

9 Susannah Cahalan, "The shocking truth about America's mental health crisis," *New York Post*, July 7, 2018, https://nypost.com/2018/07/07/the-shocking-truth-about-americas-mental-health-crisis/.

10 Grace Dobush, "The U.S. Is The Unhappiest It's Ever Been," *Fortune*, March 20, 2019, https://fortune.com/2019/03/20/u-s-unhappiest-its-ever-been/.

11 Doyle Rice, "Tens of millions of Americans exposed to unsafe drinking water each year," *USA Today*, February 12, 2018.

12 Mark Huelsman, "The Unaffordable Era: A 50-State Look at Rising College Prices and the New American Student," Demos, February 22, 2018, https://www.demos.org/research/unaffordable-era-50-state-look-rising-college-prices-and-new-american-student.

13 Diana Hembree, "New Report Finds Student Debt Burden Has 'Disastrous Domino Effect' On Millions of Americans," *Forbes*, November 1, 2018, https://www.forbes.com/sites/dianahembree/2018/11/01/new-report-finds-student-debt-burden-has-disastrous-domino-effect-on-millions-of-americans/#68bda61d12d1.

14 Abby Haglage, "Life in Prison for Selling $20 of Weed," *Daily Beast*, February 27, 2015.

15 David Voreacos, Andrew Harris, and Bloomberg, "Former Trump Campaign Chairman Paul Manafort Sentenced to 47 Months for Bank, Tax Fraud," *Fortune*, March 7, 2019, https://fortune.com/2019/03/07/manafort-sentenced-trump-campaign-chairman-mueller-investigation/.

16 Thomas B. Edsall, "No Hate Left Behind," *The New York Times*, March 13, 2019.

17 "America's Third-Party Prospects," *The Daily Show with Trevor Noah*, Comedy Central, August 18, 2016.

18 David Morris, "How to Make a Political Revolution," BillMoyers.com, July 19, 2016, https://billmoyers.com/story/make-political-revolution/.

19 John D. Buenker, Ph.D. "Progressivism Triumphant: The 1911 Wisconsin Legislature," *Wisconsin Blue Book*, 2011-2012.

20 James Rickards, "Repeal of Glass-Steagall Caused the Financial Crisis," *U.S. News & World Report*, August 27, 2012, https://www.usnews.com/opinion/blogs/economic-intelligence/2012/08/27/repeal-of-glass-steagall-caused-the-financial-crisis.

21 Emily Stephenson and Steve Holland, "Trump vows military build-up, hammers nationalist themes," Reuters, February 24, 2017, https://www.reuters.com/article/us-usa-trump/trump-vows-military-build-up-hammers-nationalist-themes-idUSKBN1630HH.

22 Dan Merica, "Trump: I will ask Congress for a $1 trillion infrastructure bill," CNN, February 28, 2017, https://www.cnn.com/2017/02/28/politics/trump-infrastructure-trillion-congress/index.html.

23 John Laloggia, "6 facts about U.S. political independents," Pew Research Center, May 15, 2019, https://www.pewresearch.org/fact-tank/2019/05/15/facts-about-us-political-independents/.

24 Ibid.

25 For more on this, check out *The Fourth Turning* by William Strauss and Neil Howe, http://www.fourthturning.com/.

26 Aileen Zimmerman, "America's Mental Health Crisis," *Dialogue & Discourse*, June 24, 2018, https://medium.com/discourse/americas-mental-health-crisis-ddd8dc95a328.

CHAPTER TWELVE

1 Martin Gilens and Benjamin I. Page, "Testing Theories of American Politics: Elites, Interest Groups, and Average Citizens," American Political Science Association, September 2014, https://scholar.princeton.edu/sites/default/files/mgilens/files/gilens_and_page_2014_-testing_theories_of_american_politics.doc.pdf.

2 "Beyond Distrust: How Americans View Their Government," Pew Research Center, November 23, 2015, https://www.people-press.org/2015/11/23/beyond-distrust-how-americans-view-their-government/.

3 "Wisconsin Ready to Amend: Completed Resolutions and Referendums in Wisconsin," Wisconsin United to Amend, https://wiuta.org/resources/wisconsin-ready-to-amend/.

4 Jessie Opoien, "Republican bill would significantly reshape Wisconsin's campaign finance law," *The Capital Times*, October 8, 2015, https://madison.com/ct/news/local/govt-and-politics/republican-bill-would-significantly-reshape-wisconsin-s-campaign-finance-law/article_3ca3dc4a-4c77-5168-aefb-e1756b054a0d.html.

5 Ben Casselman, "A Big Night for Minimum Wage Increases," *FiveThirtyEight*, November 5, 2014, https://fivethirtyeight.com/features/a-big-night-for-minimum-wage-increases/.

6 Maureen McCollum, "Voters Pass Referenda On Raising Minimum Wage, Accepting Medicaid Funds," *Wisconsin Public Radio*, November 5, 2014, https://www.wpr.org/voters-pass-referenda-raising-minimum-wage-accepting-medicaid-funds.

7 Wendy Weiser, "Voter Suppression: How Bad? (Pretty Bad)," *American Prospect*, October 1, 2014, https://www.brennancenter.org/our-work/analysis-opinion/voter-suppression-how-bad-pretty-bad.

8 Check out https://whytuesday.org/.

9 Michael D. Shear and Matthew Rosenberg, "Released Emails Suggest the D.N.C. Derided the Sanders Campaign," *The New York Times*, July 22, 2016.

10 Robert Reich, "Does Hillary Get It?" Robert Reich blog, July 23, 2016, https://robertreich.org/post/147866112730.

11 James Fallows, "How America Is Putting Itself Back Together," *The Atlantic*, March 2016, https://www.theatlantic.com/magazine/archive/2016/03/how-america-is-putting-itself-back-together/426882/.

12 Harry Enten, "Americans' Distaste for Both Trump and Clinton Is Record-Breaking," *FiveThirtyEight*, May 5, 2016, https://fivethirtyeight.com/features/americans-distaste-for-both-trump-and-clinton-is-record-breaking/.

13 Anthony Salvanto, Fred Backus, Jennifer De Pinto, and Sarah Dutton, "Donald Trump and Hillary Clinton viewed unfavorably by majority – CBS/NYT poll," CBS News, March 21, 2016, https://www.cbsnews.com/news/donald-trump-and-hillary-clinton-viewed-unfavorably-by-majority-cbsnyt-poll/.

14 "Hillary Clinton's 'honest' and 'trustworthy' numbers are lower than ever. It might not matter." *Washington Post*, March 8, 2016.

15 Chris Cillizza, "Hillary Clinton has a likability problem. Donald Trump has a likability epidemic," *Washington Post*, May 16, 2016.

16 Ibid.

17 H.A. Goodman, "Bernie Sanders Is Almost Tied Nationally and Ahead of Clinton in Three Democratic Primary Polls," *Huffington Post*, April 15, 2016, https://www.huffpost.com/entry/bernie-sanders-is-almost-tied-nationally_b_9700610.

18 Chris Cillizza, "The 13 most amazing things in the 2016 exit poll," *The Washington Post*, November 10, 2016.

19 Jon Ward, "Big government gets bigger," *The Washington Times*, October 19, 2008, https://www.washingtontimes.com/news/2008/oct/19/big-government-gets-bigger/.

20 "GOP's Favorability Rating Edges Lower," Pew Research Center, April 28, 2016, https://www.people-press.org/2016/04/28/gops-favorability-rating-edges-lower/.

21 Kevin Huska, "We are a republic, not a democracy," Letter to the Editor, *Wisconsin State Journal*, October 1, 2016.

22 Greg Stohr, "Bloomberg Poll: Americans Want Supreme Court to Turn Off Political Spending Spigot," *Bloomberg News*, September 28, 2015.

23 Allen C. Guelzo, "'Sublime in Its Magnitude': The Emancipation Proclamation," *The Cupola*, Gettysburg College, August 2007.

24 "Donor Demographics," Center for Responsive Politics, https://www.opensecrets.org/overview/donordemographics.php.

CHAPTER THIRTEEN

1 Norman Stockwell, "'It's a Scary Time': Matt Taibbi Reflects on His Travels on the Trump Campaign Trail," *The Progressive*, March 25, 2017, https://progressive.org/magazine/%E2%80%98it%E2%80%99s-a-scary-time-%E2%80%99-an-interview-with-journalist-matt-taibb/.

2 Jacob S. Hacker and Paul Pierson, *Winner-Take-All Politics: How Washington Made the Rich Richer – And Turned Its Back on the Middle Class* (New York: Simon & Schuster, 2010), 252.

3 "Record $35.8M Spent on Fall Legislative Races in 2018," Wisconsin Democracy Campaign, March 6, 2019, https://www.wisdc.org/news/press-releases/126-press-release-2019/6316-record-35-8m-spent-on-fall-legislative-races-in-2018.

4 Pamela Parker, "Nielsen: Consumer Trust in Traditional Media Ads Fall, While Confidence in Mobile, Social, and Online Rise," *Marketing Land*, April 10, 2012, https://marketingland.com/nielsen-consumer-trust-in-traditional-media-ads-fall-while-confidence-in-mobile-social-and-online-rise-9712.

5 Yuyu Chen, "84 Percent of Millennials Don't Trust Traditional Advertising," *ClickZ*, March 4, 2015.

6 Danielle Kurtzleben, "2016 Campaigns Will Spend $4.4 Billion On TV Ads, But Why?" *NPR*, August 19, 2015, https://www. npr.org/sections/itsallpolitics/2015/08/19/432759311/2016-campaign-tv-ad-spending.

7 Sarah Snow, "What Kinds of Advertising Do People Trust the Most? (Nielsen Poll)," *Social Media Today*, September 29, 2015, https://www.socialmediatoday.com/marketing/sarah-snow/2015-09-29/what-kinds-advertising-do-people-trust-most-nielsen-poll.

8 Stephen Ansolabehere and Shanto Iyengar, "Winning, but losing: How negative campaigns shrink electorate, manipulate news media," Political Communication Lab, Stanford University, 1996, https://pcl.stanford.edu/common/docs/research/iyengar/1996/goingneg.html.

9 Denise-Marie Ordway and John Wihbey, "Negative political ads and their effect on voters: Updated collection of research," *Journalist's Resource*, September 25, 2016, https://www.npr.org/2019/04/03/709567750/radically-normal-how-gay-rights-activists-changed-the-minds-of-their-opponents.

10 "Honesty/Ethics in Professions," Gallup, https://news.gallup.com/poll/1654/honesty-ethics-professions.aspx.

11 "Congress Less Popular than Cockroaches, Traffic Jams," Public Policy Polling, January 8, 2013, https://www.npr.org/2019/04/03/709567750/radically-normal-how-gay-rights-activists-changed-the-minds-of-their-opponents.

12 "Shankar Vedantam, Parth Shah, Tara Boyle, and Jennifer Schmidt, Radically Normal: How Gay Rights Activists Changed the Minds of Their Opponents," *Hidden Brain*, *NPR*, April 8, 2019, https://www.npr.org/2019/04/03/709567750/radically-normal-how-gay-rights-activists-changed-the-minds-of-their-opponents.

13 Edward-Isaac Dovere, "How Clinton lost Michigan – and blew the election," *Politico*, December 14, 2016, https://www.politico.com/story/2016/12/michigan-hillary-clinton-trump-232547.

14 Katie Delong, "Record number of Wisconsin voters went to the polls on Tuesday," WITI-TV, November 5, 2014, https://fox6now.com/2014/11/05/g-a-b-record-number-of-wisconsin-voters-went-to-the-polls-on-tuesday/.

CHAPTER FOURTEEN

1 Jacob Pramuk, "Trump spent about half of what Clinton did on his way to the presidency," CNBC, November 9, 2016, https://www.cnbc.com/2016/11/09/trump-spent-about-half-of-what-clinton-did-on-his-way-to-the-presidency.html.

2 "State of the News Media," Pew Research Center, June 15, 2016, 19.

3 Erin Keane, "The U.S. newspaper crisis is growing: More than 1 in 5 local papers have closed since 2004," *Salon*, October 16, 2018, https://www.salon.com/2018/10/16/the-u-s-newspaper-crisis-is-growing-more-than-1-in-5-local-papers-have-closed-since-2004/.

4 Riley Vetterkind and Kelly Meyerhofer, "'In Tony Evers' 'liberal wishlist,' some potential areas for compromise," *Wisconsin State Journal*, March 3, 2019.

5 Scott Bauer, "Poll shows strong support for Evers priorities," Associated Press and *Minneapolis Star Tribune*, January 24, 2019, https://apnews.com/5c3d2c4130f24e37adc72444f847f0b4.

6 Bruce Murphy, "The Voucher Lobby," *Urban Milwaukee*, May 9, 2013.

7 "Unbreaking America: Solving the Corruption Crisis," RepresentUs, February 2019, https://represent.us/unbreaking-america/.

8 Robert D. Hershey Jr, "F.C.C. Votes Down Fairness Doctrine in a 4-0 Decision," *The New York Times*, August 5, 1987.

9 "How a top conservative radio host took on Trump," *Los Angeles Times*, January 30, 2017.

10 Will Worley, "These are the world's most ignorant countries," *Independent*, December 17, 2016.

11 John Nichols, "State poised to renew progressive legacy this summer," *The Capital Times*, June 29, 2011, https://madison.com/ct/news/opinion/column/john_nichols/john-nichols-state-poised-to-renew-progressive-legacy-this-summer/article_e80def6c-df6f-5646-9488-966ceca6d825.html.

12 Amanda Erickson, "Trump called the news media an 'enemy of the American people.' Here's a history of the term," *Washington Post*, February 18, 2017.

13 Spencer Woodman, "Update: Lawmakers in Ten States Have Proposed Legislation Criminalizing Peaceful Protest," *The Intercept_*, January 23, 2017, https://theintercept.com/2017/01/23/lawmakers-in-eight-states-have-proposed-laws-criminalizing-peaceful-protest/.

14 William Saletan, "Of Course It's a Muslim Ban," *Slate*, January 31, 2017, https://slate.com/news-and-politics/2017/01/trumps-executive-order-on-immigration-is-a-muslim-ban.html.

15 Molly Beck, "DPI: 73 percent of statewide voucher students already enrolled in private schools," *Wisconsin State Journal*, October 30, 2013.

16 Molly Beck, "Report: State to spend $258M on school vouchers next school year," *Wisconsin State Journal*, September 1, 2015.

17 Kristin Durst, "Voucher Students Perform Slightly Worse Than Public School Students on Standardized Tests," *Wisconsin Public Radio*, April 8, 2014, https://www.wpr.org/voucher-students-perform-slightly-worse-public-school-students-standardized-tests.

18 Danielle Dreilinger, "Louisiana voucher students did worse at new schools, study says," *New Orleans Times-Picayune*, February 23, 2016.

19 Bill Lueders, "The selling of school choice," The Wisconsin Center for Investigative Journalism, September 18, 2011, https://www.wisconsinwatch.org/2011/09/school-choice-part-1/.

20 Jon Marcus, "The Demise of Private Schools," *The Atlantic*, September 2, 2015, https://www.theatlantic.com/education/archive/2015/09/parochial-schools-demise/403369/.

21 Erin Richards and Kevin Crowe, "Vouchers a boon for private schools in Milwaukee, Racine counties," *Milwaukee Journal Sentinel*, May 4, 2013, http://archive.jsonline.com/news/education/vouchers-a-boon-for-private-schools-in-milwaukee-racine-counties-rr9pa6l-206122011.html.

22 "U.S. Education Slipping in Ranks Worldwide, Earns Poor Grades on CFR Scorecard," Council on Foreign Relations, June 17, 2013, https://www.cfr.org/news-releases/us-education-slipping-ranks-worldwide-earns-poor-grades-cfr-scorecard.

23 Rebecca Klein, "These Are the States With the Best and Worst School Systems, According to New Rankings," *Huffington Post*, December 7, 2017, https://www.huffpost.com/entry/wallethub-education-rankings_n_5648067.

24 "Why Class Size Matters," Parents Across America, http://parentsacrossamerica.org/what-we-believe-2/why-class-size-matters/.

25 Ronald Brownstein, "America's Growing Pessimism," *The Atlantic*, October 10, 2015, https://www.theatlantic.com/politics/archive/2015/10/americans-pessimism-future/409564/.

26 Matt Egan, "America more pessimistic than poor nations," CNN Business, October 9, 2014, https://money.cnn.com/2014/10/09/news/economy/poor-nations-more-optimistic-than-united-states.

CHAPTER FIFTEEN

1 Joe Gelarden, "Political insults 101," *Boothbay Register*, June 15, 2016, https://www.boothbayregister.com/article/political-insults-101/71701.

2 "The Supreme Court Ruling That Led to 70,000 Forced Sterilizations," *NPR*, March 7, 2016, https://www.npr.org/sections/health-shots/2016/03/07/469478098/the-supreme-court-ruling-that-led-to-70-000-forced-sterilizations.

3 Sarah Pruitt, "The Night of Terror: When Suffragists Were Imprisoned and Tortured in 1917," History Channel, April 17, 2019, https://www.history.com/news/night-terror-brutality-suffragists-19th-amendment.

4 Diane Atkinson, *Rise Up Women! The Remarkable Lives of the Suffragettes* (New York: Bloomsbury Publishing, 2018).

5 Václav Havel, *Disturbing the Peace* (New York: Vintage Books, 1991) 181–182.

6 David Maraniss, *When Pride Still Mattered: A Life of Vince Lombardi* (New York: Simon & Schuster, 2000).

7 James Michener, *Sports in America* (New York: Fawcett Crest, 1987).

8 "The Powell Memo: A Call-to-Arms for Corporations," Moyers & Company, September 14, 2012, https://billmoyers.com/content/the-powell-memo-a-call-to-arms-for-corporations/.

9 Mike McCabe, *Blue Jeans in High Places: The Coming Makeover of American Politics* (Little Creek Press, 2014).

10 Wendy Davis, "Why I Caved on Guns When I Ran for Governor of Texas," *Politico*, December 8, 2015, https://www.politico.com/magazine/story/2015/12/wendy-davis-open-carry-gun-rights-texas-213423.

11 David Ross with Don Yaeger, *Teammate: My Journey in Baseball and a World Series for the Ages* (New York: Hachette Books, May 2017).

12 "Cubs curse: Bartman, 1969 black cat, curse of the billy goat," *This Day In Chicago Cubs History,* http://www.thisdayinchicagocubshistory.com/Cubs-curse.html.

13 Roger Cohen, "The Great Unraveling," *The New York Times*, September 16, 2014.

14 Paul Krugman, *The Great Unraveling: Losing Our Way in the New Century*, (New York: W.W. Norton, 2014).